PELICAN BOOKS

BELIEFS IN SOCIETY

NIGEL HARRIS teaches at the Centre for Urban
Studies (University College, London) in a post-
graduate course in urbanization in developing countries. Educated at Magdalen College, Oxford, and
the London School of Economics, he spent a year in
sociological research at the Indian Statistical Institute, Calcutta, was a visiting lecturer at the International Christian University, Tokyo, and worked
as a journalist in south-east Asia and China. He
formerly taught modern political ideas and Asian
politics in the University of York. He has been the
editor of *International Socialism* since 1965.

NIGEL HARRIS

Beliefs in Society

PENGUIN BOOKS
in association with C. A. Watts & Co. Ltd

Penguin Books Ltd, Harmondsworth, Middlesex, England
Penguin Books Inc., 7110 Ambassador Road, Baltimore, Maryland 21207, U.S.A.
Penguin Books Australia Ltd, Ringwood, Victoria, Australia

—

First published by C. A. Watts 1968
Published in Pelican Books 1971

—

Copyright © Nigel Harris, 1968

—

Made and printed in Great Britain
by Hazell Watson & Viney Ltd
Aylesbury, Bucks
Set in Intertype Plantin

CONTENTS

PREFACE

THE topic of this book is vast, and a multiplicity of themes is touched upon in a way that can only be, at best, irritating to numerous specialists in different fields. Yet it is important to try sometimes to put together some of the elements in order to comprehend the whole. Little of the book is original, but in an effort to relieve the text of dreary lists of citations I shall often have failed to give the necessary credit to major work in the field. Citations have been included to signpost quotations, and can be properly located in the brief bibliography at the end.

Some of the argument in Chapter 2 was originally presented in different form in 'The Owl of Minerva', *Soviet Studies*, xviii, 3 January 1967. Parts of Chapters 5 and 6 have featured in three articles in *International Socialism*: 'India, a First Approximation', Part I in *IS 17*, Summer 1964, and Part II in *IS 18*, Autumn 1964, and 'Marxism: Leninism-Stalinism-Maoism', *IS 26*, Autumn 1966.

The term 'conservative' is used in this book to refer to people who defend the existing nature of society, whatever that society is and wherever it is. The term 'Conservative' is used to refer to members or supporters of the British Conservative Party.

I am most grateful to three people who have read the book in manuscript and made most useful suggestions for its improvement: Tirril Harris, Jim Kincaid and Robert Looker. The errors are my own.

N. H.

1968

I

The Problem:
The Jumbled Catalogue

These times are times of chaos; opinions are a scramble; parties are a jumble; the language of new ideas has not been created; nothing is more difficult than to give a good definition of oneself in religion, in philosophy, in politics. One feels, one knows, one lives, and at need, one dies for one's cause, but one cannot name it. It is the problem of this time to classify things and men. . . . The world has jumbled its catalogue.

ALPHONSE DE LAMARTINE,
Declaration of Principles, cited Geertz, 1964

'IDEOLOGY' is fashionable. In our daily diet of words, the bombardment of press, radio and television, this word has a complex significance.

If we read 'This decision is not guided by practical reality, but by pure ideology,' what are we likely to infer? First, that the decision was irrational, inappropriate to the problem faced. Second, and underlying our first inference, we would probably know that the writer assumed that the problem was relatively easy to identify, that most sensible people could see what range of decisions would be appropriate. However, in contrast to the range of decisions sensible people might take, this decision was foolish. There is also the implication that the decision is related systematically to other ideas, so that this system is related to the current decision, and the decision is not itself an isolated act of foolishness. One can reasonably infer, also, that the writer thinks the system is foolish. Thus, we can infer that the writer means the decision 'flows' from an irrational system of thought, and the system can be seen to be, not just undesirable (that is, we disagree with the aims of the system), but incorrect (that is, all reasonable men can see, almost as a technical matter, that the system is logically or empirically invalid).

In this context the label 'ideological' is particularly damning, for it damns the decision-maker on a whole range of judgements not present in the example. We have to take it on trust that the critic knows accurately what these other statements are.

If our first example of the usage is the most common, and heavily derogatory, there is also a commendatory one. Thus, 'The decision is not guided by selfish economic interest, but by pure ideology,' gives us a mirror image of the first use of the word. The implication of a system reoccurs, but this time it seems to be an ethical rather than an irrational and mistaken system — 'ideology' seems to mean a framework of ideas which is sharply or clearly at variance with obvious material interests. Thus, we could insert in our example some phrase such as 'systematic un-selfishness' in the place of 'ideology', implying a series of other unspoken judgements, all of an ethical kind. The first and second uses might not be mutually exclusive if we believe that morality is irrational or mistaken where it conflicts with a man's material interest. We must assume, however, in both uses that it is reason-ably easy to identify what the contrast with 'ideology' is – that is, in our two examples, 'practical reality' and 'selfish economic interest'. For 'ideology' takes its sense in these two usages from its contrast, and it is presumed that we all know what 'reality' or 'interest' is in practice, so that we can readily identify the oppo-site. Much of this book will be concerned to express some doubts about these assumptions, and, in particular, doubts as to whether we can separate two compartments, 'reality' and 'ideology'. For our reality is the next man's ideology, and vice versa.

Common Sense

An underlying philosophic problem in discussions of this kind concerns the relationship of men's thoughts to the world at large and to the actions they perform. The common-sense explanation of these relationships does not get us very far. There are at least two such explanations which we might crudely put forward as:

1. We look at the world carefully and closely, gathering and measuring all the facts, and then we work out the most obvious

solution and execute it. There are, by implication, a limited number of facts, these are unambiguous and relatively easily identified, and, if we have done our preliminary work adequately, the solutions follow. All reasonable men will follow the course of reasoning involved, and voluntarily approve the solution since it is 'obvious', given the factual information. At an extreme, this view can imply that the range of choice open to sensible men is virtually nil. The facts, as it were, dictate their own solution, and sensible men merely act as passive catalysts in this process. At a generalized level, if history is made by sensible men it becomes inexorable and inevitable, an unfolding process in which the sensible men are passive connecting links between the facts and action. Of course, history is not strictly like this because from time to time men who are not sensible make decisions. The connecting link is devious because the nonsensible men have 'clouded' judgement or imperfectly examine the facts. The elements which 'cloud' judgement are seen as emotion or prejudice or subordination to one of the vested interests at work in society or the influence of factors other than those 'in the facts of the situation'.

2. We have ideals, and we set out to achieve them. It is usually suggested that 'ideals' are the kind of aim which is, in pure form, unrealizable. However, in seeking to realize them we do succeed in changing the world a little towards them, in achieving some approximation. The 'ideals' are given. They come from nowhere, but are a datum. It is often suggested that it is good to have ideals, although in this rudimentary explanation it is not clear why.

The first argument is much the most common, although many people advance both at different times. I would suggest that both models of the relationship between ideas, the world and action are a bit nonsensical, not least because in no single respect do they fit what we might, on reflection, see as the process whereby we reach certain conclusions and seek to act upon them. For most of us, making a decision is an extremely complex matter, in which accidents, *ad hoc* considerations, play a role, and where a multitude of different, often implicit, considerations come into play.

We need not pursue this very far, but it is useful to note certain specific weaknesses in both models. In the first, the 'facts' give no answers. To a multitude of men the infinity of possible facts gives a multitude of different answers, of choices. What is a 'fact' is not obvious, for we have to approach the world with some preconceptions of what it is we are looking for, with some framework for analysis which indicates what we are to consider 'facts' and with some purpose which indicates what we are to consider as relevant facts. Characterizing the facts is a separate problem, for in the way we do this so we illuminate different relationships between them. In general, they only exist for us when we have some purpose, some reason for calling something a 'fact', and that purpose is crucial in deciding what are facts. Of course, men who make decisions like to present them as obvious, what any sensible person would have done in the circumstances. To convince people that one's decision was obvious is to prevent open discussion of the criteria involved in making it, to safeguard one's own authority from challenge. But if we accept this piece of propaganda as the way the world works we merely decide to align ourselves with decision-makers, whatever their decisions might be. Then, whatever has happened, had to happen; whatever happens, must happen; what is to be, will be. Since society is organized in a particular way, whatever authority is making decisions, is making the right ones. Implicitly, we are saying we are conservative or apathetic.

The second explanation is not much more satisfactory, since it is not usually worked out in sufficient detail to be taken very seriously. It certainly allows men to choose – the 'inevitability' of the first argument is not present. But it does not offer any grounds for judging the rightness of decisions. Something called 'ideals' comes from nowhere and has no justification, and is imperfectly related to the world. No reason why men have ideals is given, why they pursue them, and why this is good.

Any account of the relationship of ideas to the world must indicate where ideas come from, how they are created and changed, and how they relate to the things we do – and, even more important, to the immensely different things which different men do. If 'ideologies' are systematic organizations of ideals, or of 'interests' which cloud judgement, we need to know why they exist. But perhaps the problem would be better approached at this stage by examining how some prominent social scientists have identified ideologies.

Social Science

It was noted in the earlier 'common-sense' definition of 'ideology' that the term carried a greater or lesser connotation of condemnation, and relied on a sharp contrast with 'reality'. The same elements tend to recur in social science definitions, only a few of which can be examined here. Thus, for example, even in Julius Gould's relatively neutral formulation – ideology is a 'pattern of beliefs and concepts (both factual and normative) which purport to explain complex social phenomena with a view to directing and simplifying socio-political choices facing individuals and groups' (1964, p. 315) – the implicit condemnation of simplification is attributed to ideology.

Talcott Parsons identifies very specifically the contrasting 'reality'. He says that the 'essential criteria of an ideology' are 'deviations from social science objectivity'. 'The criterion of distortion is that statements are made about society which, by social scientific methods, can be shown to be positively in error, whereas selectivity is involved where the statements are, at the proper level, "true", but do not constitute a balanced account of the available truth' (1959, p. 25). Thus, 'reality' here means what social scientists, presumably collectively (since, as individuals, they are likely to disagree), say it is, and ideology is ideological in so far as it diverges from the account of reality offered by social scientists. Ideology is thus defined explicitly as false, although the falsehood may take many different forms. We must presume that a social scientist, as social scientist, cannot participate in an ideology – the truth is reserved to one class of men, and what they collectively say the truth is, defines what is false.

A number of social scientists have been less concerned with the substantive definition of ideology, more with criticizing the style of men they identify as ideologists. Ideology, Edward Shils (1958, p. 450) says, is full of distrust, is aggressive, undermines existing political institutions, is dogmatic, doctrinaire, totalistic and futuristic. This is an impressive list of sins, but Shils does not explain very explicitly why they *are* sins. Perhaps distrust or aggressiveness are appropriate responses in certain situations; perhaps existing political institutions need to be undermined, and so on. Implicitly, political judgements are being made here, rather than argued explicitly. Stark (1958, pp. 90–91) raises the condemnatory definition to new heights of abuse; for, he says, ideology is 'a mode of thinking which is thrown off its proper course ... something shady, something that ought to be overcome and banished from our mind', something psychologically 'deformed'; thought related to 'the *facts* of reality' is 'like a pure stream, crystal-clear, transparent; ideological ideas [are] like a dirty river, muddied and polluted by the impurities that have flooded into it'. This is all very jolly, but does not show very specifically how we can discriminate the virtuous truth from the vicious falsehood, nor does Stark show much compassion for those poor victims of error who are snared in ideological delusion.

Erikson (1958, p. 22) does not pursue this baroque sense of sin, but rather focuses on the psychological element. He says that ideology is 'an unconscious tendency underlying religion and scientific as well as political thought: the tendency at a given time to make facts amenable to ideas, and ideas to facts, in order to create a world image convincing enough to support the collective and individual sense of identity'. Reality is, it seems, bent to suit the wishes of the ideological, and wish-fulfilment is the dominant motif; it is not clear why people need to go to such lengths to attain a 'sense of identity', why they lack such a sense, but the implication is that the personality of the ideological person is inadequate, and the evidence for its inadequacy lies in the person's adherence to an ideology. Others have developed the psychological interpretation very much further, so that social movements as a whole seem to reduce to curiosities of personality. Talcott Parsons (1951, p. 357), indeed, says that 'ideologies have functions directly homologous with those of rationalization in the personality system'. The rationalization may cover some inadequacy, some inherent personality drive, or console one for one's troubles, 'a patterned reaction to the patterned strains of a social role' (Sutton *et al.*, 1956, p. 307).

Now, just as in an earlier example reasonable people were able easily to identify 'reality', so here the nature of good health, of the 'normal', is assumed to be clear, for only thus can the 'abnormal' be identified. The 'normal' identify reality in, it is suggested, a particular way, so that those who identify it in ways outside this range are, by definition, 'abnormal'. Ideology, on an individual plane, is a problem for psychiatric treatment rather than serious intellectual consideration. It was noted, in connection with the first common-sense definition of ideology, that the usage implied a clear mistake had been made by the ideologist. Here, it is implied, one need not argue with the ideologist for he is clearly sick, and sickness is answered with treatment, not argument.

Quite clearly, in relationship to these last definitions ideology is what Geertz calls 'radical intellectual depravity' (1964, p. 50). The term is wholly condemnatory, and can be paraphrased in terms like 'false', 'incorrect', 'invalid'. Less pejorative usages still presume the clear (and relatively obvious) distinction between 'reality' and 'ideology'. Mannheim, whose pioneer work (*Ideology and Utopia*, 1936) provides a most important framework for most modern discussions of ideology, defines his particular ideology as beliefs which express the interests of a particular social group; as such, it provides only a partial and distorted view of reality, for what can be known of reality is only available by synthesizing all the partial views of particular groups.

Apter links ideology to some prior psychological need, presumably not ideological – the need for 'honour' or 'dignity'. Thus, he says, ideology 'links particular actions and mundane practices with a wider set of meanings, and by doing so lends a more honourable and dignified complexion to social conduct' (1964, p. 16). He does not say why men need this linkage, where it comes from and whether or not it varies. Otto Hintze develops the same idea in more detail:

Wherever interests are vigorously pursued, an ideology tends to be developed also to give meaning, reinforcement and justification to these interests. And this 'ideology' is as real as the real interests themselves, for ideology is an indispensable part of the life process which is expressed in action. And conversely: wherever ideas are to conquer the world, they require the leverage of real interests, although frequently ideas will more or less detract these interests from their original aim. (1931, cited Bendix, 1960, p. 69)

Again this is rather difficult because we have no idea why ideology is 'an indispensable part of the life process', why men choose to disguise their interests and to muddle the pursuit of those interests with extraneous, apparently superficial, elements. In the context of our earlier discussion, 'reality' appears here in the guise of 'interests', and seems somehow to be things people would have done, regardless of what they believe. The statements become irrelevant to the real guiding motives of the person concerned. As Geertz (1964) says, ideological statements are like saying 'Ouch!' when we bang a toe; the actual sound or form of the term 'ouch' has no direct formal relationship to the pain in the toe. Similarly in some modern ethical theories, statements of morality express inner feelings rather than proper processes of reasoning.

Once again, also, these definitions assert the clear distinction between 'reality' or interests and ideas. Yet we may legitimately disagree about what our interests are, and 'interests' are only identified within a general framework of ideas that might also include what is being called 'ideology'. Men cannot see their 'interests' clearly, nor can those interests be identified outside general considerations of ethical, political and social values. Interests are no more than the ideas some people have, so that they do not stand clearly contrasted to 'ideas'. It is not too paradoxical to say that people's ideas are their interests, and ideologies express interests as people see them. Nor is it clear why interests are normally 'meaningless', so that ideologies have to be created to 'give them meaning', any more than it is clear why men need decorative forms to make their interests respectable. Perhaps the development of ideologies is precisely the development of people's awareness of their 'interests' or their discovery of what they think their interests are.

Some other writers on this topic see action as peculiarly related to 'ideologies'. Friedrich (1966, p. 612) sees ideologies as 'syndromes of action-orientated ideas'. To appraise this properly one would need to know what the contrasting kinds of idea were, for whether or not action is the implication of a given statement of an idea depends very much on the person making the statement and the context in which it occurs. Bell (1961, p. 394) goes much further with his curious metaphor: 'Ideology is the conversion of ideas into social levers'. Ideology here seems to refer to the *implication* of certain statements in particular contexts, or it may be (as it seems to be in Bell's general case) that ideology means the use of ideas for manipulative purposes. Thus, ideas are merely ideas until someone uses them, more or less cynically (or such is the implication of Bell's account), to make other people do something, at which point ideas become 'ideology'. Now it is not clear at all why action is more closely related to ideology than is inaction, why other studies of the world are seen as 'action-free', nor why cynical propaganda is the sole example of ideological statements. *People*, rather than 'ideas', undertake action, so that ideology can only refer in this context to certain uses to which some people put ideas, rather than to the ideas themselves.

Bell's definition is given as part of a wider argument. He argues that intense political faith existed in the inter-war period but has now declined in Western countries. There has thus been an 'end of ideology'. The model is almost an erotic one – passion in Bell's youth in the inter-war years, followed by disillusion but comfortable security in the post-war world. Indeed, if we were unkind, we might call his idea of the 'end of ideology', the *post coitum tristis* definition. Perhaps the polemical nature of Bell's case for Western conservatism should not be taken too seriously, but it has been influential in offering justification for some Western trends. Yet to identify 'ideology' with the activities of charlatans is to miss the most important area of all, the audience. The question is not how or why unscrupulous men work – they are still with us, whether Bell wants to call them ideological or not – but why audiences respond. On this, Bell has less guidance to offer – 'Ideologies, because they somehow (sic) catch up one's passions, move people to action. This is the source of their initial power.' (1965, p. 591.) But just *what* is this source? Bell's circular description leads back merely to the same repetition, misleadingly expressed as a causal sequence.

The dimension Bell omits is the meaning of the statements involved for the audience. For to examine such statements would be to admit the dimension of rational comprehension, would compel Bell to state explicitly his political priorities in a clear form and to use this commitment to argue against certain other opinions. Bell would thus have to enter the political arena he is trying to condemn implicitly. For it is not the *style* of ideologies which is crucial, but the content of some, and only some, ideologies (most notably, for Bell, communism, and secondarily, fascism). In contemporary terms, the shadow of the Cold War lies across the debate. Because Bell's argument is offered in isolation to an already committed audience the opposition presents no answers. It is not a 'debate' at all, not an examination of the real issues at stake, about the different purposes of two groups of people (some Russians and some Americans), but rather about the psychological abnormality of the other side. One does not argue with the insane; one interns them (or so the logic implies).

The general language of the discussion indicates the kind of condemnation involved. Consider for example Bell's statement: 'For the hierophants, the interpreters of ideology, the strains [of facing 'reality'] are masked, for one of the chief tasks of these pulpiteers is to provide a seemingly unbroken line of continuity in the validity of the doctrine.' (1965, p. 597.) Now this is really just name-calling, of the same vintage as Stark's earlier account of 'ideology', disguised at points in pretentious pseudo-scientific language. Bell does not seek to justify his terminology, for he takes it for granted that his audience shares the same political commitment. The condemnation of style is a substitute for an argument against political ends, and conceals a commitment in the side issues of methodology.

However, other social scientists have sought to come to grips with the thorny problems of beliefs in a much more serious manner. Mannheim's study, already cited, does introduce the wider context of culture which will be our concern in the next chapter. Geertz also provides a more general perspective when he argues that 'symbol systems' (within which he includes ideologies) are

extrinsic sources of information in terms of which human life can be patterned – extrapersonal mechanisms for the perception, understanding, judgement and manipulation of the world. Culture patterns – religious, philosophic, aesthetic, scientific, ideological – are 'programs'; they provide a template or blueprint for the organization of social and psychological processes. (1964, p. 62)

Debunking

In some of the definitions of 'ideology' cited in the preceding section, the aim of the writer seems to have been less the identification of an occurrence in the real world, of the beliefs of men, and more the illumination of the writer's own rationality. The term 'ideology' is used as a synonym for 'false', but in a disguised way so that the authority and objectivity of the writer emerge by implications rather than arrogant assertion. The 'ideological' statement is examined thus not to assess its validity, but rather to dismiss it on grounds not explicitly specified. Indeed, the aim goes further: to deny the statement possible consideration at all within rational discourse. The statement is not the expression of a view of the world at all, but rather a symptom of sickness, an expression of the diseased nature of the 'ideologist'. As a symptom it requires medical examination, not argument. Thus, those who believe in what these writers call 'ideology' are denied rights of debate, rights of democratic participation. They are isolated in an intellectual ghetto, treated at most to amazed pity, but not offered the response of being taken seriously.

Freud – himself a person sometimes tempted to listen to other people's statements as no more than the confused symptoms of underlying illness in the 'unconscious' – also noted the approach which denies a person any hope of being taken seriously. If we meet someone, he says, who argues that the centre of the world is made of jam, we will probably object in a special kind of way. 'The result of our intellectual objection will be a diversion of our interests; instead of their being directed on the investigation itself, as to whether the interior of the earth is really made of jam or not, we shall wonder what kind of man it must be who can get such an idea into his head.' (1933, cited Merton, 1957, p. 458.) We thus come to ask, not 'Is it true?', but 'How could such a thing ever be believed?'

In ideologies, however, the question is more difficult – not some simple oddity like the world being made of jam. Rather is the disagreement likely to arise between different perceptions only narrowly separated, but touching on most sensitive issues of power and influence. 'All reasonable men', that cosy assumption of the secure but vulnerable, suddenly disintegrates into a multitude of unreasonable men, and the basic assumption of consensus disappears.

'Debunking' – not taking statements at face value, but merely as symptoms of some hidden motive – is the mark of an age of doubt, of scepticism, of central social cleavages sustained over a long period of time and exacerbated by the extensive use of propaganda and advertising that seems to devalue the very words we use, the coinage of the market in ideas. Cynicism, the belief that all men are 'on the make' and their statements must be viewed accordingly, is one defensive escape. But other, more intellectual, forms of debunking are even more common. Thus, whatever one says becomes no more than a symptom of inherited psychological drives, one's childhood, fears or secret wishes, socio-economic status or class, a cynical struggle for power, or, finally, one's 'blood' or 'race'.

The 'reality' offered is said to be an unseen but underlying condition, the 'real basis' of the surface chatter. The 'reality' is a substitute for certainties eroded by time and circumstance. The fading of a common framework of assumptions about how we should live and what we should pursue has been described by many commentators on the appearance of modern industrial society. The process, it is suggested, produces a sense that the old certainties have become not merely invalid but meaningless. In his superb book, *The Hidden God*, Lucien Goldmann speaks of the transition between two dominant 'world visions' as producing a sense of the meaninglessness of existence in great writers :

... all forms of consciousness [he says] express a provisional mobile balance between the individual and his social environment; when this balance can fairly easily be established and is relatively stable, or when it can pass fairly easily from one form to another, men tend not to think about the problems raised by their relationship to the external world. On a social as well as an individual plane, it is the sick organ which creates awareness, and it is in periods of social and political crisis that men are most aware of the enigma of their presence in the world. (1964, p. 48)

In such conditions of malaise, then, morality, religion and philosophy become matters of doubt. Politics reflects the confusion of men's direction. Sense and nonsense become difficult to distinguish, the catalogue is jumbled. Confusion prompts men to seek new guides, to examine the old, and in the process of examining past beliefs they come to be aware of the social and personal roots of their beliefs, the historical relativity of opinion and knowledge, the existence of 'ideologies' in what had formerly been 'common sense' or 'reality'. Those most closely integrated into the old ideology are the least self-aware, the least able to see the ideology as a relative response to a particular range of problems. Weber remarks that major innovations in existing belief systems tend to arise not in the major centres of a cultural system but on its periphery, for 'The possibility of questioning the meaning of the world presupposes the capacity to be astonished about the course of events.' (1952, p. 206.)

In this context, then, 'ideology' does not stand contrasted to 'reality' or common sense. On the contrary, 'ideological' is just how common sense appears when seen in a particular and relative historical and social situation. To say of a man's view of reality that it is 'ideological' means here that it is related to his position in the social structure or in the course of history. But to say this is to deny the absolute validity people tend to attribute to their view of the world, and it is this denial which has been seen as subversive. For it undermines the assurance of a man that he believes the truth and the sole truth, and subverts the established order which claims to embody the truth. This is not strictly a correct judgement, for it implies that the word 'ideology' has been used only by radicals to attack the *status quo*, whereas a history of the word shows this not to be so. As Napoleon used the word against one of its earliest users, Destutt de Tracy (*Eléments d'idéologie*, 1801, 1803, 1805), it was a defence of the newly established imperial order against the republicanism of the 'ideologists'. Again, today, the word 'ideology' is used in the West largely to refer to the views of the leaders of the Soviet Union, contrasting with the 'realistic' and common-sense views of the West. In this case, 'ideology' describes no more than the false views of the given opponent.

It was in the hands of Marx and his followers, including Karl Mannheim (although not, strictly speaking, a Marxist himself), that the concept is properly subversive, a means to challenge the validity of statements used to defend the *status quo*. Marx boldly affirms this radical perspective thus:

> The ideas of the ruling class are in every epoch the ruling ideas: that is, the class which is the ruling *material* force in society, is at the same time, its ruling *intellectual* force. . . . For instance, in an age and in a country where royal power, aristocracy and bourgeoisie are contending for mastery and where, therefore, mastery is shared, the doctrine of the separation of power, proves to be the dominant idea and is expressed as an 'eternal law'. (1845–7/1965, pp.60–61)

Terminology

If we accept, then, that particular beliefs cannot be labelled 'ideological' (so that other beliefs are 'non-ideological'), it is similarly clear that neither terminology nor particular beliefs belong exclusively to one side or another in the debate between Right and Left. Semantics summarizes the historical fluctuations of the meaning of words, and thus the shifting fortunes of words involved in that debate. A not uncommon element in that struggle for supremacy is the erosion of key concepts used by one side. This is not necessarily a deliberate tactic by one protagonist to rob his opponent of a concept, but it follows from the nature of the controversy, and is a very great hazard in picking one's way through the complexities of political history. Mannheim notes the same point in the following observation: 'The variation in the meaning of words and the multiple connotations of every concept reflect polarities of mutually antagonistic schemes of life implicit in these nuances of meaning.' (1936, p. 74.) Similarly, definitions of words or apparent generalizations can be offered in political controversies which are not merely means to identify the meaning of a concept but means to persuade, means to rule out of reasonable discourse certain kinds of events. In terms of apparent generalizations, we can note the frequently asserted statement that 'nothing is ever achieved by violence'; John Strachey reasonably replied to this that history demonstrated that nothing was ever achieved without violence. Consider also that favourite conservative observation: politics is the art of the possible or of compromise, both of which are designed to rule out of politics' figures such as Napoleon or Lenin.

We can see the shifts in political power implicit in the ambiguity of certain central concepts. For example, the word 'democracy' has been used and abused for much of recorded history, as demonstrated in the collection of definitions prepared for UNESCO (cf. Naess *et al.*, 1956). The definitions vary over an immense area, ranging from 'control of the State or society by a popular majority' to merely 'popular' or, in modern terms, 'liberal' or 'what exists today in Britain or the United States or somewhere else'. It was certainly not irrational for the Victorian upper-middle class in Britain to be frightened of the first conception, but it would have been to fear the anodyne senses. The complete identification of 'democracy' with, say, the British House of Commons at any given moment of time robs the language of effective criteria with which to judge that institution. The real is redefined to become the ideal. Opposition, logically, must therefore always be 'antidemocratic', even if it seeks a greater popular participation in the House of Commons.

The word 'socialism' has been involved in the same process. Indeed, it might be hazarded that the word 'socialism' occurs historically because the word 'democracy' is being robbed of effective meaning. Originally 'socialism' was quite rightly feared by the propertied, since it promised majority control of the economy, and equality. A reply was formulated that liberty depended upon the possession of property, and that therefore socialism was incompatible with liberty (to which the socialists replied that liberty was impossible where only a minority held most of the available property, so that socialism was the sole means to achieve liberty for the majority). But the same processes of erosion which affected the concept of 'democracy' blurred the notion of 'socialism'. Equality became 'equality of opportunity', an aim which presupposed, as the British Conservative writer, Mallock, quite rightly pointed out, a system of social inequality – equality of opportunity was equal opportunity to win unequal rewards or it was nothing. Thus, 'equality' in its qualified form symbolized commitment to an unequal society, the exact opposite of its original sense. Similarly, majority control of the economy became State control of the economy, the illusion of majority participation being retained in the tenuous mythology of representative government. But even that was insufficient, so that 'socialism' has come to mean in contemporary Social Democratic parties little more than 'popular', a sense scarcely distinguished from the anodyne meaning of 'democratic'. This last sense – socialist is what is popular – can be seen in Joseph Chamberlain's declaration in the 1870s that 'The Poor Law is Socialism; the Education Act is Socialism ... and every kindly act of legislation, by which the community has sought to discharge its responsibilities and obligations to the poor, is Socialism.'

Very little remains of a concept thus subject to the acid of political debate in which at least one side finds it useful to redefine the other side's basic demands so that they become unobjectionable. What does remain is a blur, in which anyone can identify with the concept on nearly any grounds, even though the grounds on which two people identify with the same concept are mutually contradictory. The changes are not arbitrary nor random, for they are an essential part of the struggle. If conservatives can reduce their opponents' demands to no more than an appeal for kindliness, most of the battle is over and the conservatives have won.

The subject of beliefs is shot through with such terminological hazards. Thus, the central dichotomy, examined earlier, between 'reality' and 'ideology' often overlaps and is blurred by much older dichotomies – between fact and value, reason and passion, science and faith, and so on. Many of the spokesmen for 'reality' implicitly take up the older dichotomies, and the attributes associated with them. For example, traditionally it has been argued that 'facts', 'reason' and 'science' evolve as pure description of an unambiguous world, contemplated by detached observers in isolation from any interest in what they see. Within this context, it is implied, the only reasonable use of language is description, and this is only available to an uninvolved outsider. All other uses of language are either erroneous or suspect. Where statements seem to describe the world but come from a committed position then the content of the statement should be divided into its pure descriptive element, its 'scientific component', and a 'value or ideological component'. The first is often identified as a technique, an element of methodology. But the context of this solution seems to misconstrue the problem. Some viewpoint is involved in the perspective of any observer, detached or not, and the 'values' bound up in it cannot be clearly separated out. The formal mechanics of reasoning are neither here nor there. Logic is, broadly, non-ideological, or perhaps an-ideological, and every series of connected sentences employs (or should employ) logic, as each individual sentence employs grammar, but this says nothing about the use to which the sentence is put, its content or meaning. What it says cannot be determined by the purity of its logic. There is similarly no reason at all why the outsider is more capable of enunciating the truth than an active participant, unless we suppose the truth must always acccept the situation it finds and not include a statement on how it is likely to change.

There are, of course, whole ranges of statements which do not for us at the moment have ideological implications. 'The cat is on the mat,' is not a statement that touches directly on major issues. But to think that statements on major issues can somehow be reduced to this level is to ignore the content of the major issues, to ignore the fact that what affects us is different from what does not.

But this rudimentary excursus into the much larger debate on fact and value does not bring us to the end of the terminological thicket. For crucial words and stereotyped descriptions recur all the time in discussing the beliefs of others. We might set out some of the key words, with alternative formulations:

the ideologist (that is, the person with whom the speaker disagrees) is *dogmatic* (loyal to his beliefs), *doctrinaire* (uncompromising, clear), *rigid* (principled), *aggressive* (keen, enthusiastic), *Messianic* (hopeful of a final solution), *apocalyptic* (fears a coming disaster), *totalitarian* (beliefs are coherently unified and relatively comprehensive), *brainwashed* (persuaded), *devoted to myth and illusion* (believes what he believes), and so on.

The alignments are not systematically made, but they do indicate the flavour of this acrimonious attempt to undercut the validity of what is being said, to evade the meaning of what is asserted in *argumentum ad hominem*. Often, even those most dedicated to the separation of 'fact' from 'value' make little or no attempt to carry out just such an exercise in relationship to views with which they disagree, as much United States scholarship on the Soviet Union demonstrates. The contrasting terms which the speaker offers to match these derogatory attributes can, with equal validity, be aligned with other derogatory terms. Thus:

the realist (that is, the speaker or those with whom he agrees) is *flexible* (unprincipled), *pragmatic* (narrow conservative), *cautious* (cowardly), *pursues rational interests* (empty of vision), *does not look further ahead than is justified by the evidence* (aimless, unprepared), and so on.

The game is endless, and one cannot fix any rules for debate when the issues are really vital. Courtesy only operates for most people when the issues at stake are relatively trivial, when, as British parliamentary commentators are fond of noting, the parties agree on basic issues. To our list of derogatory terms we might add also those attributes specifically applicable to individual deviations – *biased, prejudiced,* and so on, rephrased, if one wishes, as truthful, single-minded, not to be deflected, etc.

If the term 'ideology' is to be used in ways which avoid some (but not all) of these pitfalls, we ought provisionally to try to see people's beliefs in the context of culture as a whole. We will return to the problem of the definition of 'ideology' at the end of this book, for it cannot finally be defined in a way which omits the purposes of the user. We shall, here, try to locate 'ideology' as the language of the purposes of a social group, recognizing that one's estimate of ideology turns on whether or not one thinks those purposes are reasonable. 'Purpose', the word substituted here for what others have called 'interest', cannot however be identified separately from an ideology. It is not the case that in the beginning there were purposes, and men created ideologies to relate those purposes to the world they faced. Rather does the definition of purpose arise during men's exploration of the world; they locate what purposes they should pursue, just as they discover what their interests are, at the same time as they learn more about the world in trying to overcome specific problems. Ideologies are not disguised descriptions of the world, but rather real descriptions of the world from a specific viewpoint, just as all descriptions of the world are from a particular viewpoint.

But how are we to speak of a specific viewpoint of the world without simultaneously postulating another viewpoint with which it contrasts? We cannot. We thus must postulate something referred to hitherto as 'reality', but in doing so we must also admit in all honesty that this other viewpoint is itself only one among many. It is not 'reality' at all, but *our* reality, contrasted to *their* reality which, for the immediate purposes of discussion, we are calling an 'ideology'. Thus what is said in the following pages takes for granted a specific, evaluative and, if you will, 'ideological' perspective on the world and on other ideologies. To say that this perspective is specific is not to say that it does not adhere to the ordinary criteria of truth and falsehood, but rather that it is related to only one committed viewpoint. The lines of that viewpoint will emerge in the following chapters, but perhaps it does need to be said at the outset that whereas in many accounts of ideology the social group which is taken to be the final framework for the analysis of beliefs is the nation-State (usually identified as 'society') here it is assumed to be social classes. From the first viewpoint the 'national ideology' is identified with society as a whole – the beliefs of subgroups within society are seen as relatively marginal – whereas here the group supporting the so-called 'national ideology' has to be specifically identified; in the first, conflicts between nation-States are seen as the crucial area of conflict, whereas here inter-State conflicts are seen as taking place between dominant groups in different nation-States and as only one kind of conflict, for equally important is the conflict within society. There are a number of reasons for this assumption, and its selection will, I hope, be validated in what follows. However, the assumption is part of a more general theory of society which cannot properly be explored here but which identifies social classes as the product of a competitive struggle for scarce resources and a social division of labour; the most important beliefs within society are seen as related to this basic struggle, and thus to class. This does not prevent attempts to identify the beliefs of subgroups or beliefs held in common by the majority of the population of society, but it does imply that such beliefs can be best seen in relationship to the continuing theme of the central rivalry within society. Goldmann, in the context of the analysis of literary works, expresses this methodological assumption clearly : 'there are certain social groups (and empirical research has shown that during the course of history, these groups have most often been social classes) whose aspirations and needs correspond either to the total re-structuring of all interhuman relations and relations between man and nature, or to the total preservation of social structures and existing values.' (1967, p. 904.) There is one important implica-tion in this assumption, for the conservative view of an integrated and harmonious society is deliberately relinquished for the radical perspective of society as an arena in which social groups conflict on roughly equal terms (equal in the sense of the attention which should be devoted to them, not in terms of actual power). However, here it is necessary only to suggest the broad direction of this account – the relative 'reality', in contrast to which other ideologies, other 'realities' are to be seen – but we shall return to this theme at later points in the book.

Mannheim's 'particular' and 'general' ideologies will not be differentiated, since every 'general' ideology is simultaneously a 'particular' ideology: the views attributable to society as a whole are also the views formulated by the one dominant group in society, and the views of each subordinate social group could, in principle, become a 'general' ideology in certain circumstances. It will be possible to separate different emphases in the use of the word 'ideology' in this connection, but for immediate purposes this should not detract from the association of these emphases in a common concept.

It is also assumed here that ideas are things had by men. Ideologies do not exist, only people who have ideas, or groups which share ideas, many of which can have no significance at all for an isolated individual, only for someone who can presuppose membership of a group. Thus, ideas are seen as part of the history of men, not as extraneous elements, imperfectly tied to what men would have done in any case. Inevitably, ideas treated in isolation seem to be ritual, only accidentally related to what men do. Thus, explanations have to be offered suggesting that ideas are decorative features of an on-going process, or concealments of *real* drives. Here the *real* drives are seen as not prior to ideology, but as partly embodied and partly discovered in ideology.

Detaching ideas from the people who have them includes the mistake of attributing a particular group of ideas to the whole of society. The mistake is analogous to that involved in describing nation-States as if they were people. Thus, newspapers sometimes make proclamations like 'Britain is angry with Germany,' even though possibly most people in Britain are quite unaware of the most elementary details of the dispute. To attribute a group of ideas to society as a whole is not merely to conceal the immense divergencies always present within society, the continuity of heresy and objection, it is also to align oneself with the group that formulates that belief-system. The dominant group within any nation-State has a natural interest in presenting a picture of national unanimity both to the outside world and to its own citizens, for that unanimity or, in modern terms, consensus, is said to legitimize the dominant group's rule, to show that it is right. It is because we often take the datum point of history as the viewpoint of such groups that we often feel the past was dominated for long periods by great unified and unchanging orthodoxies. We fail to note that the orthodoxies are often no more than what the dominant group would like to believe, its ideal image. The orthodoxy ignores the revolts which punctuate its rule, and seeks to conceal the steady change which takes place, which can convert the orthodoxy into its opposite while its protagonists firmly maintain its unchanging loyalty to its original postulates. Christianity began as the doctrine of the poor, of artisans (free and slave), essentially outsiders or aliens in Roman society, hostile to wealth and social differences, without a priesthood and, for some believers, synonymous with small communist communities where goods were held in common and the community loomed larger than the family. Yet it became the doctrine associated with maintenance of imperial power, of the rich, of insiders, happy to live with pockets of wealth amid poverty, with social differences, synonymous for some important believers with the *status quo*. One cannot see such a transformation if one thinks Christianity has been a continuous and unified orthodoxy, if one accepts the words recorded historically by the great without seeking to discover what the audience felt.

The chapter which follows seeks to pursue some of the themes briefly introduced here in greater detail as a prelude to examining certain beliefs in history, and a selection of beliefs in the contemporary world.

2

Culture:
Virtue and Nightmare

We are afraid to put men to live and trade each on his own private stock of reason; because we suspect that this stock in each man is small, and that individuals would do better to avail themselves of the general bank and capital of nations and of ages. . . . Because prejudice with its reason, has a motive to give action to that reason, and an affection which will give it permanence. Prejudice is of ready application in the emergency; it previously engages the mind in a steady course of wisdom and virtue, and does not leave the man hesitating in the moment of decision, sceptical, puzzled and unresolved. Prejudice renders a man's virtue his habit; and not a series of unconnected acts.

EDMUND BURKE, *Reflections on the French Revolution*, p. 95

The tradition of all dead generations weighs like a nightmare on the brain of the living.

MARX, *The Eighteenth Brumaire of Louis Napoleon*

THE study of ideology can most usefully be undertaken in the context of a consideration of culture as a whole rather than in an isolated fashion. But to suggest even a rudimentary view of the role of culture in our lives is not only well beyond the confines of this small book, but is finally impossible since we can only view culture from 'within it'. In an analogous way, we cannot give a complete acccount of language as a whole since, to do so, we must use language, we must describe in terms of language.

However, some more or less useful generalizations do have to be risked, granted that they can only be made by someone who is at the same time culturally relative. The history of ideas must take for granted the historical reference point of the observer. My assertions – about, say, ancient Greece – take for granted that the vantage point which I occupy in my judgements is Britain in the 1960s, or Western culture, or some such base as that.

Culture

We might suggest provisionally that culture consists of an immense series of systems of concepts, many of them in constant change and interpenetration. These systems stand in symbolic relationship to our experience as well as fashion it so that we discriminate what is important for us. In the first instance, we see the things we do see, we identify objects, because we have the cultural background we do have.

To say this, however, is to say very little. For there is an immense number of different systems, some of very great generality and some of very narrow specificity. Some, and perhaps all, of the specific systems are distinguished by the fact that they can be rendered inconsistent with our immediate experience – what we believe and what we see do not match. If this inconsistency affects something we feel is important, then we do seek to adjust one or other element – we change what we believe, or we change what we see. This occurrence of inconsistency is thus the ideational dimension of change, the source of changes in belief. If the adjustment is sufficiently radical it will perhaps carry implications for some of the more general systems, not themselves directly subject to being rendered inconsistent with experience.

Now it would take this account too far afield to begin a proper discussion of the distinction suggested here between general and specific systems, between what we might call 'higher-order' and 'lower-order' systems, but some suggestion of the nature of the distinction is important. One such has already been made – lower-order systems are directly related to our immediate experience, subject to the test of consistency with that experience. What I mean by 'higher-order systems' are those conceptual schemata which make experience possible at all, which organize the raw, unidentified perceived data in forms comprehensible within lower-order systems. Thus, for example, taxonomy classifies the data whereas subsidiary theories offer accounts of the relationships between the objects named. Then the separation between the higher and lower orders is only partly made, for the system of classifying objects is already a rudimentary account of the relationships between the objects. However, a number of different and contradictory lower-order systems are consistent with the one taxonomy.

The higher-order systems, historically, have been refined by past generations of men relative to their experience, but we have long since forgotten why they chose to identify objects with the terms they have bequeathed to us. What we know of the higher-order systems comes to us in the form of logical postulates, of axioms, of apparently arbitrary rules, without which we can undertake no examination of the world at all. Thus, to the question, 'Why do we call white things "white"?', there is no answer. We do not know why some men formulated a particular kind of sound to refer to a particular quality, that sound ultimately being refashioned over an immense period of time to become the 'white' we know. All we can say is that, given we use the word 'white', these are the rules for its use, and without these rules, we are incapable of identifying white objects.

Thus, higher-order systems include the systems of logic, the rules for the use of which we acquire at a very early age. Lower-order systems concern rather the particular ways we use this logic, the associations we make and unmake. By and large, people are aware of the lower-order systems, for these must be constantly checked against experience lest they prove mistaken. It is the lower-order systems about which men argue, which change, which vary between social groups, between different kinds of studies, between historical periods. Of the higher-order systems, philosophers examine perhaps the tip of the iceberg, giving an account of some of the rules presupposed by our ordinary use of lower-order systems.

Why do we need such systems of concepts? They organize our experience very quickly so that we do not have to work out consciously from scratch an attitude to immediate happenings. Such organization is vital if we are to know how to act or to refrain from acting in order to survive. For Burke, in the citation at the head of this chapter, 'prejudice' covered some of these systems. Talking, writing, discussing, arguing, the experience of reading or watching drama or films or seeing paintings, are often directly the process of relocating ourselves in new systems or strengthening old ones, finding what we call 'the truth'.

Kenneth Burke describes culture as 'forms of symbolic action' (1941, p. 8). The symbols embody the meaning we, or our ancestors, attribute to events or to objects which are part of events. However, it would be wrong to see symbols as in any sense unreal reflections of a reality with which we should grapple directly, a substitute for reality, for we can know no other reality than the one which presents itself to us in terms of culture, in terms of the symbols we use to identify it. In higher-order systems reality is the symbols we use.

In lower-order systems the symbolic role is much more clearly apparent to us. A community is symbolized by its chief, a king or assembly, or by a group which is propertied or plays some specific role, holds titles and so on. Kenneth Burke suggests that a social crisis is the time when what we thought symbolized the whole community appears as a major obstacle to the community, when the symbol of unity becomes a symbol of disunity.

It has been suggested earlier that we need the systems we have in order to locate the actions we need to take to survive. Yet, once the problems of sheer physical survival have been overcome in a society – the technique of exploiting the soil, weather and seed permits a more or less large surplus above the needs of the existing community – then 'survival' comes to mean very much more complicated and varied things. What is considered 'survival' can vary between individuals, groups, classes and societies, just as what is considered to be 'poverty' can also vary very widely. Since the nature of 'survival' varies socially and historically, then all the associated concepts also vary. Thus, what particular men regard as a 'problem' or a challenge varies in relationship to what they regard as the prerequisites for survival. What the problem is, indicates what men will identify as their interests or their purposes.

As a result of the sheer diversity of possible cultural systems, each tailored in part to a unique configuration of events, natural and geographical features and history, then the diversity of possible responses by men to a given problem becomes immense. Of course, those responses do, in another sense, fit along a determinate scale, for there are in fact only a limited number of solutions to each concrete problem, and people who undertake solutions which lie outside this range either have to demonstrate a new and startling innovation which takes up and supersedes past solutions or have to be protected from the possible results of insanity. The man who quenches his thirst with poison is either demonstrating a new way of overcoming the effects of a liquid formerly classified as poison or is committing suicide (or is just mistaken).

Each new problem which arises, then, is tackled by men who are part of a long accumulated cultural tradition, a tradition which is, by and large, an unconscious possession of each one of us and not at all unambiguous in its entirety. Gramsci (1957, p. 59) describes men as 'the product of the historical process which has left you an infinity of traces gathered together without the advantage of an inventory'. We do not know – or we do not have time to explore – the cross-references, the allusions, the hints, that occur in our own speech or that of others. We employ literary critics and psychoanalysts, among others, to suggest possible meanings for these things. Thus authors are not necessarily very good guides to their own work, and literary critics are, or can be, vital commentators. It is not impossible at all that an author will not know the meaning of his work, but that a shrewd critic can tell us why we respond in the way we do.

The purpose of Gramsci's 'traces' is to supply us with an answer to a problem, and we can never predict beforehand what that problem will be. It is because we cannot predict that mankind collectively collects the answers of the past, even though it may long since have forgotten what were the questions the answers were formulated to meet. Lévi-Strauss (1966, pp. 16–36) most fruitfully develops this idea in his metaphor of the *bricoleur* (the nearest equivalents in English are 'handyman' or 'odd-job man', although these do not entirely convey the meaning). The handyman collects oddments and stores them, even though he may not know either what function the 'oddment' fulfilled in its original form nor to what use he will put it in the future.

We can witness the operation of lower-order systems, or fragments of systems, 'traces', when we meet any particular problem and are required to solve it, to – as it were – thumb through our mental card index of possible solutions. Say we get an electric shock while repairing a plug, or we find all the lights go out, then we set out to explore different hypotheses, explanations of the fault in order to direct our repair activities most fruitfully. And the hypotheses will range over many different systems, theories of mechanical breakdown, of electrical circuits, of water leakages, of temperature changes or decay. We will call both on our experience and on what we are no longer conscious of, 'traces'. Perhaps those 'traces' will provide the 'hunch', the source of which we cannot recall but which will solve the problem. We may even be reduced to the salutary kick, and we may reach very remote hypotheses, traces from a pre-electrical culture – that the spirit in the machine is injured or insulted, that we have sinned and this is a punishment. We may compare notes with other people, to expand the range of possible hypotheses by borrowing on someone else's 'traces', and they may argue with us that their hypothesis is more appropriate, trying to substitute a different system for our own. And so on; the whole process will rapidly travel over a very wide range of different systems of meaning, different assumptions about the nature of the world.

The central role of culture, then, is to present us with a diversity of partial or coherent systems with which to organize our experience, so that, by identifying objects and attributing systematic meaning to them, we shall be able to overcome the problems we face in seeking to survive. Of course, the same object may be identified in a host of different ways within different systems. The chair is only a 'chair' in a system that incorporates a wide range of specific conventions, namely those of sitting, of domestic and social behaviour. Within another system the chair can be a meaningless object because it is irrelevant to the purpose of that system, either because the people who use it have no experience of chairs and their allied conventions of use, or because the system is one – for example, the complex called nuclear physics – in which chairs as chairs have no role (although they may be useful to physicists as people). The chair can be a commodity (similar to any other commodity) in a market, or an antique at Sotheby's, or part of a set of furniture, or a work of craftsmanship (within the context of the history of furniture, of carpentry or metalwork, or of general history – part of what, say, we understand by the 'Louis XIV period', and so conjoined with modes of dress, hair-styling, literature, and even wars), part of the corpus of work of a famous artist, an example of technological development, a philosophic example, old metal to be melted down for the war effort (so that its associated objects are iron-railings, bronze monuments, and so on), or just a bundle of sticks for making a fire. The question: 'What is a chair *really*?', is a meaningless one if it asks: 'What is a chair outside of any system?' For it is the system in which the concept of a chair is involved at any given time which renders it meaningful, which classifies it with comparable items. The systems in which the concept of chair might play a role are as endless as the needs we have, or rather the needs to the satisfaction of which a chair might contribute in any form. However, the question could mean: 'What is a chair in the most general system we have available?', and then it becomes an empirical question: 'What is the general state of people's opinion about chairs at this moment of time?' At this level we can say without quibbling that, for us, a chair is an object for sitting on, even though other people in the world and in the past might see in a chair no more than a bundle of sticks, meaningless for sitting on but perhaps appropriate for lighting fires or beating enemies around the head. If objects are transferred between cultures then they can become 'meaningless' in terms of their original function – a recent cartoon portrays primitive tribal women wearing brassières as hats.

On the other hand, the word itself – rather than the object identified by the word – can operate in many different systems simultaneously. To return to the 'chair', we know its meaning quite well in a number of other systems; for example, a Chair of Philosophy, chairman of a meeting (and chairing a meeting), chairing the victorious soccer team home and, slightly removed, a seat in the House of Commons.

The examples cited here are relatively simple, since they suppose the existence of clear and specific objects symbolized by the word: chair. But a vast number of other systems do not presuppose such determinate objects and, indeed, the symbol is all we have. There is nothing we can locate as we locate a chair when we use terms like God, society, gross national product, the unconscious. Yet many of these concepts are no less essential and, indeed, with the development of modern society become very much more essential. Some of the concepts symbolize the interaction of vast collectivities of men and for this reason it would be quite wrong to put them on a par with concepts like 'chair'. The systems we employ in order to understand social existence are different in kind from those we use to understand other forms of existence. People do tend to treat all systems on the same level, so that when societies break down they experience the same sense of shock and bewilderment as they would if inanimate objects took on suddenly an unpredictable life of their own – the electric plugs really do have a spirit that needs to be placated. When government becomes as changeable as the men who constitute it, when the apparent objectivity of institutions dissolves into no more than the contradictory subjectivities of an uncoordinated mass of individual men, it is no wonder that some onlookers feel a 'sense of meaninglessness'. The stability of the social order is taken for granted no less than the stability of the natural order.

The nature of what constitutes a 'system' is obviously problematic, and it would perhaps be a just criticism to say that I am using the word to cover so many items that it becomes itself almost meaningless. I have earlier suggested that systems of logic and classification are part of higher-order systems even though, in some classifications, they are intimately related to lower-order systems and immediate experience. The problem in relationship to lower-order systems is that each system is framed at a certain level of generality in relationship to a particular range of problems, so that although one might expect to find common patterns recurring, one might be able to say little *in general* about these systems precisely because they are related to the nature of very different kinds of problem. One might be able to identify certain patterns accepted by people as subsequently embodied in a lower-order system – social relationships which people felt to exist in a fragmentary fashion in a number of different systems might subsequently, in relationship to a particular problem, be portrayed in one specific theory which attained such widespread adherence that it constituted a lower-order system within general culture. The constraints which hold a given range of variables in a certain relationship, a 'system', obviously derive in part from the objects the system is supposed to analyse, but it is also true that such systems are not static. They are constantly adjusted by new experiences. An innovation in motor technology might adjust a multitude of systems concerned with cars, road haulage, holidays, mechanics, sales representatives, and so on.

These systems are not, as will be clear, matters of individual creation. We inherit most of them when we grow up, the systems created by past generations, even though the society we live in may adjust them and even abandon them as explicit elements. 'Strictly speaking', Mannheim says (1936, p. 3), 'it is incorrect to say that the single individual thinks. Rather it is more correct to insist that he participates in thinking further what other men have thought before him ... on the one hand he finds a ready-made situation and on the other he finds in that situation pre-formed patterns of thought and conduct.' Men do not start from scratch, from a *tabula rasa*, a sort of Cultural State of Nature, but rather under circumstances transmitted from the past. Lévi-Strauss (1966, p. 95) has a rather fruitful analogy in this respect:

... man is like a player who, as he takes his place at the table, picks up cards which he has not invented, for the card-game is a datum of history and civilization. Second, each deal is the result of a contingent distribution of the cards, unknown to the players at the time. One must accept the cards which one is given, but each society, like each player, makes its interpretations in terms of several systems ... we are well aware that different players will not play the same game with the same hand even though the rules set the limits on the games that can be played with any given one.

We can thus exercise some choice and discrimination, and in relationship to some lower-order systems we can accept some and reject others, stress certain elements and ignore others. We are not trapped in a scheme of ideational determinism. The nature of our experience is certainly meaningful because of the systems we have, but it is not the system which determines the movement of the objects we experience. Certainly we have the purposes we do have because of the cultural tradition of which we are a part, but in relationship to many lower-order systems we can also reject what we inherit. Culture is not some external strait-jacket, but rather multiple suits of clothes, some of which we can and do discard because they impede our movements. This metaphor perhaps implies, wrongly, that there is a basic substratum, the individual, beneath the clothes, but in the systems what is the individual develops in relationship to the clothes. We learn what our purposes are through the systems we use, just as we learn what is required for survival through the interaction of systems and our experience in trying to do things. In one age to light a fire is an essential element in securing survival; in another it is building nuclear power stations, and quite different systems are involved in both.

Experience is not, it is implied here, in essence passive or contemplative, but shaped by what we want to achieve. It has already been suggested in the first chapter that the reverse assumption is a major element in vitiating some definitions of ideology. Obstacles to action or achievement operate to reshape our lower-order systems, to restress some elements or create others. More to the point, our success or failure in the attempt to achieve given ends can revalidate the system's 'meaning', its appropriateness for the purposes we have, or it can ratify innovations or invalidate them. It is essential for most lower-order systems that they are 'successful' in practice.

Now what 'success' is, its definition, returns us to the same series of mutually defining terms we have mentioned earlier – survival, purpose, interest and problem. In general the terms can only be seen in a specific historical context, relative to a particular man or group, for all of the terms have different immediate references in different circumstances. On the other hand, one must guard against the formulation becoming merely tauto-logical: beliefs, a particular lower-order system, disappeared because they were 'inadequate', the sole evidence for their in-adequacy being that they disappeared. Thus, if a society is destroyed by earthquake, one cannot deduce from this event in isolation that the beliefs of the members of the society were 'inadequate'.

Yet it is also difficult to locate specifically the purposes to which a given system was put, so that here again 'success' becomes problematic. Men can change the purposes to which they put particular systems, can pursue different purposes while appar-ently adhering to the same system, so that the circumstances required to validate the system also vary. Again, different sorts of belief stand in greater or less proximity to practical tests, and some lower-order systems are scarcely open to invalidation in the normal course of events. Once a system has been created, if its use becomes associated with certain established institutions, with the maintenance of the prestige, power and status of particular groups, then almost inevitably those groups will, as part of secur-ing their own power, seek to render the system invulnerable to disproof. Of course, in so far as they do this they tend to make the system less and less useful as a means of comprehension.

Practical tests must be differentiated from logical disproof, for the second is only partly relevant here. For example, because the roots of ideology lie in the existence of a social group, not an individual, critique in terms of logic may be of relatively little relevance. What destroys the ideology is the destruction or trans-formation of the group or the disappearance of the purposes to which it was originally wedded. For example, the modern decline in mass adherence to Christianity is not the result of religious scepticism, but religious scepticism is itself another symptom of the decline. The arguments which cast doubt on the validity of the Christian viewpoint are very old, much older than any modern decline in faith. Rather is the decline in faith part of a long-term change in beliefs, a shift in people's view of the means to achieve the things they think important and perhaps a change in those things themselves. The purely logical critique is relatively ineffective, for the intellectual defences of the Churches can, with time, accommodate such objections. The Christian can disentangle himself from earlier Christian positions which can be shown to be empirically doubtful, yet cling even more loyally to the central positions which cannot – God exists, Christ was his son, the first man (now more carefully defined in terms of spiritual grace) was Adam, and so on.

An analogous case in the contemporary world is the status of Marxism-Leninism in the Soviet Union. For some Western commentators favour the argument that Marxism-Leninism comes face to face with 'reality', is thus shown to be invalid, and is successively abandoned by the leaders of the Soviet Union. It is all somewhat dramatic and anguished, although few commentators say very specifically why 'reality' has been so long delayed in presenting itself (it is, after all, more than fifty years since the revolution). But the postulates of Marxism-Leninism, no more than those of Christianity, do not meet some direct logical or empirical invalidation; rather, as with all declining ideologies, the beliefs fade gently away as the originating group disappears, leaving only incoherent memories. After due lapse of time, men look back to the past and marvel at the oddities their predecessors believed without understanding at all why they believed them, and thus are unable to see why they themselves believe something different.

Of course, one must also utilize wherever possible the ordinary criteria for invalidation. If postulates can be shown clearly to be inconsistent with either logical criteria for deductive proof or with what empirical evidence is available, then there is a *prima facie* case for disbelieving the postulates involved. Yet, if other people continue to believe these postulates, one must inquire further, for it is likely that the postulates mean something other than what one thinks, or serve purposes where the truth content of the postulates is only of marginal importance. One must also see that a large number of postulates are not open to this kind of approach. Thus, the postulates of astrology continue to be accepted in some parts of the world, and to be accepted by intelligent men who are aware of Western scepticism. Astrology has disappeared in our own society not as the result of disproof – in fact, it is logically possible, though implausible, that a set of viable astrological theories could yet be worked out – but rather for reasons which are matters of detailed historical research: men turned to other things.

Ideologies

From what has preceded, then, it will be clear that it is suggested that 'ideology' be seen as one sort of lower-order system or complex of systems within general culture. Ideologies are differentiated by the feature that they provide us with organization for social experience, that is experience comprehensible only in the context of a society rather than in the context of an isolated individual or the relationship of inanimate objects. More specifically, ideologies relate to the arena of social conflict, to the purposes of groups competing for scarce resources. This is a slightly arbitrary simplification of the problems, but one necessary to say anything at all. The relationships of ideologies to other kinds of systems, to, for example, sciences, or the implications they might carry for the treatment of inanimate objects, are being deliberately left out of account.

I am indebted to Geertz for the general lines of this conception. He describes ideologies as 'most distinctively, maps of problematic social reality and matrices for the creation of collective conscience' (1964, p. 64). Thus, within society, ideologies provide a more or less coherent organization for our experience, experience and organization which are directly related to conscious action or inaction in the pursuit of continuing purposes. The most important social groups provide the stable foci around which ideologies are formulated. For new recruits to such groups, ideologies shape their experience, offer a form of coherent organization for fragmentary experience, identify objects of approval or disapproval in relationship to the dominant purposes involved, and provide an appropriate perspective. Purpose, experience, terminology, future action are all, in the most developed ideologies, coherently synthesized in one perspective. Thus ideology, strictly, does not *give* meaning to events which exist independently, it *is* the events as we perceive them, or at least, as we perceive them if we are full participants in the ideology concerned. If we are not full participants we may delay saying what we perceive until we have received an authoritative description from a source we trust. Our prior susceptibility to describing sensitive events in a particular way seals our description, our commitment, in language: 'if you size up a situation in the name of regimentation you *decree* it an essence other than if you sized it up in the name of planned economy' (Kenneth Burke, 1941, p. 7).

The nature of the group which provides the basis for the ideology – which makes it an 'ideology' rather than an individual's eccentric philosophy – arises from any of an infinite variety of influences. The existence of a problem common to a number of people (and the definition of what is a problems reveals a purpose shared by that number of people) can create a group. It has already been suggested that in modern society such groups are ultimately subordinate to certain specific structural features in society which create major classes. However, a group discovers a common purpose in seeking to overcome a common problem, and in this process of discovery it creates appropriate theoretical formulations of what it is seeking to do, why it is doing this and what differentiates it from other groups; it creates an 'ideology'. With an ideology the group can become almost a separate community, discriminating more or less sharply between members and non-members. The justification for the identification of the members may be more or less elaborately developed, but it will obviously be central to the belief-system concerned – God has chosen the group, distinguishing it from gentiles (or barbarians or foreigners or aliens or laymen or primitives or the stupid, the ignorant, the inferior, the arrogant), raising it above all others to provide an example or, perhaps, authority and leadership for all others. Now, depending on the structural features of society within which the common interest of its members is identified, the group may argue that its particular interests are its guiding framework, or that its particular interests are in the interests of all. For example, the Nazis and the Zionists both claimed to affirm the interests of particular groups – German and Jews – but other social groups may claim to affirm the interests of mankind as a whole, to be universalist; thus, industrial workers, in creating social democracy, claimed to be embodying not just the interests of industrial workers, but of all mankind (of course, enemies of social democracy did counter-attack by saying social democracy was merely a 'sectional interest', implying that they themselves were not).

But what is true of a social group may not be true of its individual members. Mannheim (1963) notes that each individual participates only in certain fragments of the group 'thought-system', the totality of which is not in the least a mere sum of these fragmentary individual experiences. Within any such group, Bendix suggests, some will be naïve, some cynical about the ideology, but the majority will just take it for granted, using it much as we all use language, without reflecting on its meaning (1956/63, p. 342, footnote). Ideology is for the group what consciousness is for the individual, and as the individual will not know the full meaning and origin of what he himself believes (it has been forgotten, not by him, for he probably never knew, but by his group or by mankind), so a group will not know the significance that we, outsiders from the group situation, might attribute to its beliefs.

Within any complex society a number of different tendencies will coexist, perhaps posed within a common terminology that derives from a dominant ideology. The discriminations which identify in-group and out-group cannot be foretold in advance and some may seem quite arbitrary. There is not, so far as I know, a society which discriminates between red-haired and non-red-haired people but one could imagine one where this was so, and one can imagine the host of correlations that might be 'discovered' between colour of hair and kinds of behaviour. A general structure of popular assumptions could grow up around the discrimination, and the social sciences might well be enlisted to verify those assumptions – one can imagine the learned textbook which asserts that 'Over a number of exhaustive tests, no association could be found between red hair and violent behaviour *per se*, but then our definition of "violent behaviour" covers only the more extreme kinds of such behaviour. It could be that, given the sensitivity of skin associated with red hair (cf. Smorg and Hausen, 1432), there is greater irritability, particularly during hot weather, which in its turn makes for a higher propensity to be moderately violent.' Other men would write novels, plays, poetry and filmscripts which, if the discrimination was at a very general level, would take for granted that hair colour was crucial. If the discrimination was at a lower level there might be thrillers that experimented with the themes of insecurity – the orphan who discovers his parents had red hair, the mysterious man who was bald or who was unmasked wearing a wig, the villain who dyed his hair, and so on. The colour of hair would be part of our 'common-sense' notions about the world and other people, and those with red hair (since this is the quite arbitrary discrimination I have selected) would probably also constitute themselves a group in opposition, a group that might come to worship the colour of its hair (if it was confident) or be systematically ashamed of it (if it was not) – God had blessed his peculiar people with hair the colour of the rising sun so that men might reflect on his goodness and, accordingly, a lock of hair should adorn each altar as its centrepiece; or a curse had fallen upon the people of red hair, such that each child should be shaved at birth, and all men should wear head covering all their lives.

Now, while one can see the logic in this arbitrary distinction, it has not, in fact, existed in this form, since to achieve powerful group identification requires a number of overlapping discriminations, each strengthening the other and at least one of which relates directly to the general structure of society and its division of labour. However, if my example seems too far-fetched, one has only to consider the role of skin colour to see how easily an arbitrary distinction can play this kind of role, and how white domination and the cult of negritude go together as matching variables (as do Zionism and anti-Semitism). In the case of skin colour, a host of discriminations coincide – between imperialism and the oppressed, the rich and the poor, the powerful and the weak, the developed and the underdeveloped; in the United States, the discrimination divides the employed, and in part, the unemployed, the educated or skilled and the uneducated or un-skilled, the inhabitants of outlying residential areas and the cen-tral slum-dwellers. Colour is thus only one small symptom of a major social cleavage.

Underlying the formation of more important groups, then, is the total organization of a society, its differentiation in terms of classes and its division of labour within the economy. One can postulate a limiting case where the group and the whole society are nearly the same, although the society must be, by definition, a relatively small and primitive one, living by means of a com-mon occupation, perhaps a relatively static subsistence agricul-ture. But even here one would expect differences of emphasis to arise between men and women, between the active and the aged and any small variation in the conditions of the community would upset its stable pattern of beliefs.

Ideologies, then, can most usefully be seen as one of many different sorts of system created to overcome a given range of problems, problems within society. In an analogous way the sciences are themselves systems generated by general culture, focused upon particular narrow areas of experience (natural phenomena) and defined to overcome a certain range of specific problems within those areas. Once created, a science can have its conclusions read back from its narrowly restricted premises to general culture, redefining important concepts in our everyday language, redirecting the non-scientist's attention in new ways and providing him with new models to analyse his experience in areas quite remote from the science itself. One can see an example of this in the term 'body', taken from ordinary usage to be incor-porated in Newtonian physics as a specialized term, and then returning to ordinary language – so that non-physicists have at least two quite separate notions of 'body' to use.

Ideologies can travel the same kind of circuit. A term can be taken from general culture for use in a specialized sense by a particular social group, and then return to general culture. The circuit conceals the actual fortunes of the group concerned, for it may begin as one among many groups, and yet end as the dominant group in society, providing the dominant ideology for society in terms of which most other groups formulate their views. Ideologies can, in this way, begin to pervade a very large area of the inherited culture, rewrite the history of their own people, society and world, and spread out into a diversity of different pursuits. How far this process can go requires empirical investigation of particular examples, but one can be sceptical of the claims of particular rulers to have transformed the entirety of culture. The life of ordinary people often remains much the same, despite the propaganda and the new terminology used to describe old practices. Often the 'new' men are just the old men writ large.

Because the social sciences deal with the same area of interest as ideologies, they have many common characteristics. However, the social sciences rarely constitute a coherent perspective since they are not based upon a single social group – rather do different social scientists embody the divergent views of divergent social groups, even though, as with the views of each major social group itself, these are usually offered as in the interests of all or the product of pure reason. This does not imply that the social sciences are pure repetition of views held by social groups. On the contrary, by narrowly specifying a given area of inquiry and intensively exploring it, the views already held can sometimes be substantiated or invalidated. But the field for the debate is already selected and refined, and, in major questions, the social sciences cannot provide new answers so much as a sifting of the old ones. It is, in principle, impossible to see how this could be otherwise.

Ideologies as such can only be seen in diversity: for there to be a 'yes' there must be a 'no'. If only one belief system is present in a society the members of that society cannot be aware of it except through some other ideology outside that society. Without this second condition then the function of the word 'ideology' lapses for the members of that society – there is only the truth or common sense. Thus, ideologies can only properly be observed if there is more than one available, even if the other is only an historical occurrence. But, as suggested earlier, it is slightly illusory in relationship to any complex society to speak of one ideology, since it is likely that what social differentiation there is, the division of labour or an arbitrary distribution of power, will be operating to stress different elements in the given orthodoxy. Orthodoxies have an elastic quality to cover very different social groups, to unite them within a common terminology, but inevitably the version of the orthodoxy held by different social groups will be different, incorporating each group's specific perspective. For the poor of Europe Christianity is and was the religion of the poor; for the rich, it is not. Every major orthodoxy, to survive, must be sufficiently ambiguous to allow this kind of multiple interpretation – it is the price of hegemony in a society which has not been changed so that it accords with one version of the ideology. If all men were rendered poor (or rich) in a Christian society, if there were equality, then one element in the necessity for multiple interpretations would be removed.

This 'plasticity' in an ideology when it is seen in general (rather than as related to a particular group where the ambiguities may be clarified in one interpretation) makes it particularly difficult to examine. It is made even more difficult by the fact that, in relation to one group, some of the ambiguities may *not* have been clarified or inconsistencies may exist, simply because the people concerned have not had to act – that range of problem has not occurred yet, so that the clarification which action needs or entails has also not occurred. Of course, there are also some people who manage to act, once at least, without working out clearly what it is they are doing and how this relates to what they believe.

Looking at ideologies from the outside it is extremely difficult to see always what elements are really operative – would in fact guide action in the event of a challenge – and what are elements merely carried along because they originally occurred in the same context as the operative element. We cannot always accurately locate at what points action might validate the system, nor do we have the opportunity always to infer from the actions of men what system is actually operative. Where large social aggregates are concerned the problems are compounded, for if the people do not act we do not necessarily know what they think. For example, given the history of Christian morality concerning the right to kill other men, would we be able to infer the history of wars, murder, the death penalty and so on which has actually happened? On the other hand, it would be equally wrong to infer from the actual history of Christians killing each other that the precept was meaningless, that it had no operative value at all.

What tends to happen in this situation is that we construct what we think an ideology is from a kind of lowest common multiple of a number of authoritative figures, a flat enumeration of what look like platitudes, unilluminating because they have no context, no speaker and no audience. We have no guide to the meaning of the statements, their meaning at different times and to different people or groups, what is implied for the audiences by the statements, the distribution of the statements in terms of priority, their multiple functions at the same point of time, the action (or inaction) or the policies suggested by the speaker or to the audience which precede or follow the statements, and the different relationships between what is said and what is in fact done. We have instead the appearance of an unchanging monolith, based upon dreary trivialities or a ritual, a functionless creed.

It is scarcely surprising that this kind of exercise often serves to do no more than illuminate the observer describing the subject who has chosen to describe it in terms which assume its incomprehensibility or irrationality, and thereby exclude rational comprehension. Some Western commentators on Marxism-Leninism are peculiarly devoted to this kind of exegesis, the condemnation with which they conclude their account is no more than the reiteration or explication of an assumption already implicit in their method. For a critical reader the observer's rationality rather than the irrationality of the observed emerges as the most emphatic element.

A more fruitful approach is to examine the work of a particular representative, even though he is necessarily only one of a group that formulates an ideology or supplies different elements, even though such people are usually of above average cultural sensitivity, of fine ideological training, more or less aware of strict canons of logic and scientific method and what it is reputable to believe out of a heterogeneous cultural tradition (or at least, reputable to say one believes). He may thus not be a representative figure in the sense that he provides an accurate guide to the detail of the beliefs held by the members of his group, he may make those beliefs 'respectable' to non-group members, make the necessarily unspecified specific (and therefore distorted), make the implicit explicit, integrate in one way what is integrated in another by his associates. Goldmann (1964, p. 104 footnote) suggests that 'An ideology never, in fact, affects more than a larger or smaller fraction of a particular class to which it corresponds, and it is often the case that this fraction is only a minority, and even a small one at that.' Bendix (1956/63, p. xii) says that:

the attitudes of individuals do not become the public opinion of a group merely by the process of addition. Instead, public opinion is formed through a constant process of formulation and reformulation by which spokesmen identified with a social group seek to articulate what they sense to be its shared understandings. A study of ideologies deals with these formulations and reformulations and hence with those attitudes which have proved strong enough to gain adherents.

Thus, the check on the statements of 'representative figures' is whether or not they carry the group concerned: 'The consent or dissent of the masses for an ideology is the means by which real criticism of the rationality or historicity of modes of thought make itself apparent' (Gramsci 1957, p. 73). Above all, one needs to understand something of the multiple motives summarized in the expression of an ideology, for although statement A by the 'representative figure' may receive the assent of the group, statement B, which the 'representative figure' feels to be naturally associated with A, may not.

Indeed, the 'representative figure' may be remarkably unrepresentative in his actual social position, and it may be necessary in part for this to be so. Perhaps only someone from outside the social group who fully identifies with its problems can make the required appraisal of its position. In an analogous way, Weber suggests, as earlier cited, that it is not major centres of culture which produce religious innovation, but rather peripheral centres. Goldmann (1964, p. 117) goes on to suggest that an ideology is first formulated by outsiders, 'a few professional politicians and, essentially, ideologists', and it is outsiders or relatively peripheral members of the group concerned who are likely to assume the leadership of the group. Thus, neither Burke nor Disraeli, the two most important formulators of the British Conservative tradition and the spokesmen for the British landed interest up to the 1850s, were themselves members of the landed interest, gentry or aristocracy.

It would be a mistake to see such figures as necessarily fraudulent; on the contrary, it is perhaps inevitable that, as Marx suggests (1845–7, p. 61), the major and most important part of the group concerned is immersed in actually doing the job, so that intellectuals from outside the most important part have to be employed to formulate the views of the group. On a rather more calculating basis, we do, after all, employ as separate personnel, public relations men who are initially, at least, 'outsiders'. However, this mundane standard should not be used to infer that great writers stand in this simple salaried role, nor should it conceal the difficulties in interpreting what a social group effectively believes, the relationship between the work of an individual and his group. Goldmann asserts unequivocally that it is the mark of great literature that it presses the disparate views of a given social group to a new level of 'coherence' or brings into simultaneous comprehension the contradictory position of a social group. Great literature poses common problems in their essential form, crystallizes matters, presents them unmuddied by extraneous elements, by the qualifications and doubts which afflict other people. He says:

... in certain exceptional individuals, the structure of certain private areas of activity, or the structure of works produced in a certain field (writing, painting, conceptual thought, faith, etc.) coincide entirely with the mental structures corresponding to one of the trans-individual subjects [groups, *N.H.*] with which it is linked.... the work does not in any way appear to this point of view as a reflection of social reality but, on the contrary, as the particularly coherent expression of its aspirations, an expression that the members of the group never attain except in circumstances that are both short-lived and exceptional. (1967, p. 904)

Of course, historically this requires different sorts of explanation in each period, for the appeal of Shakespeare to his Elizabethan audience might depend on a different range of factors to those underlying his nineteenth-century popularity.

Thus, if we accept Goldmann's method, the great writer does not merely embody the purposes of the group with which he is associated, he identifies those purposes for the group. By analogy, the audience does not merely supply the raw material for the dramatist's art, it decides what is or is not great drama, it learns about itself. In this process of learning it finds again strands and elements of its culture, 'traces', that had remained submerged or implicit, and it recreates the great themes of human history.

It is thus hardly surprising that new ideologies rework the material of the old, repeating themes that have recurred for many hundreds of years. The systems originally formulated to answer one set of problems are recaptured and restored, in, no doubt, a radically transformed way, to answer a different and new set of problems. Thus, when writers remark that the main focal points within the work of Marx correspond to focal points in Christianity (the millennium, the party as the Church, the suffering proletariat as the suffering Christ, etc.), we should not be surprised, and certainly not deflected from considering the validity of the theories concerned on their merits.

What is essential in appraising an ideology is to know the problem or series of problems it is designed to help answer: 'if Christianity had never been attacked', de Maistre observes, 'it would never have written out its dogma in order to determine it: but also dogma has never been determined by writing unless it existed previously in its natural state, which is the spoken word' (1966, p. 155). The questions answered and the way in which they are answered follow in part from the kind of attack, just as the attack itself takes part of its shape from the pre-existing nature of the orthodoxy. Thus the *status quo* in Britain has been alternatively symbolized by the monarchy, the House of Lords, the system of property distribution, etc., depending on the kind of attack launched. Kenneth Burke in discussing literary works says: 'Critical and imaginative works are answers to questions posed by the situation in which they arose. They are not merely answers, they are *strategic* answers, stylized answers' (1941, p. 3); and the 'strategies size up the situations, name their structure and outstanding ingredients, and name them in a way that contains an attitude towards them.'

Without knowing the target we cannot know how accurate was the shot which was fired at it. Despite the obviousness of this point, it is not true that the prescription is always followed – Lenin's *What is to be Done?* has been the target of numerous Western attacks, and many of them have not tried to understand what Lenin's slight pamphlet was a reply to even though this would put his remarks in a different light. It is as if one day, seeing that it was raining as I prepared to go out, I said, 'I must wear a macintosh,' and that by some mischance these words were recorded so that some future archivist exploring the mysterious sect of Macintoshists was able to assert authoritatively that 'Harris was always all his life a profound believer in the virtues of the macintosh; for example, he said at one stage "I must wear a macintosh." ' The parallel is not exact, but the point is true. Western commentators have been nearly as unscrupulous as Stalin in quoting Lenin out of context, devoid of the questions to which he was formulating an answer. The logic of debate disciplines, reshapes and, indeed, creates the positions of an ideology, even though the essence of those positions derives from a given social situation. That social situation is also crucial for understanding the ideology, for people do not at all have the same perception of events: a flat disc may appear circular from one position, but a thin strip from another.

This point is perhaps illustrated in relationship to a most interesting study, *The American Voter* (Campbell *et al.*, 1960). This seeks to examine levels of mass involvement in national Presidential elections by locating the conceptual ability of people to participate in considering national policies. The study suggests that at one extreme, at the 'bottom of society' (the least educated and, by and large, the poorest), there is fragmentary consciousness; the criteria for appraising political issues in the light of old principles is just not available to a large section of the population. Consciousness is here not a system in the sense used in this book, but an apparently undiscriminating collection of unrelated elements, perhaps sustaining logical contradictions. The point is not new, although it has not previously been examined so systematically. People often maintain unreconciled contradictions in their viewpoint, contradictions expressed in different contexts. An obvious example is in some responses to questions about racial discrimination – 'I am against coloured people in this country'; 'Jack, the man next door, is very likeable and an excellent neighbour,' and Jack is coloured. A less obvious example might be the argument, 'Russia has the H-bomb, so we must have it,' and 'More should be spent on hospitals and less on bombs.'

Of these contradictions, the first operates over two levels: national policy and immediate perception. The second perhaps also does (if the speaker's second statement is the product of a recent stay in a hospital), but may not. It is in this linkage between an opinion about national policy and immediate experience that many of the most obvious contradictions arise. For people's intellectual participation in a large number of topics thought crucial by national politicians may be exceedingly tenuous. A study of some Indian peasants just after the Sino-Indian border dispute in 1962, when the urban intelligentsia felt national unity and consciousness had never been higher and was spread throughout the whole country, suggests just how remote the idea of 'India' was to the people concerned, and perhaps was and is today to a majority of Indians (cf. Thakur *et al.*, 1963).

Converse (in Apter, 1964, p. 206) cites a number of studies to demonstrate how remote are some political ideas thought to be held by the vast majority of the people concerned. Thus, Znaniecki suggests that the vast majority of Tsarist peasants in the nineteenth century were quite unconscious of the fact that they were supposed to belong to a Russian society united by a common culture. A report of a 1934–5 survey in the Pripet marshes argues that nearly half the inhabitants, ethnically members of the White Ruthenian nationality, were unaware of that nationality. Stouffer (1955) found during the McCarthy hearings in the United States that thirty per cent of a cross-section of the United States public were unable to name a senator or Congressman investigating domestic communism. And, finally, at the height of the Berlin crisis in 1958 sixty per cent of the United States public did not know the city was encircled by hostile forces. Converse estimates that some seventy per cent of the United States electorate will not know which party controls Congress.

We might generalize from this fragmentary evidence that, in times of relative social stability, a substantial proportion of the population, even a majority, is not aware of the national political arena, and does not give even, what Edmund Burke called, 'a sort of heavy lumpish acquiescence' to government, representative or not. Rather are the State and its agencies much like the weather, something one must tolerate as part of the natural order of things, not something one can 'accept' or 'reject'. Many people feel this is a distasteful verdict, precisely because our theories of government include powerful justifications in terms of popular representation – witness the endless Talmudic disputations over whether a government has a 'mandate' for something or other.

However, the case can be pushed too far, and has an implicitly authoritarian undertone. It is only a hair's breadth removed from the argument that, since the mass of the population is too stupid or ignorant to comprehend political issues, an élite or a dictator must do it for them. Implicitly, the argument asserts an arbitrary decision on what politics is – these are the issues and permitted responses and people, since they are not interested in them, must be ignorant or stupid. But the argument can be turned round: since people are not interested in these issues, it is clear either that they really know they can do nothing about them or that these issues embody very little that is important for them. In the first case, the politicians are given more power for we trust them to decide for us; in the second, they should be deprived of power because it is clear they do not represent the majority.

It has already been suggested that action is a validating condition for delineating an ideology, and although, at any given moment of time, we can see in the passive beliefs of an individual no coherence or continuity, and large gaps, this does not mean that he will not respond to a given problem in a series of ways which, in sum, add up to an attitude which can be consistent only with one coherent ideology. There is no more sense in the question 'What is your real opinion?' than there was earlier in the question 'What is a chair really?', if the context about which the opinion is held is remote from the person asked. Where the context is remote the person feels powerless; nothing he can do can change things so that his opinion is of no importance. It is powerlessness which underpins what is called 'apathy', the knowledge that no action taken by oneself can change matters. However, interviewers still expect people to have opinions, and people themselves feel slightly ashamed if they do not have opinions about what the newspapers say is important, but the 'opinion' here is merely a decorative feature, like wearing a respectable hat or having combed hair; it is not an 'attitude'. By contrast, where important matters are concerned, then opinions denote attitudes, and attitudes are consistent – an electrician is consistent about electrical matters, as a plumber is consistent about plumbing, for these are important to the people concerned. Opinions become inconsistent about things which do not matter or cannot be affected. The role of citizenship is, for the majority, one of the least important, subject to contradictory pressures which remain unreconciled because power and the demand for action is lacking.

There are few studies of behaviour over time and in relationship to the spectrum of political experience, but only this would offer a tentative basis (tentative because someone might in the future change his mind) for saying what the political beliefs of some people were in an operative sense – that is, what they might do when faced with certain alternatives. We cannot tell by merely asking someone whether the demands of action will compel the integration of his beliefs, their reformulation, the abandonment of some and restressing of others. The definition of politics which asserts that if a man is not interested in which party controls

Congress, he is ignorant of politics, accepts one arbitrary perspective on reality, and in particular, the perspective of Congress itself, the press and universities, upper-middle-class opinion. Now upper middle classes in industrialized countries are characterized by their role in society, a role which means their consciousness tends to be of the society as a whole. The national boundaries supply important perimeters to their consciousness.

But a man who, by nature of his work and life, is bounded by the perimeter of his city or town or village will tend to possess an appropriate consciousness. What happens outside those perimeters is beyond his control and therefore often beyond his need to comprehend. This is worth saying since it is perfectly possible for someone to be very politically active, to be committed to a particular perspective, within his local environment. Daily, some workers in some factories go on strike, that is, voluntarily give up a part of their income thereby imposing considerable hardship on themselves and their families (as well as exposing themselves to immense social hostility from the press, government and employers) in order to assert some principle or position against their managers. Nor will it do to dismiss such action as 'merely economic', because often it is not related to specifically economic ends, and even if it were, this does not alter the case since national politics is also largely 'merely economic', and no less crucial for that. Yet some of those strikers will perhaps be people who do not vote – on the one hand they are prepared to take, in terms of their lives and livelihoods, major if temporary steps to assert their viewpoint; on the other they are indifferent. It would be quite wrong to say that one could classify them solely on the second characteristic. To do so would be merely to line up with one side rather than the other. Of course, one might want to say, quite rightly, that in certain major disputes the workers concerned would not be able to secure an improvement without 'going national' – railwaymen cannot do very much at a local level and need to comprehend the lines of national transport policy to wage a proper battle. But the process of education, the transition from a localized to a national consciousness, comes precisely from trying to do something: from using the system appropriate to one's immediate environment, finding it does not work, and extending it outwards to incorporate more and more remote elements, until, perhaps, one reaches the universal: 'Workers of the world, unite!'

One could perhaps plot this process in a major dispute – how sailors, for example, in the 1966 seamen's dispute, were prevailed upon by events to extend their awareness first from the particular ship they worked on to the company for which they worked; and then to the shipping industry as a whole (when they faced the shipping employers' federation) and finally, given the government's intervention in the dispute, the government itself, the arena of national politics, and Britain as a society. The process of extension can, of course, be stopped at whatever stage the dispute is settled, and the people concerned will resume the context they held formerly. The conditions of cooperative action with other groups of people has ended, so the system of analysis which rendered action possible is no longer of relevance. People act when they can hope and, being in general fairly realistic, do not normally see sufficient grounds for hoping they can act – others will not move, so that if they move on their own, disaster is inevitable. It is the groping process of education that is omitted in any once and for all classification of consciousness, the ebb and flow of people grappling with problems, failing or succeeding, going on or falling back in the continuous attempt to understand the world, to frame a perspective that will guide action consistently towards goals worth achieving. Bendix captures something of this fragmentary process in his account of a culturally much more homogeneous group, employers (a homogeneity appropriate to the role of employers and their size as a group):

Ideologies often help to create a cohesive group out of more or less diverse elements. In the case of employers, such cohesion may arise because the conflicts of interest among employers give way to an overriding unity by virtue of their common encounter with a hostile social environment. Under these conditions ideologies help to define and to advance certain core interests of the group. And this on-going definition of material interests helps to persuade and unite the members of the group in the process of defending their

interests against opposing groups. Without such continual ideological reinforcement the class consciousness of a solitary group cannot persist. (1965/63, p. 199)

It is part of the definition of a social crisis that larger numbers
of people enter the area of comprehending society as a whole,
precisely because so many things formerly taken for granted as
'common sense' are losing their meaning, are no longer capable
of offering the justifying assumptions they did. The furniture of
the mental room no longer supports the inhabitants. Much of
what was so obvious that it was never mentioned or even considered, suddenly becomes doubtful or problematic – even one's
'interests' no longer seem clear. The confusion forces men to
grapple with their reality in new ways, or even revive antique
ways as a comfort or a guide to creating order out of new anarchy,
to reach for what seems still secure and cling to it. Thus, surveys
of public opinion, if done carefully, can only tell us what a given
group of people said they believed at one moment of time in
answer to one question, not what they believed later nor what
their range of responses might be if they were presented with a
specified range of alternatives. This is necessarily so since, by and
large, people do not know beforehand what their future response
will be. And they do not know, not just because they do not have
specific and stable 'attitudes', but because they cannot know the
concrete details of the decision they will have to take, what the
alternatives will be nor what persuasive influences they might be
subject to. On a lesser level, in terms of given beliefs, people do
not know what exceptions might be available from an authoritative source, exceptions which are sufficiently strategic to transform the context of possible action. 'When the existence of the
Church is threatened', the Bishop of Verdun is reported to have
said in 1411, 'she is released from the commandments of morality'; of course, the Bishop does not say who is to decide when
the 'existence of the Church is threatened'. On a more humorous
level, it is said that on Japan Air Lines the menu for Friday
includes a note that a Papal dispensation has been gained so that
Catholics travelling on that day may eat meat.

This account has at various points touched upon the ascending order of comprehensiveness of ideologies. The greatest encompass the entirety of social life within a given society, or at least they seem to envelop it for old practices are redefined in terms of new terminology – the family mores of the nineteenth-century German middle class becomes the new 'Nazi family morality', and the Puritan code of family organization, usually advocated by middle-class people in the early phases of industrializing a predominantly peasant society, becomes the new 'communist morality' of Stalinist Russia. But in terms of the general intellectual pursuits of society, a major ideology can reorganize the dominant patterns in most areas, much as medieval Christianity seems to have provided the basis of 'common sense' and the structure for intellectual disciplines in the Middle Ages. Nineteenth-century liberalism provided, on a slightly lower level (since it was relatively brief in time, and challenged by the effects of continuous social change), an analogous pattern of beliefs – a code of politics, behaviour and ends, a theory of knowledge, comprehensive philosophy and methodology, a code of ethics and a perspective on the law, a system of economics, administration and a view of history that differed sharply from what had preceded it. It contributed the concept of the 'individual' as the primitive unit of society and the analogous 'atom' as the basic element in the cosmology. Broadly, it provided what had been necessary up to that time, a comparable model for the individual, society and the cosmology, the three levels of comprehension that needed to be integrated in a common view. Earlier suggestions about the three levels of comprehension had evolved a simple and effective duality of each, and the model can be seen in writers as diverse as Plato and Edmund Burke. Within the individual, beast (or passions) struggled with soul (or reason), in society the masses (anarchic) were ruled by the aristocracy (embodying both reason and divine order), and in the cosmology man was ruled by God. The three ends of each equation were neatly linked together for the individual's soul should govern his passions by reason and in conformity with divine will, as did the aristocracy in society and God in the universe. Even the divine world was restructured to accommodate the same model – heaven (itself a closely regulated hierarchy of status) ruled like an aristocracy, while beneath it the dreadful fumes of hell, the beastly masses, rose to frighten the virtuous; with the growth of a middle class some middle estate appeared in the cosmology, purgatory, although there was no scriptural warrant for this *via media*.

However, at the opposite end of the spectrum one can see the beginnings of ideology wherever any social group faces over a more or less extended period of time a common problem, purpose or the need for common action. The definition of a group, its creation, has already been discussed, and part and parcel of its awareness of itself as a group is the formulation of some embryonic ideology. We are all members of groups of all kinds – football clubs, gardening associations, housewives' leagues, church associations, and so on – and each does not necessarily create any general ideological form, except where it is engaged in conflict with other groups that compel it to define itself and sustain that definition. Since the division of labour creates groups bound by a common work role and a common experience, it is thus also a powerful compulsion towards the definition of these groups in ideological terms. Occupational groups likewise offer examples of embryonic ideologies.

Thus, the material of the National Union of Teachers will show us how teachers, or at least some of them, regard themselves and their role in society; or the publicity of the British Medical Association will create the aura of the mission of doctors, how vital they are, their role in the past (again, rewriting history in relationship to the contemporary perspective of doctors) and what they should do in the future; or the National Union of Farmers will portray the hard life, the selfless devotion and sacrifice of farmers, indicating how crucial they are for the survival of the rest of us. Indeed, the farmers' picture may be more fully developed than many because farmers have a greater opportunity to be autonomous, independent: in the division of labour their product can sustain life longer than that of the enmeshed complexity of interdependent industrial output. It is interdependence which constantly tends to erode efforts to refine a separate ideology. Groups are constantly 'reimmersed' in the wider culture because they cannot operate as an independent unit, because they depend on a large number of other people playing their part – teachers on administrators, on suppliers of food and clothing, on builders, on the State for their incomes, and so on. And modern farmers depend heavily on suppliers of seed, of machinery of all kinds, on chemical fertilizer, and on buyers of commodities to offload their output. Thus the first tentative steps towards refining a separate view of society relative to the purposes of a given group are checked at every stage, although these checks may be partially overcome where a major dispute activates all members of the group and creates the need for common and sustained group direction. To make an ideology sharper, to deepen its assumptions, requires the continuation of just such a major problem, and usually a threat to the existence of the group through great deprivation or sustained hostility by the rest of society. The classic examples here are religious sects or ethnic minorities (for example, the Jews), and here the basis of the group need not be a simple occupational one, but a complex identification. Where the group concerned is also isolated, then the ideology can achieve a clarity and an intensity not otherwise seen, and perhaps best exemplified in millenarian sects like the Cargo Boat Cults.

The earlier discussion took it for granted that people can believe things which do not help them to understand the world, can have 'passive' beliefs: that is, beliefs which are asserted or acknowledged but which do not lead to action or conscious inaction. These are 'traces' which are not operative. The original source or meaning has been forgotten, but, of course, sometimes men cling to the symbol for other reasons even though the simple substance has gone. When the Labour Party Conference of 1959 decided to retain in its Constitution Clause IV (committing the party to the nationalization of the means of production, distribution and exchange), there was an element of this since although the symbol was retained, no effort was devoted to making it have practical implications. Converse cites a similar example from the United States when he says that voters in his study were loyal to a party, not to its policies – 'The party and the effect towards it are more central within the political belief system of the mass public than are the policy ends that the parties are designed to pursue,' (in Apter, 1964, p. 241). The symbol has consumed the object symbolized; we love the name of our beloved but have forgotten the person named, we recite the Ten Commandments, but they in no way influence our behaviour. Gramsci cites an analogous although further advanced condition in terms of language which, he says, 'is at the same time a living thing and a museum of fossils of life and civilization'; when we use the word 'disaster' we do not indicate a belief in astrology, nor with 'by Jove!' a love of pagan gods (1957, pp. 110–11).

The traces of the past remain part of present language, just as the ruins of the past's great monuments and buildings remain part of our present landscape. However, the decay of belief systems is particularly accelerated by the association of popular beliefs and the maintenance of authority. When rulers utilize the elements of popular beliefs to justify their rule, a rule which is popularly disliked, then what we have called an inconsistency between a lower-order system and experience exists. The inconsistency may persist for a very long time, particularly if the ruler controls powerful resources of physical force, but it may also precipitate certain changes in beliefs. Thus, men may just withdraw their voluntary adherence to the original doctrines, retreating into cynicism or boredom while, when necessary, paying lip service to the letter of the doctrines. Others may cling to the terminology although the original content has gone. How many atheists thank God for survival from a crisis, silently or explicitly? The expression does not, as priests sometimes like to suggest, show a 'natural' belief in the divinity, so much as the slowness of the process whereby men supersede past 'traces'. The occurrences are in part examples of what has been called 'false consciousness', and a fuller discussion of this notion is postponed to a later chapter.

I have tried here to argue that in the examination of particular groups of beliefs we have to see them as some sort of response to a real problem, and that in doing so we cannot assume the meaning of the ideological statements for all members of the group concerned, nor can we assume irrationality – except at the cost of historical truth. If we do presume irrationality we abandon any criteria of the rational in the subject examined and presume our own rationality. The aim of the exercise degenerates into self-adulation by a rather elaborate means, or if not *self*-adulation praise for the group of which we are members. Again, ideologies have to be seen properly in context, as part of the general description of events, not as a kind of extraneous factor imposed on a reality that, somehow, does not need ideas except as decoration. If we are to see ideas in this way we must understand the purposes of the groups concerned, either in their own terms or in terms which we from our relative standpoint create; not as the actual substratum of reality, but as the expression of our perspective, also part of an idelogy, competing with other ideologies, in a given society at a given time. The posture of God, defining his reality, is too easily assumed by those who examine other people's ideas, and in doing this the texture and subtlety of beliefs are destroyed. Beliefs are men's attribution of meaning to events and, as such, must be examined as carefully as the events themselves, or else we can not understand why people responded to events in the way they did.

3

Primitive and Traditional
Mediators

There is always a mediator between *praxis* and practices, namely the conceptual scheme by the operation of which matter and form, neither with any independent existence, are realized as structures, that is, entities which are both empirical and intelligible.

LÉVI-STRAUSS, *The Savage Mind*, p. 130

ONLY a very small part of the immense variety of complex but systematic ways in which men have examined the world has been explored even now, and the systems, as systems, are imperfectly understood. Yet it would be inappropriate to continue this account without even some cursory glance at that variety, allowing that whatever can be said here can only be relatively superficial in relationship to the space available, the wealth of basic material and my own ignorance. On the other hand, generalizations that compare what fragmentary information there is tend to distort the unique character of each belief system by lifting it out of the unique conjuncture of a peculiar culture, the purposes of a given group of men and the precise nature of the problems they face. There are, however, crude guide lines, provided we retain some conception of the common nature of many problems, the common 'reality' (as suggested in the last chapter) which we postulate as the backcloth. This is an arbitrary procedure, but provided its implications are spelt out it does provide us, from our relative position, with a rough compass.

The rough compass is important here, for the purpose of this chapter is to suggest the continuity of some themes, the religious appearance of some problems which face us today in secular guise. Bendix (in Apter, 1964, p. 294) suggests that the word 'ideology' only properly applies to beliefs in the period since the seventeenth or eighteenth centuries. Before then, he argues, men's view of the world was dominated by the assumptions of an objective morality, a divine moral order, which even the most eccentric thinkers did not question. There is something to be said for this view, but it does place very great stress on one element, that element which is perhaps most different from beliefs today, and in doing so, it tends to obscure the continuity of responses, the similarities before and after the industrial and French revolutions. God can take many forms, and there are many things which God might have been in the past.

The division between the religious and the secular, so important in European history as, among other things, the conceptual demarcation line between two forms of rival power, Church and Prince, has today tended to become the division between nonsense and sense. Thus, in the ungodly age to hope for salvation, to seek seriously to achieve salvation either in this world or the next, is to be taken as foolish, and it is a condemnatory judgement to be called 'religious' on any questions except those that can be quietly shuffled away into the mausoleums of decaying churches. It should be noted that this is a conservative move to defend a certain kind of society or policy against the kinds of radical criticism that a dedicated Christian might want to make : religion can only be permitted to exist as 'a matter of private conscience', a psychological toy with which the believer may play in the solitude of his own house provided it has no implications for the world outside. Christianity is, of course, 'millenarian' and 'Messianic', much of its message is 'apocalyptic', that is, it is quite straightforwardly a prime candidate for the kinds of condemnation levelled at certain secular creeds, and sometimes quite rightly so, for such creeds have borrowed those elements from Christianity.

They are part of the formalization of hope, and it is hope, in its active rather than passively consoling guise, that rulers have always feared among the ruled. Hobsbawm notes in this connection that :

'The essence of millenarianism, the hope of a complete and radical change in the world which will be reflected in the millennium . . . is present, almost by definition, in all revolutionary movements of whatever kind, and 'millenarian' elements may therefore be discovered by the student in any of them, in so far as they have ideals.' (1959, p. 57)

Hope is the essence of all the major innovations in belief systems, hope that all is not lost and something can be done to realize those ideals which are at other times secluded from action because they are 'unrealistic', made matters of 'personal taste', private eccentricity, or isolated in obscure rituals performed privately by devotees, themselves no longer sure why they once hoped.

The Primitive

Many of the issues discussed in the last chapter reappear in considerations by anthropologists of the multiplicity of so-called primitive societies. For here, within much more narrowly circumscribed limits:

. . . natural conditions are not just passively accepted. What is more they do not exist in their own right for they are a function of the techniques and way of life of the people who define and give a meaning by developing them in a particular direction. . . . On the other hand, even when raised to that human level which alone can make them intelligible, man's relations with his natural environment remain objects of thought: man never perceives them passively; having reduced them to concepts, he compounds them in order to arrive at a system which is never determined in advance: the same situation can always be systematized in various ways. (Lévi-Strauss, 1966, pp. 95–6)

Models linking the individual, the group and the cosmology must be integrated with one or more overlapping systems for classifying mankind, the weather, flora and fauna, parts of the body, the symbols that represent families, clans, kinship units, and so on: the multiplicity of discriminations men must make in order to grapple with the world. The system of classification, the attribution of an identity (and thus a meaning within a system) to entities, is the root consideration, for it is in identification that men 'understand' or comprehend the world, that they announce they are able to pursue specific strategies to survive. Classification, the ordering of experience, is never ending, since new events constantly recur, and some events can cast doubt on the efficacy of the classificatory system – a new discrimination is required to accommodate an unexpected occurrence. For example, suppose we pursued an example favoured by philosophers: here is a cow, and hitherto it had been assumed that 'cow' was defined by, among other things, the fact that it did not eat meat; yet, we see, this cow is carnivorous; then we must reflect on a number of related questions. Is this in fact a cow? Does it correspond in every way, except its diet, with the characteristics we have hitherto associated with cows? Alternatively, are we quite sure that other cows do not eat meat? So we check all the determinate points in our assumptions until we reach the point of the decision, whether or not to revise what we have believed ('all cows are herbivorous' to 'most cows are herbivorous, except X type') or create a new species ('all cows are herbivorous remains true, and X is therefore not a cow, but a separate species').

The importance of classification is explored most illuminatingly, particularly its overlapping character in primitive symbolization, in Lévi-Strauss's *The Savage Mind*. But, of course, mere classification at a point of time is a relatively simple phenomenon. It becomes extremely complex over a long period of accumulated experience, when the original principles that guided the taxonomy have been forgotten or lost:

Mythical thought ... is imprisoned in the events and experiences which it never tires of ordering and re-ordering in its search to find them a meaning. But it also acts as a liberator by its protest against the idea that anything can be meaningless with which science at first resigned itself to a compromise. (ibid, p. 22)

At this stage, the classification of the natural and human world is the same act as designing the codes by which men will live, and the whole is an activity determined by the group. It permits relatively little scope for individual reflection which is not part of group-guided activity.

It takes a very much more complex society to permit the separation of these elements, and even then it is relatively rarely achieved. The appearance of a separate minority within the original group, a minority that most often controls both the means of power and of culture, generates the first kind of major differentiation within the belief system; and that differentiation already presupposes a more developed economic system, one which is capable of supporting the minority. The culture of that minority for the first time delineates clearly the lack of culture of the majority – as Redfield says (1954, p. 220), the precivilized hunter or villager is 'preliterate', but the peasant is 'illiterate'. The appearance of towns, foci for separate cultural development, for the first time divides the original tribal or clan cultural unit. Henceforth, the culture has to span two social structures, town and country, where the first is economically dependent on the second, and the second comes to be culturally dependent on the first. Redfield goes on:

> There is a cultural *élite*, whose ultimate basis of power is their control over the central symbolic resources of the society (religion, philosophy, art, science, and most crucially in the more complex civilizations, writing); and there is a subordinated practical hardworking peasantry, whose ultimate basis of power is their control over the central material resources of the society, its food supplies. The two become symbiotically dependent upon one another, their two variant traditions reflecting back and forth within one another as in two etched mirrors, each catching dimly the other's reflection. One cannot have a peasantry without a gentry or a gentry without a peasantry.

And the necessarily very different ethos of gentry and peasantry provides one of the themes of the culture of early traditional societies. As Cora Dubois (1949) says:

> Here was a class (the gentry) whose ethos was deeply at variance from that of the peasantry. It conceived of life in terms of hierarchy and power rather than in terms of simple communal democracy; in terms of private rather than mutual obligations; in terms of ostentation and aggrandizement rather than subsistence and communal obligations.

Geertz (1960, pp. 234–5), who cites this observation, goes on to say that as one descends the social structure in Java, so one notices that:

> Mystic practices tend to turn into curing techniques; a vague and abstract pantheism gives way to a vivid and concrete polytheism; a concern for individual religious experience is replaced by a concern for group religious reciprocality.... [The top and bottom groups] have very similar world-views and although they share many concrete items of religious belief and practice, the ethics which can be deduced from these underlying world-views and which the items are arranged to symbolize differ rather markedly.

Religion

However, differentiation between different groups sharing the same belief system (or claiming to do so) is not the sole source of changes in emphasis. Changing circumstances can achieve a similar shift in stress. For example, Weber suggests in his study of Judaism that the worship of Baal became more important in times of peace for the Israelites, the worship of Yahwe in times of war or foreign invasion. The two gods presumably co-existed, even though now, retrospectively, we identify one as the essence of orthodoxy and the other as a notorious heresy.

The major religions spanned (and span) vast and complex societies, so that the complexity of relationships can become very great. For sometimes the religion of the local group is merely a formal ritual, itself incorporating ancient practices that existed before the dominant religion appeared and which have been renamed in terms of the new dominant religion (much as the pagan festival on 25 December was reidentified within Christianity as Christmas), a system partly of magic, partly perhaps expressing or seeking to secure the tangential end of the security and stability of communal relationships. At other times, at the opposite end of the spectrum, religion comes to embody directly the real and immediate hopes and aspirations of people. It becomes a system designed to understand both this world and its relationship to other worlds of meaning.

Virtually every separate community perhaps had at one time its own peculiar rites and beliefs, and these in turn possibly reduced further to the rites of constituent clans or kinship units. The belief system corresponded at its boundaries to the actual and historical existence of the members of the group, related by direct blood ties or marriage. The content of this multiplicity of 'embryonic religions' (corresponding in part to what were described in the last chapter as 'embryonic ideologies') must also have varied very widely. Yet overall certain dominant motifs probably prevailed – from the relatively simple, perhaps monotheistic, beliefs of desert and nomadic peoples, to the luxuriant complexity of rites and interpretations within settled agricultural communities. Such belief units were both part of a wider ideational context – they shared common beliefs with, and were influenced by, innovations from the communities around them – and yet found their main source of strength in the immediate group. The examples of such religions are often dismissed in accounts as 'animism', but perhaps the religion of the ancient Greeks is a more fertile example. Hinduism perhaps embodies the major survival from this period, and its complexity, its amazing degree of localized variation, makes it relatively distinct from the other, later developed, major religions. One might also detect elements of the same forms in Shintoism, despite the fact that this group of beliefs was consciously refurbished by the Japanese State for modern secular and nationalist purposes.

The propensity to analyse the world in particular ways probably varies among different groups of people, depending upon their way of life. As a result, one group will reshape imported religious doctrines in quite new ways, and this is one reason why older beliefs are reincorporated. Islam, a religion of desert peoples and one of considerable severity, became a different sort of religion in India and Indonesia, countries of fertile and densely settled agriculture. Indeed, the doctrines that constitute Christianity also changed very radically from their Palestinian source. Consider only the relationship between its pristine monotheism and its subsequent Trinity and hierarchy of saints. Different elements within each religion made a separate appeal to each group, and to each group at different times – the Judaic elements in Christianity, Yahwe as the dark god of war shielding an Israel threatened on every hand by enemies, had an especial appeal for threatened groups. Lanternari (1965, p. 26) suggests this in a multitude of cases where people were dominated by foreign imperialism: black Davids faced white Goliaths, and black Christs rose despite the physical death imposed upon them by alien authority.

Weber (1965, p. 80) was particularly concerned with the differing propensities of different groups to grapple with their environment in different religious ways. Peasants, he suggested, were so tied to nature, so little used to rational specialization, that 'in general, the peasantry will become a carrier of religion only when it is threatened by enslavement or proletarianization', a judgement which Marx had earlier affirmed in relationship to secular political beliefs. What religious revolt might be precipitated by peasants would be where some institutionalized communal ownership was threatened, and then the response might be some form of agrarian communism. More normally, the peasant was trapped in the variations of the weather and the seasons, given to a belief in magic, animism and ritual. By contrast, those engaged in commerce, handicrafts and industry were not dependent on the seasons and natural processes, but rather on calculated returns and cooperative interdependence with others – which in part leads, Weber thought, the modern proletariat to be hostile or indifferent to the religions of the bourgeoisie, 'the sense of dependence on one's own achievements [and thus the importance of spiritual grace, N.H.] is supplanted by a consciousness of dependence on purely societal factors, economic conjunctures, and power relationships guaranteed by law' (ibid, p. 100). Early Christianity, he suggests, was essentially a religion of artisans, with an overall trend towards congregational religion, a religion of salvation and, finally, a rational system of ethics. While retaining this element for its original audience, it also became a host of other things for the imperial order which adopted it, and for the peasantry which subsequently adhered.

Because of the complexity of the world's greatest religions it does not necessarily make sense to analyse them as single entities. Of course, one can analyse the central doctrines as expressed in one or two major texts, but such an analysis scarcely throws much light on what people in a given locality believe. Here, the concrete detail may be only most remotely connected with what one interprets the text to mean. For similar reasons, comparison between the world's major religions is even more difficult, and one might find surprising similarities of content despite immense differences in form. Gramsci (1957, p. 91) pinpoints this multiple appearance of religion when he suggests that: 'Every religion, even the Catholic one (or rather, especially the Catholic one, precisely because of its efforts to remain "superficially" unitary in order not to break up into national churches and social strata) is in reality a multiplicity of religions: there is the Catholicism of the peasants, the Catholicism of the *petite bourgeoisie* and of the town workers, the Catholicism of the women and the Catholicism of the intellectuals', compounded with the flotsam of past beliefs, popular heresies and superstitions. Thus, although one may know what religion a country claims to adhere to, one may know very little about the operative beliefs involved in a particular section of the population, town occupational group or village district. Of course, this is too sweeping in relationship to industrialized countries today where as a result of the simplifying process of industrialization itself which makes us all more similar to each other, religion, now a minority pursuit, does seem to retain much greater uniformity. For example, the occupational differentiation (leading to, for Catholics, the association of particular saints with particular occupations) seems today rather more like a slightly eccentric addition to a form common to others outside the occupation than itself a peculiar version of the religion concerned. When the shaping bonds of a peasant life are released, urban industry tends to manufacture us all in the same mould, and the existence of rival cults spanning many social groups prompts our own to enforce a higher degree of unanimity between groups than might otherwise arise.

However, an important area of differentiation between major religions, which can perhaps be located rather more easily, is the internal organization of the religion at the level of the most important princes or empires, and the relationship of religious belief to the maintenance of authority. There is, on one characteristic, a sort of descending scale of association, beginning with Confucianism and ending with Buddhism. In China, it seems, there was no real religious mass orthodoxy uniting rulers and ruled. Confucianism was less a religion in the ordinary sense of the word, it was rather the ethics associated with a gentlemanly administration, designed not for the achievement of salvation or even truth, but rather 'tranquillity'. As such, the Confucian mandarins tolerated a great multiplicity of popular cults among the people without seeking to systematize the doctrines of such cults, to reconcile them with Confucianism and incorporate them. The official orthodoxy included no elements of metaphysical speculation and no ordinary person performed the high ritual acts of State – the princes and high officials alone had the prerogative of offering sober, unadorned, unecstatic and unascetic prayers on behalf of the political community. The worship of great deities was a matter of State, and the people were required to worship their own ancestors in like manner. The popular cults were merely tolerated as aberrations, the price of administrative peace. It is true, of course, that the literati, who sustained Confucianism, also produced Taoism, almost along division of labour lines for those outside the imperial civil service. Taoism tended to oppose the holding of office, it permitted withdrawal from the world and led towards mysticism : the ideal of the mystic saint replaced that of the cultivated gentleman.

Thus, in Confucianism religion became the doctrine of the Emperor but broadly excluded the mass of the population, themselves organized from the point of view of the State in clan units, each with its own system of clan deities worshipped in the ancestor cults. Necessarily, religious devotion which went beyond this formalized system had to operate without official recognition, as Taoism for the literati or popular cults, including Buddhism itself, for the mass of the population. For the State these deviations were perhaps distasteful, but no action was required except where such cults came to threaten the established order, and that,

Bendix suggests from Weber (1960, p. 150), could not be a matter of doctrine, since the official doctrine could encompass almost all conceivable variations – but of direct action – where a new cult came to embody popular aspirations against the dynasty and its servants, as Christianity did in the T'ai-p'ing rebellion (1850–64).

By contrast, Islam was a popular religion and one of great severity and simplicity, but without a centrally organized and controlled priesthood. Its relationship to authority was singularly simple since the edicts of the prince were, *ipso facto*, the will of God, and there was no provision for independent priestly interpretation that might check the prince. In some conditions the *ulama* or priestly scholars might seek to check the prince – as influence was brought to bear in Pakistan after partition – but the final scriptural authority had little to say except that subordination to the wish of the true prince (of the faith) was appropriate. Nor did this permit the tactful division of private and public duties that is characterized in Christ's 'Render unto Caesar' – religious belief was not a private world untouched by public observances.

Christianity faced immense problems as soon as it developed centralized forms, since it had simultaneously to reconcile the immense divergent pressures of an agricultural population and the wills of a number of different (and competitive) princes, from a position outside the State, or rather as a State within the State. It did so in a number of different ways, the exploration of which would take this account too far afield. Suffice it to note that the Church became at various points committed to fighting the princes, which, sometimes, led to its own expropriation; that it operated often as a kind of middle class, a buffer-state between rulers and ruled, sometimes representing the prince's will to the people, sometimes the people to the prince, and it had so to act in order to survive, for if it became solely identified with one side or the other, it was threatened with destruction.

These tensions shaped the doctrines of the Church, its political 'tact' and made some doctrines which had formerly been clear ambiguous. On the other hand, 'after-life' became singularly important as the receptacle for all that had to be denied in this life, an advantageous exit denied to subsequent authorities. Ossowski (1963, p. 188) notes that 'the ideology of the bourgeois democracies did not have at its disposal the world after death, into which the realization of the principles of social equality could be transferred without endangering the estate structure'. The tensions within Christianity grew steadily greater as commerce increasingly disorganized the inherited pattern. The strains produced breaches that were overcome by the formation of new popular mass movements, subsequently absorbed by the new mendicant orders of the Middle Ages. But later developments meant that the dominant Christian orthodoxy could no longer absorb the strains within it. The Reformation broke the unified whole, to create a diversity of religious responses, each more closely tailored to the immediate needs of different sections of the population. Indeed, the old Church was saved only by a new, much more highly disciplined and repressive organization, embodied in the Counter-Reformation and, in some parts of Europe, the Inquisition.

But even a religion like Hinduism which did not have a centralized organization and which tolerated a localized variation so great that from the outside even the notion of a common shared religion might seem doubtful, experienced major ruptures at various points – Jainism, Buddhism, the religion of the Sikhs and so on. The Brahmin advisers to the princes had little external discipline to enforce common adherence to a single position (they relied on the existing social structure). Yet under the exigencies of the caste system, they did tend to operate as a group which enforced its own peculiar view of society upon the rest of the population, while according with the principle that the *dharma* of each caste, its natural role in the world, should be performed even if it contradicted what the Brahmins saw as necessary for salvation: each group must fulfil its role, not seek all to be Brahmins, or rather, follow a Brahmin way of life. The system permitted maximum flexibility and demonstrated the power of Hinduism to absorb, digest and neutralize both divergent trends and extraneous influences. More relevantly in relationship to authority, it ensured doctrinally if not in practice the maximum stress upon performance of inherited duties. Any individual who did not perform the duties incumbent upon his caste was damned not only for this life or a relatively simple next one but for eternity – for the sinner would slide down the scale of existence to lower and lower forms of life. Whatever disabilities one might have in this life could not be the fault of other men or the environment, but were the result of sins committed in the past life. In terms of ensuring social conformity, 'faith through works' achieves its apotheosis here.

It will be clear from what has gone before that while perhaps a number of observations can be made about religion in general (and I have omitted reference to Buddhism, a major religion, and Judaism, a religion with specific peculiarities of considerable importance for European religion), ultimately only by looking at beliefs in the context of their appearance or operation, can accurate statements be made. Each of the major religions has generated divergencies at some stage, either open splits or sectarian organization within the religion like the Zen within Buddhism, or the Nicheren sect in Japan. The ease or importance of such developments depends upon the organization of the parent. Such is the organization of Hinduism, for example, that it was able to absorb Indian Buddhism (Buddhism originated in India), and alter substantially the Buddhism which flourished outside India, contributing elements of Hindu mythology to the life of the Buddha, recreating some of the pantheon of Hindu gods as Boddhisattvas (reincarnations of the Buddha) and so on. Hinduism had the same effect on other religions imported into India. For example, many Indian Christians accept and adhere to caste discriminations, or accept food prohibitions, the justification for which exists solely in Hinduism.

Capitalism

As was suggested in the second chapter, understanding beliefs involves understanding the context in which they were held, the problems facing the men who formulated the beliefs and the purposes they had in relationship to those problems. But often the paucity of historical material makes the comprehension of the changes in great religions no more than speculation, an unsubstantiated inference from the change in beliefs to some conjuncture of events that might explain it. The history of the rise of capitalism in Western Europe, conjoined with the Reformation, has provided an area for major debate in this connection, and an area where the historical material is relatively abundant.

The controversy has lasted a very long time, and it would be inappropriate for us here to enter a field already so elaborately explored. The debate, very crudely, concerns the balance of factors which precipitated industrialization, and, more specifically, the psychological features of the pursuit of private profit. Can entrepreneurial motives be taken for granted or do they also need an explanation which shows the relatively autonomous existence of motives, and, in particular, the spiritual influences involved?

A position is attributed to Marx which suggests that no separate account of motives is required. Religious changes, it is said, are seen as the results of changed economic opportunities. The counter position is attributed to Weber, in particular to his *The Protestant Ethic and the Spirit of Capitalism* (1930). Weber, it is said, argued that men's motives were relatively autonomous, and provided a separate source of drive in the development of capitalism.

The two writers themselves only imperfectly fit this dichotomy. Marx's writings contain substantiation for a number of different positions, and it is perhaps unfair to use him in a debate, the main lines of which were only formulated after his death so that he had no opportunity to clarify what might have been his reply. On the other hand, Weber explicitly rejected any attempt to provide a causal explanation, and offered a large variety of different kinds of explanation for the connection he saw between the *later* stages of industrialization (the early stages he did not seek to explain at all in *The Protestant Ethic*) and the development of Protestantism. Again, Weber shifted the emphasis of his analysis through his life's work, so that his later work stands much less clearly contrasted to that of Marx.

Marx certainly at times drew a sharp contrast between interests and beliefs, similar in stress to the contrast between 'base' and 'superstructure' (an unfortunate separation for the clarity of later Marxists), but then Weber also distinguished between what he called 'ideal interests' and 'material interests'. In fact, in the main body of both writers' work, their views often seem complementary rather than contrasting, particularly if we ignore the later interpretations of Marx by Kautsky or Plekhanov, for here the contrast with Weber is much sharper. A crudely materialist interpretation of Marx can support a debate which will fit, not altogether comfortably, along one side of the schism between the philosophic doctrines of materialism and idealism. But this does less than justice both to the work of the two writers and to the detail of historical material.

At its worst, the controversy can degenerate into a debate between a cynical view of history and an idealistic one (the 'idealism' being of the ordinary sort, not relating to the philosophic doctrine of idealism) – were entrepreneurs selfish or not? This is a slightly trivial question, and certainly not one for which there is one answer. Marx, writing from an explicitly committed viewpoint described the motives of his opponents in relationship to that commitment. Thus, an employer might well feel sincere and honest – and be in his daily life, a kindly man – while working his employees for fifteen hours per day for a subsistence wage, but his sincerity and honesty are irrelevant from the viewpoint of his employees. The 'sincerity' of a man is of little concern when he is wrong, but 'sincerity' has been used as a pretext for moderating criticism, as if only the corrupt could be properly wrong. Thus, if Stalin was sincere, then his errors are not crimes, but 'mistakes'. That Hitler sincerely believed the Jews were the root cause of all Germany's troubles should be of relatively little concern, since he was profoundly wrong, and it is his wrongness that should occupy the centre of the picture, not his degree of cynicism or sincerity.

Marx was, rightly, I think, more concerned to see what was wrong than to see whether or not those who were wrong were also sincere. Of course, it might be argued that man, as a moral being, ought to see what is right, and what is right is what everyone sees, but the truth of this rests upon our all being equal in fact as well as in principle. What may seem legitimate, indeed obvious, to the king, will not be the same for his prisoner, and only when they are equally powerful, and therefore equally powerless, can an approximation to such unanimity be envisaged.

On the other hand, Weber did at times make simplifications which although they may have helped his analysis did obscure important points. His 'ideal' portrait of Confucianism is neither that of the literati (except in terms of their wishes and daydreams) nor of the non-literati. As a picture it inhibits the examination of the complexity and counter-trends inevitably generated in any belief system held by many people over a long period, it tends to direct attention not at what happened to men, what they did and how they related the two, but rather at certain doctrinal formulations, inevitably taken out of context and therefore robbed of their specific meaning. Bendix (1966, p. 262) qualifies Weber's approach in his examination of the role of the samurai in Japanese development, but to such a degree that, while Bendix's study is sensitive and illuminating, little of what might have been Weber's substantive case is left. Weber's work was incomplete, and perhaps when he finally came to examine the impact of economic and social events upon religious beliefs the wheel would have come full circle. Perhaps 'ideal' and 'material' interests would have been reintegrated as attempts to understand the world in certain ways. Perhaps also we would have seen how the same doctrines can lead to apparently contradictory results – some Catholics entered monasteries, some became businessmen; some Moravian Protestants remained relatively remote from the world in Germany, others conformed to the logic of capitalism in the United States (Gollin, 1966).

The term 'social change' as used here hitherto is so unspecific that it could mean virtually anything, and it is true that there are no absolute conditions for the identification of such change. What is or is not 'social change' depends in part on what the people concerned see as change. However, it has been most commonly observed that the immense long drawn out process of development in Europe, beginning perhaps before the tenth century in some respects, prompted men to begin anew the attempt to understand their changing world and their position within it. The process of change included the movement from village to city (for many, from village to slum), from the relative economic independence of the peasant to the necessary interdependence of the town worker. For some people rapid social mobility was also involved, so that their perception of both their physical and their social worlds changed rapidly. Change in the social order confuses and alarms men, induces an extreme insecurity, as would arbitrary or random change in the natural order; the two are closely related, and Shakespearian drama contains many examples of characters inferring disorder of the social from the disorder of the natural world, 'unnatural portents'.

The new migrants moved from the land, from a seasonal work pattern in which great skill and fine discipline were less appropriate for the labourer than sheer hard work (punctuated with periods of idleness), to the urban work place where work was continuous and as skills increased the discipline and application required steadily intensified. All moved also from a context where perhaps the exchange of goods took place in large or small measure without the intervention of money. Choice was limited by the nature of the kind with which the labourer was paid, by the availability of goods, by the conventions of barter. But the town and the city very early had to find the means to lubricate exchanges more rapidly without having to find an owner of exactly the goods needed. The cash economy opened up new alternatives for expenditure as simultaneously the abundance of retail outlets became great. The village labourer, torn from the relationships that gave his life order and meaning and working without the pause of winter, was and is vulnerable to spending his wage on the means of oblivion (drink, drugs or gambling). Family, community, and self could pursue a course of tragic self-destruction which new religions could check by bringing the collective discipline of a new religious community to strengthen the will of the isolated individual, giving him power he otherwise lacked, hope and a perspective of salvation from the new anarchy in which he threatened to drown.

The responses at different stages in this very long process (long, at least, in European history) were immensely varied. Walzer speaks of those educated migrants to London who experienced an immense fearfulness in the face of urban life, particularly at the end of the sixteenth and beginning of the seventeenth centuries, a fearfulness that perhaps drew them to Calvinism as a code which identified what should be feared, what was the nature of evil, and the means to overcome it by strict order and control, tightly organized self-discipline.

These people felt themselves exceptionally open to the dangers about them and this must have been, in part, because they were cut off, as were the men who succumbed to chaos – beggars and vagabonds – from the old forms of order and routine. It is this sense of being cut off, alien, that is expressed in the endless descriptions of the saint as a stranger and pilgrim which are so important in Puritan writings (1961/1966, p. 56).

But if middle-class men reacted thus in one context, another middle class, much more heavily white collar and much later in time, could perhaps turn to the Nazis and their version of *Blut und Boden*, the sacred sentimentalized German village, as consolation for the anarchy of the 'bourgeois' Weimar Republic. Others, perhaps rather more sons of the lower gentry, in Tsarist Russia, became Populist, sought to rouse the peasantry to an awareness of their oppression, and most successfully organized the murder of prominent men. Yet others retreated from the world into a mystical pursuit of personal holiness or disassociation from society, or formed secret societies or revolutionary brotherhoods with elaborate ritual, structured play, to contrast with an unstructured world of work.

More generally, almost all societies dragging themselves out of a predominantly agricultural state have experienced a pervasive and romantic sense of loss about the village. The romantic reconstruction of medieval life, favoured by some European writers, expresses both nostalgia and current alienation. In the romantic writers, this mood is conjoined with a new discovery of the things

of nature and the relics of the past and perhaps a kind of pan-
theism – from Wordsworth to Young England, the themes are
reiterated. And in Rousseau personal anarchy in his life contrasts
with the idealized order of the small community guided by a
common ideology, the 'general will', what T. H. Green described
as 'impalpable congeries of hopes and fears of the people, bound
together by common interests and sympathy' and which supplanted former religious beliefs.

European post-Reformation history is studded with attempts
by ordinary people to come to terms with their own experience
in ways that would include the purposes they had once seen
clearly: the pursuit of God and virtue. The attempt was not
restricted to new city dwellers, for the influence of the cities
encompasssed the villages. E. P. Thompson (1963) has superbly
documented some of the subterranean history in this area for
England in the early nineteenth century, the spectrum covered
ranging from political radicalism to millenarian sects. He tends
to see the appearance of millenarian sects as following the failure
of political radicalism, whereas Hobsbawm's study of a number
of different rural revolts in southern Europe portrays religious
and political activity as going together. Hobsbawm characterizes
the sects, particularly in relationship to the Primitive Methodists
in England, as distinguished by their great fervour, sense of
drama and high congregational participation, features which perhaps helped to console the worshippers for the insecurity, the
drudgery and the isolation of industrial life. The sectarians were,
he says, untheological, unintellectual and emotional, for in passion and morality each man is the equal of the next. But many of
the sects tended to regard economic conditions as matters of fate
(or, at most, a test), not something which could be changed by
their own efforts. The consolation they offered, they offered only
to the few. Thus, when the Primitive Methodists became too
large to sustain a face-to-face community, they splintered into
new groups (1959, pp. 132–3).

At the opposite end of the spectrum, Cohn (1957) has outlined
some of the responses of early medieval Christians to earlier
economic change, the response, for example, of some of the

unemployed weavers in northern France and Benelux (as it now is), the nucleus of developing Europe. Others have outlined the significance of separate phases of change, spanning an immense period of time. Thus, for example, Williams (1962) documented the great variety of responses subsumed under the name of the Reformation, some of those responses repeating in religious forms many of the subsequent variations reproduced in secular political terms in modern times. The Reformation was not a single simple rupture, but rather was it the disintegration of a formerly unified faith into a multiplicity of faiths. The peculiar features of diverse communities broke the uniformity of orthodoxy.

Imperialism

In the developing countries of the world the impact of industrialization – or at least urbanization – has been further complicated by imperial rule or domination. Change has been muddled by a class structure identified in terms of colour of skin, language and culture. The religious responses have been even more diverse than those in Europe, although common problems do permit the identification of some similarities.

Often, revolts in favour of a restoration of some previous state, revolts of princes as in the Indian Mutiny, or in favour of the Manchu dynasty as in the Boxer Rebellion (in Hobsbawm's terms, a sort of archaic movement, for king and country or Church and king, against the new order that had displaced them), later merged imperceptibly into a rejection both of the pre-colonial and the colonial régimes. Within these limits, movements for the reform of the indigenous culture appeared, its degeneration being measured against Western culture. In India the Hindu renaissance and the reform sects, for example the Arya and Brahma Samaj, sought to purify a new Hinduism in accord with, indeed more perfectly expressing, the highest morality. In Java the reform of Islam became the central purpose of one group, the creation of a more severe Islam, purified of the extraneous elements of Hinduism and native beliefs. The Permai sect sought to purify popular traditional beliefs by removing Islamic accretions, and to give them new meaning, to restore and rejustify traditional curing techniques, much as in India *ayurvedic* medicine, and in China acupuncture, have been refurbished in modern terms (Geertz, 1960, p. 113).

Some groups spanned a number of areas simultaneously. Permai, for example, united its 'original' Javanese beliefs with the populist nationalism of the Indonesian Communist Party; and Gandhi devoted much of his life both to a pursuit of a purified Hindu peasant life and Indian independence. 'Uplift' of the downtrodden took many forms, from campaigns to wear village-woven cloth, eat the same diet as the peasantry, to fostering temperance among the urban workers; spiritual and physical healing were part and parcel of the same process. At the same time the area of the identified community came to be spread wider and wider to link together all the oppressed – from citizens of Bombay or villagers of the Deccan, to Indians, and finally to Asians; from villagers to Ashantis to Ghanaians to Africans; from a clan to a tribe to all Red Indians. Pan-Arabism, pan-Africanism, indeed, the 'Afro-Asian peoples' and the tri-continental Third World may have had very tenuous roots in reality, but it was and is an important tendency in relationship to a common threat (cf. Lanternari, 1955, p. 87, *passim*).

But within this area there were many other possibilities, including from our viewpoint the suicidal, what we might call 'the lemming syndrome'. In practice, this is a relatively rare phenomenon, although Lanternari (ibid) mentions a number of examples. Nor is it always clear how accurate a suicidal interpretation is, as is shown in the disputes over the meaning of the Cargo Boat Cults of Melanesia. However, in principle it may be possible for men to identify the problems which face them in terms of their inherited culture so that the problems are incapable of solution for the community as a collectivity (even though individuals may escape disaster), so that withdrawal or suicide seems the sole course of action available. The Ras Tafari of Jamaica seem to have withdrawn, to have escaped their dilemma by the 'inward pilgrimage', or to have given up practical action in favour of awaiting salvation from outside (for them, salvation at the hands of the mythical figure, the Emperor of Ethiopia). Beliefs, system-building for analysis, seem to have become irrevocably separated from possible action.

Embryonic Religions and Differentiation

Analogous to the second chapter's 'embryonic ideologies', 'embryonic religions' have already been mentioned, but it is worth examining the topic again in the light of the tensions of change which men experience. We have not so far separated the religious cleavages which occur within an established orthodoxy and those which are promoted from outside it. For the purposes of understanding major religions, however, it is important to see something of the tensions *within* them, the plasticity of belief systems that cover a multitude of divergent experiences within one code.

Thus, each major religion implicitly permitted a greater or lesser degree of differentiation within itself. As earlier suggested, differentiation in China permitted each clan or kinship unit to distinguish itself by the worship of its own peculiar ancestors. In India each caste – or rather, each sub-caste (*jati*) – supported some differentiation, most marked in the village where appropriate rituals existed. The lowest castes might perform some special subordinate role within the rituals of the upper castes, so that the division of labour within the community was repeated in ritual form, and interdependence was emphasized. Such ritual interdependence perhaps constitutes the 'reimmersion in general culture' which was mentioned in the discussion of embryonic ideologies in Chapter 2: the means whereby the 'embryonic' is prevented from becoming the full grown.

In Java no centralized or uniform system of worship encompassed all believers. Religious differentiation remained without common form. Leaving aside what was discussed above – localized or occupational or kinship differentiation – Javanese peasants tend towards a polyglot combination of traditional beliefs with Hindu and Islamic revisions; the merchants towards

Islam (the term 'merchants' is used loosely here to avoid going into Geertz's rather more careful characterization); the aristocracy towards Hinduism. But each group overlaps the other, and itself is also divided in various ways. Geertz suggests that the merchants showed at least two trends, one towards a revival of traditional beliefs (within a nationalistic framework), one towards a more highly purified Islam. Geertz suggests a possible division within what is left of the former nobleman, between the modernized Dutch-style intelligentsia, immersed in the bureaucracy and politics of the State, and those who retained something of the Hindu mystic and courtly perspective of the past (Geertz, 1964).

Finally, in Europe the Church permitted national differentiation (although seeking at various times to combat it as part of the battle against the territorial princes): occupational, town, city and village distinctions (and distinction by urban districts). The multitude of patron saints, descending to us in the form of crests, shields, flags and other symbols (a custom the large business corporations have also adopted), indicates the wide variety of this differentiation.

This 'internal tailoring' of the religious forms to the actual contours of the society was vital to preserve unity. Perhaps the term 'embryonic ideologies' (or religions) is misleading, for such beliefs are, of their nature, incapable of becoming general ideologies. The limits of the audience are fixed by occupation, residence or ethnic criteria, and there is no possibility of an evangelical movement outwards to convince outsiders to join. This both limits the nature of the beliefs, and makes intense the nature of the community concerned, but it can also affect the wider ideology in some circumstances. The beliefs of the warrior can be transposed to the entire society in time of war; and with mass mobilization, all receive entry to the microcosm. Furthermore, identification along ethnic or kinship lines includes many unpleasant attributes that become disastrous when transferred to the level of a society. Racialism, and commensurately, the idea of racial hygiene to preserve the purity (or potency) of the blood group, the 'familial charisma' as Weber calls it in relationship to the kinship group (cited Bendix, 1960, footnote p. 162), can become identified with the nation-State.

Another kind of differentiation, rather more sporadic, lies in the identification of enemies (internal and external), the threat to the group and the means whereby the solidarity of the group can be more sharply portrayed. In evangelical movements in the early phases of a religion, it is often the breaking down of barriers which is remarkable – as both Buddhism and Islam initially sought to break down the caste differences in India, as Christianity first broke down the distinction between Jew and Gentile, and as Judaism unified disparate kinship groups and tribes to form Israel. But within a stable religion, when people are subject to increasing hazards of a kind not previously encountered, then some individuals within the group can be identified as the source of all evil, whether they are witches (Walzer notes that witchcraft developed suddenly and more extensively in south-east England at the same time as London grew and many new migrants turned to Calvinism), Jews or, outside the group, other nation-States. In a rapidly changing social structure the fantasy search for scapegoats provides focus for anxiety and the frustrations arising out of the insecurity of changes. A state of high nervous tension means that the audience is relatively easily directed at certain targets – Calcutta Hindus turn on Muslims as Lahore Muslims criticize the Indian government; Indonesian Muslims slaughter communists and quite innocent Chinese traders; Jews turn on Arabs and Arabs on Jews; Pekin youth on any who seem to slight the national name, and all on the legacies of European and now American domination.

'Such anxiety and aggression', Geertz suggests (1960, p. 365), 'arise not only out of realistic social fears, of which there are enough, but also out of the psychologically wearing process of rapid social change.' The scapegoat proper is the community's sacrificial object, whose sins must be read back into history of the portents of fate or ethnic origin, and his role is to seal the solidarity of the community, to safeguard the leadership against challenges that might otherwise become directed against it. The criminal in similar manner is an agent to cleanse society, to expunge evil and more brilliantly illuminate the virtue of the good. The villain has no role but to create the hero just as heresy's function, provided the authorities do not permit it to 'get out of hand', illuminates the truth of orthodoxy. But this interpretation offers only one gloss – everything, even opposition, favours the powers that be. One can also see that the Indonesian Chinese traders do represent something inimical to the Indonesian peasant – they buy cheap and sell dear, lend at high rates of interest at the end of the slack season when the peasant has no alternative but to borrow, and they foreclose when the harvest is poor. Thus, the 'scapegoat' can be very much more than merely a symbolic figure; he can also be a real threat.

The ambiguity of the status of the criminal in a peasant society – like the ambiguous status of the policeman in almost all societies – indicates a similar situation. The criminal can symbolize the evil which more sharply illumines the non-criminal's virtue, but he can also symbolize the hero who has escaped from the drudgery of ordinary existence. The policeman may symbolize the security of 'law and order' or the racket which threatens not merely the criminal himself, but also the peasant. For those not brave enough to be criminal themselves, sheltering him and refusing information to the police about him is one small gesture of defiance. Hobsbawm (1959, p. 16) sees 'social banditry' as one part of the defiance expressed by 'pre-political people', those who have not found or are just finding language to express their aspirations. Through the spectrum of the blood-vengeance brigand of Corsica, the man who fights with and for his kin against common enemies of members of his kin, to the classical Robin Hood hero, the peasants are in fragmentary revolt against the landlords and their agents, the police. Such protest, Hobsbawm says, is strong in so far as there are not other, overtly political, movements of protest. When such overt movements begin, the bandit may become a political militant or merely a parasite. If he becomes a militant, his banditry can be transformed into guerrilla warfare as happened in inter-war China and modern Latin America.

Popular Heresy

We have already noted in passing the differentiation within an orthodoxy between the rich and poor, the ambivalent nature of doctrines as a result, and the generation of new movements within the orthodoxy to supply what had been robbed from the original. Ossowski (1963, p. 190) makes an interesting comparison in this respect between the evolution of Christianity and Marxism-Leninism:

After the words and practices that had served the revolutionary movement had been accepted, they were given a different content or their application was restricted to situations without relevance for everyday life. The sharing of bread and wine continued to bear the name 'communion' when it was transferred into a sacrament given at the altar. On Maundy Thursday, the Bishop continued to carry out the ritual of washing beggars' feet, but this action did not involve any risk of lessening the gap which divided him from them nor help to make the relations between the Church dignitaries and the Christian population more democratic. Again, every worker who had the opportunity of making a direct approach to Stalin was able to address him as 'comrade', while a charwoman or porter would be called 'porter' by those who had unlimited bank-accounts, could shop at special stores and had access to special social services for themselves and their children.

It was suggested in the last chapter that the association of a doctrine with the maintenance of authority tends to rob the doctrine of its original meaning. In religious terms the identification of a doctrine of salvation with an authority which permits little or no actual salvation, emasculates the doctrine, and prompts popular attempts to formulate the essence of the doctrine in a new form. Something of the popular reaction to deprivation of this kind is known, but the continued response has few historical records. When responses become explicitly heretical or defiant, even then only fragments of evidence survive the passage of time, usually contained in the reply of authority rather than the original challenge. 'Our map of [archaic movements]', Hobsbawm says, 'even in Western Europe, is as uncharted as that of the world in the period before proper cartography' (1959, p. 9). But the physical world before cartography was much the same as after, whereas the records of heresy and revolt have been lost or destroyed by authority, lest the self-created image of a universal orthodoxy and a happily supported authority be spoilt.

However, some of the common characteristics of the known movements do emerge, although how general they are – how much European experience within the Christian tradition is peculiar – is less clear. A revival of popular hope is the most important feature, a hope which is shared and thus itself becomes encouraged. One of the commonest forms for this hope in the Christian tradition is a belief in the real possibility of a redeemer, a Messiah, who will uplift the downtrodden. Such trends must be distinguished, however, from the whole development of the liberal ethic of 'self-help': man displaces his substitute, Christ, as intermediary between existence and truth, and simultaneously dispenses with all mediating elements – in Luther's heroic formulation, 'All Christians are priests,' and, we might add, 'are Christs'. But this is a much later more radical turn. More commonly, self-dependence has not replaced dependence on some outside force. 'The lower the social class,' Weber argues (1965, p. 102), 'the more radical are the forms assumed by the need for a saviour, once this need has emerged.' One individual comes to represent or, hypothetically, symbolize the oppressed community, and in his life or the legends woven about that life the experience of the oppression of all is retold in symbolic form. Sometimes the individual is a new prophet who has assumed magical powers of invulnerability or resurrection through his acquired relationship to God or the source of magical powers – he can resist the weapons of men or survive death. In his words and teachings he enunciates a new lower-order system to unite the oppressed and embody collective hope. The hope cannot be permitted to die once awakened, and so the hero also never dies; he only lies sleeping, awaiting the call to return and save his people. The theme repeats itself all over the world in different contexts – from Drake in Plymouth, Oleksa Dovbush or Jesse James (Hobsbawm, 1959, p. 25), Subhas Chandra Bose, still awaited by his own political group in Bengal, to, perhaps today, the elusive Che Guevara. The hero brought the message of salvation, the word, 'what had hitherto been a hidden, hopeless aspiration seemed capable of realization because the peasants had had a revelation, brought to them by good and noble men' (Hobsbawm, ibid., p. 99). What formerly had been a private or family tragedy, a problem isolated in silent misery, suddenly becomes the condition of the people, and the saviour is worshipped because he brings into the light what was hidden, enunciates a new system that reveals as common to all what had been formerly only private. In the commonality of the problem lies hope, for the strength of the collective can overcome the private problem not soluble in isolation.

The simple response can generate not merely worship of the symbol of communal coordination, it can also produce worship as a substitute for doing anything – let the hero alone solve the problems of all, even though he can only act with the community's strength behind him. It is the Judaic and Puritan stress on the necessity of the individual's own action – 'It is for action that God maintaineth us and our activities: work is the moral as well as the natural end of power. . . . It is action that God is most served and honoured by' (Richard Baxter, cited Bendix, 1960, p. 82) – that makes it possible for some to dispense with a saviour as vehicle for salvation, as a projected image of the suffering unacknowledged by all.

Second, reform or revolutionary movements within major orthodoxies have tended to re-examine the *content* of beliefs and reject a stress upon the form. It is not adherence to convention, it is argued, but the meaning of doctrines which is important. Thus Paul enunciating the new Christian radicalism reproached Peter for excluding Gentiles when he ate with Jews – 'Man is not justified by the works of the law [such as those pertaining to foods and circumcision] but by the faith of Jesus Christ. . . . For if righteousness come by the law, then Christ is dead in vain' (cited Bendix, 1960, footnote p. 97). The detail and the essence, the ritual and the meaning, institutions and policies, must be separated, for the second is essence and the first merely the immediate form. In the same manner, the Buddha is said to have argued that it is not birth (and more specifically, birth as a Brahmin) but right conduct which makes a man a true Brahmin. Puritans in Europe maintained that it was not priests or bishops or a Church which ensured the path to salvation, but right reading of the scriptures by the believer. Christ himself, following earlier Judaic prophets, downgraded the forms (and those people who stressed the importance of the forms, the Pharisees) and raised the importance of the meaning of content.

The association with established authority perhaps means that every major religion tends over time to lose its essential meaning in a welter of ritual, of complex detail and forms, so that the religion can no longer supply the requisite guides to under-standing, can no longer serve as a system for comprehending the world. It becomes a kind of pageant, a show, a decoration of events, while criteria of what is to be right and wrong are directly determined by authority itself (which then rephrases its edicts in terms of the religion) instead of emerging organically from the meaning of the doctrines held. At this final stage of atrophy (which can last for a very long period of time), new problems precipitate new attempts to grapple with reality, drive reformers to try and reawaken the meaning of religion in the process of reawakening popular hope. Where religious individuals have negatively defended their beliefs against the atrophy of authority's manipulation of the religion, by withdrawing into a 'private sphere', the 'inward pilgrimage', reformers are concerned less with awakening merely the isolated meaning of the doctrines, but rather with once again revealing its public and collective promise of hope.

Syncretism

Where a group of beliefs, originally formulated to fit the needs and problems of one community, are transferred to another community, the ambivalence of the word permits not only diverse interpretations but also 'syncretism', that is the conjoining of disparate elements from different groups of beliefs without the logic of each source being permitted to work itself out in the form the original group conceived. Old beliefs and new are conjoined into something, the meaning of which is probably quite different and which does not necessarily entail the contradictions one would suppose from outside. Modern political movements have produced a host of such conjunctures – Burmese Buddhist Marxism, the Cambodian Buddhist socialism within a national framework, and so on. At a different level, Westernized intellectuals, atheists and socialists by explicit profession continue sometimes to sustain contradictory practices – taking a dip in the Ganges just to be on the safe side, or consulting astrologers on an auspicious size for the Cabinet or day for its assembly. In purely religious terms, we have noted Geertz's description of the Javanese combination of indigenous beliefs, Hinduism and Islam; of Islam before the reform movements, he says that its sense for the external conditions of life had already been blunted and introverted by Hinduism during its transition across India, and it was not reinvigorated by direct contact with its original source in Mecca or its following in Cairo so that, in Java, it 'vegetated, another meandering tropical growth on an already overcrowded religious landscape. Buddhist mystical practice got Arabic names, Hindu Radjas suffered a change of title to become Moslem Sultans, and the common people called some of their wood spirits jinns; but little else changed' (1960, p. 125). The belief system in its original form did not 'bite', did not directly locate the same sources of support as those that had originally inspired it, or if it did momentarily, people forgot and reverted to original practices, much as, it is said, Hindus on the Indian side of the Indo-Pakistan border celebrate Muslim festivals, and Muslims over the border commemorate Hindu ones. Hobsbawm cites a more activist form of syncretism where, despite surface incompatibilities, common feelings are expressed – the Pianesi in Italy prize their Albanian origin (against the surrounding Italians), their Greek orthodox faith (against the Roman Church) and the Italian Communist Party (against the landlords and the State). There is almost a division of labour between doctrines, each functioning to answer a specific need for understanding in a particular area, each constituting a separate (indeed, for the outsider, an inconsistent) system to cope with one area of problems. Even in some Western European intellectual circles some apparently insurmountable intellectual barriers dissolve to make possible Zen Buddhist existentialists, Christian socialists and Marxist Catholics, indicating that the active conscience uses any material at hand to construct an appropriate and accurate comprehension when peculiar purpose meets unique problems.

Given the diversity of situations and the differences in immediate cultural inheritances (as well as the different degrees to which men are capable of dispensing with parts of their inheritance), it is impossible to predict with much assurance how people will react to change, who will fight in what ways and who will withdraw. There are common problems and limited ranges of solutions, but the ambivalence crystallized in the formal postulates of every major belief system, the contradictory precedents in the history of each system, means that knowing a man's religion is not much guide as to likely responses. The generalizations presented here must be regarded as very qualified and tentative hypotheses, offered only to suggest some of the continuities in men's attempts to understand their world. Underlying the religious vision and the secular perspective is a common struggle for comprehension, without which control of the natural environment is no more than an accident, and the survival of men jeopardized.

4

Conservatism and the West

Tranquillity is the first duty of the citizen.

THE three chapters which follow seek to look much more closely at particular complexes of beliefs, each concentrating on one particular country but using this discussion to suggest similarities and contrasts in political thought. Implicitly, a number of traditional categories are abandoned in order to pursue the theme – in particular, the division between West and East, between capitalism and 'socialism', is ignored in order to compare the beliefs of British Conservatives (the heart of this chapter) and Marxist-Leninists in contemporary Russia. At various points, the evolution of British Conservative thought is used as a means to compare ideas in other Western capitalist countries in the hope that the British example is not so peculiar that it will not stand provisionally for them all. The discussion of Russian Marxist-Leninism concentrates appropriately on formal issues, whereas consideration of British Conservatism, where formal theorization is almost completely absent, is inferred from the statements and actions of British Conservatives. Marxist-Leninism in Russia provides an excellent foil, since it is a group of beliefs which began as the medium for revolutionaries and ended as the medium for conservatives. The revolutionary phase contrasts sharply with British Conservatism's history, but the Russian conservative phase shows interesting parallels with the British. We might almost be able to locate characteristic forms of conservative thought emerging from the radical husk. These two chapters are followed by a discussion of what happened to Marxism when it moved eastwards to the developing countries and, in particular, to China. Again, the features of a specific society are expressed through an international medium, with dramatic results. As the

98　　　　　　　　　BELIEFS IN SOCIETY

discussion of British Conservatism provides the main means of looking at Western capitalism, so the discussion of Chinese Marxism provides an entry point to political beliefs in the developing countries as a whole (or, at least, in those parts of Asia with which the author is familiar).

An important weakness in the discussion which follows is that there is little or no account of the heresies to which the orthodoxy was a reply. The heresies have to be taken for granted (inevitably, some are cited along the way), or these chapters would have to be expanded into whole volumes recounting the histories of the respective societies in the period concerned. It is hoped, however, that the account will not prompt any of the inferences criticized in earlier chapters, such as that the orthodoxy comes to mean the beliefs of all or a majority of the citizens in the countries concerned.

British Conservatism provides one kind of continuum of ideas spanning the major structural transition of all Western capitalist societies. The two transitions of particular importance here are the main one, from a predominantly agrarian rural society to a predominantly industrial urban society, and the minor one, from an entrepreneurial industrial society to a managerial or bureaucratic industrial society. The methods by which some Conservatives overcame the hazards of the first transition both set the characteristic mode of future Conservative behaviour and provided a preview of certain important Right-wing attitudes in the future. All the comparisons have not been drawn here, but, it is hoped, a sufficient number have been sugggested to substantiate the contention that common problems promote similar ideological solutions, even when those solutions seem to be expressed in the peculiar cultural inheritance of one nation-State.

British Conservatism

Both major British political parties (Whig and Tory, Liberal and Conservative, Labour and Conservative) have, with marginal exceptions, presented very similar statements of policy, similar programmes and broadly similar policies in office. If ideology were no more than a summation of policies executed or proposed, then it would be reasonable to say that Britain has been governed for much of its modern history by one ideological party, and that the Conservatives, as one of the two factions in that one party, have no peculiar ideology of their own. However, although the policies may be the same, the sociological contexts from which they derive are different, and it is the context which is dominated by a different ideological ethos, even if that ethos is at times more of a separate emphasis than a separate belief system.

Even with this, however, the ethos of the Conservatives is never very clear, for as a political agency, their historical role has been to represent the differing views of various groups commanding British society. Diverse interests have had to be unified in a common perspective, so that the party has always had a greater interest in blurring internal distinctions than clarifying them. Compromise and harmony are more important than logical clarity, since clarity engenders conflict. Thus, the Conservatives do not have an ideology which can be said to be separate historically from opinion among the more important segments of the British ruling class – Conservative ideology is British public ideology, its precise nature depending on which groups are dominant in British society at any given time and what is the nature of the radical attack upon the British *status quo*. If there is no radical attack, or if it is so marginal as not seriously to impinge on public politics, then Conservative ideology becomes 'common sense', embodying relatively few general propositions of any kind. Conservatives themselves can achieve a 'non-political' situation where administration of a *status quo* that is taken for granted is all, and controversy over the nature of the *status quo* is eliminated. In this context, important questions can be 'taken out of politics', that is, no longer seriously debated from different perspectives.

Conservative history is a microcosm of British public history as seen from the position of the ruler. The party presents a screen on which the images of different groups involved in conflict and periodically reigning supreme are portrayed in idealized terms; where the victor, since he commands the party, is always right;

where the dominant interests of each historical phase receive their political embodiment, decide the attributes of statesmanship, but also make their peace with the dominant interests of the preceding phase so that there shall be historical continuity, so that no terrible abyss will be publicly exhibited and thereby render relative the absolute claims to authority of the dominant group.

But in the phases after the battle, when one major group commands both the party and thereby British society, the ethics of the preceding dominant group tend to reassert themselves, and provide the same contrasts to new challenges of rising groups within the party as those presented when the dominant group itself began its ascent to power. The new groups rising within the party revive old themes: there is a greater possibility of progress within the existing *status quo* than is being realized by the 'oligarchy' at present in power; open competition for power in the party must be permitted – democracy and reward for merit must supersede birth as criteria for office. In matching form, the defenders of power reassert that more progress is impossible without sacrificing other priorities; open competition is unnecessary for all who have the ability may achieve office, and is undesirable, since it upsets the fragile equilibrium of a coalition party and exhibits disunity publicly to the mass of the population which needs firm guidance and unified leadership, not confusing, conflicting perspectives.

The themes of the rising groups occur in the speeches and writings of some great Conservative leaders – the young Disraeli, Lord Randolph Churchill, Joseph Chamberlain, the young Harold Macmillan – and have been summarized, since Churchill, in the phrase 'Tory democracy'. It is inevitable in a society in a state of almost continuous change that this picture of flux should emerge, for the survival of any organization of this kind through an extensive period of history is only possible if it successively embodies the different perspectives of groups thrown up by that process of change. It also follows that inconsistent or contradictory elements may co-exist in the ideology – the ethics of the past and the present.

However, this process of change can be seen as one dominated overall by two or three major transitions – the first, which created the Conservative Party, from an agricultural society and a Tory Party of the landed interest, the gentry or squirearchy, from agricultural protection to industrial free trade and competition; the second, when British manufacturing interests themselves, no longer supported by British manufacturing supremacy in the world, began to move towards economic autarchy, to protection and imperialism; the third, when the largest, now bureaucratized, firms moved towards planning and State control. In terms of general ethics the transitions span three separate phases: the world of the landed interest, of the Victorian entrepreneur, and of the modern managerial captain of industry. Each presented a different view of the ideal character, the nature of society, the future and past of Britain, but each was partially absorbed in what followed, so that what may be clear conceptually is blurred historically. If we put the conflict in terms of societies we might say the traditionalistic agrarian order was replaced by private capitalism which was in its turn superseded by managerial State capitalism, but such a formulation tends to conceal important distinctions, particularly those hidden in the phrase, 'traditionalistic, agrarian order'.

In terms of the earlier discussion the process can be seen as that in which a particular social group, formulating its perspective in an embryonic ideology, assumes a national and general social significance, assumes an ideology proper, or, in Gramsci's terms, an hegemonic ideology. The ethics of each social group can be detected. For the squire the land *was* the nation, and ownership of the land was the most important single qualification for the leadership of society. For the entrepreneur, his leadership depended not upon land, but upon his ability to secure an increase from limited resources, upon his constant drive to minimize costs and maximize output, on his 'flair', his 'risk-taking', his 'enterprise' (a term which was adopted as his slogan), all of which presupposed conditions in the economy such that he could exercise choice. For the managerial businessman, his claim to authority rests upon his claimed expertise, training, education and experience (so that seniority is important), attributes which presuppose not a jungle in which the pioneer can cut out a clearing for himself, but settled and established institutions, hierarchies with niches to accommodate the talents of the organization man. In all three schemes the attributes of the ideal person change – from a stress on culture and leisure, on wisdom acquired in meditative communion with the soil; to the person capable of surviving in conditions of rapid social change, the autonomous individual who is his own guide, needs no external authorities to shape his actions, and can, out of anarchy, win triumph, thereby fostering a system which produced expansion and progress; to the person whose status is explicit defined (even so far as to the quality of the carpet in his office) within a given hierarchy, status granted by reason of the incumbent's seniority and bearing clearly defined responsibilities. When the social groups that provided the basis for the first two perspectives came under threat and declined, then periods of confusion for Conservatives followed in which they lost the security and the certainties that had formerly been the parameters for their behaviour.

To illustrate these themes at all properly would require immense detail, and would repeat work I have done elsewhere (1963), but a number of examples are necessary. One difficulty lies in the repetition of the same terminology, or the implied identification of two different words separated by a long period of time, which blurs the distinctions which need to be made. This blurring is necessary to sustain the idea that the Conservatives have one continuous tradition, one truth consistently applied to a changing reality. For example, the 'State' in Burke's writings meant, at its most important, society in its moral guise, since both government and society were rightly headed by the landed aristocracy and no serious conflict between the two could be envisaged. But with the development of the Liberal notion of the 'individual', contrasted with the State as an external and alien agency, and the absorption of both Liberal ideas and formerly Liberal businessmen, Conservatism abandoned the mystical connotations of the term 'State'; it became merely administration.

However, in our own times the 'individual' has become increasingly less important with the rise of large corporative organizations and the immense coordinating and directing role of the modern State, so that the Liberal sense of mere administration of minimum and essentially less important activities has declined – the Burkeian State becomes once more a conceptual possibility, although in a now completely transformed sense. Some Conservatives would seek to say that the Conservative notion of 'State' was thus continuous, ignoring both the Liberal interlude when Conservatives strongly opposed the extension of the State, against Labour pressures for such extensions, and the different sense of the current usage, the different presuppositions involved. Similarly, one might object to the arguments of some Conservatives who have sought to identify in modern collectivism Burkeian organicism, or in Burke's view of the ruling order (the aristocracy) an atemporal commitment to 'leadership' as understood in modern terms; omitting to note what Burke took for granted, that that order was a corporate unity, not a collection of talented individuals, that entry to it was, by and large, by birth not merit, that it was rooted in the major industry, agriculture, in a society that did not make specific provision for continuous, let alone major, social change, where urban industry and all that it entails was only a marginal factor in society, and so on. The meaning of Burke's terms derives from the context in which the language was used, and only a profoundly unhistorical view or opportunistic need could take his terminology as meaning whatever we today can make it mean in our terms.

Most of what has become Conservatism – the shadowy fragments of competition (plus State control), free enterprise (plus nationalized industries), self-help (plus welfare provisions), imperialism (plus decolonization), individualism (plus collectivism), along with the assumed primacy of urban industry over agriculture, and a progress ethic – has been acquired since Burke's times, and is profoundly inimical to his perspective. But the acquisitions do not follow from the unfolding of a continuous viewpoint in relationship to particular events; rather are they short-term responses to specific challenges, and without the challenges there would be little that could be stated generally as 'the Conservative tradition'.

The first major challenge to what became the Conservative Party, the Tory Party, came from the new group of middle-class entrepreneurs that secured the 1832 reform of the Commons and ultimately transformed the Whigs into the Liberal Party. The response of the Tories was to dig in and seek to resist the encroachments upon their prerogatives, but without success. The Parliamentary Tories were in disarray, some, led by Peel, seeking to make their peace with the 'middle class', indeed, to help it forward, some sustaining opposition. Non-Parliamentary Tories were in even greater disarray, such that some campaigned for a restoration of the old society, were explicity counter-revolutionary, and provided one of the contributory strands for Chartism. The intellectuals ranged from wistful medievalists, nostalgic for what were romanticized as the virtues of the past, to those who wholeheartedly set out to discover how the order of the old society could be recreated in the disorder of the new. The pivotal force in the old society was identified as the aristocracy (as in Burke), the corporate embodiment of reason, divine order, a knowledge of Christian duty and charity, and thus the problem became how to refurbish the old aristocracy or find it allies to oppose change (the union of the cottage and the castle against the bourgeoisie was one favourite), or how to find a new aristocracy, whether a National Clerisy as in Coleridge, the Hero as in Carlyle, or Disraeli's 'natural aristocracy'. Disraeli in his writings reflected almost all the tendencies without excessive discrimination – a restoration of the medieval myth pervaded Young England, the group of mainly youthful aristocrats with whom he spent some time as a young politician, but he also saw other, less clearly delineated aristocracies – the rare decent employer, the Jewish mystic and so on. He both stressed the old Tory case that most misfortune was by and large the result of individual error, weakness or vice – a case, as earlier suggested, characteristic of entrenched groups since it preserves the *status quo* unchallenged, all strains being born by the solitary individual – and, its radical reply, that the condition of England was so bad, the structure so deformed, that individuals could no longer be held responsible for the misfortunes they suffered.

The ambiguity was solved for Disraeli during his life. Just as he ceased to be an outsider seeking power (he became Prime Minister), so the 'natural aristocracy' broke its links with the landed interest and became those who in fact held social power, a union of some of the landed interest and the new group of businessmen. The condition of England was not transformed, but the two nations became one by characteristic verbal sleight of hand, for the two nations had been rich and poor, but they became Land and the Millocracy. If the first two remained ununited, the second attained comfortable enough marital status, particularly with the Limited Liability Act (1862), which permitted liquefied assets formerly held in land to be converted into industrial investment without industrial duties.

But the transition left a gap, for the squirearchy had justified its rule by its proximity to the soil, by its embodiment of the true nation, something industry could not do alone, nor in alliance with Land. Disraeli performed a signal service for Conservatism by offering an alternative justification and an alternative that was not so closely tied to the interests of one social group that it could not do equal service in the future when yet new social groups arose within the party. Leadership, he said, depended not upon proximity to the land or membership of some corporate group, but rather upon the magnetic personality of particular individuals, a magnetism expressed in their ability to manipulate the national symbols in order to evoke loyalty and obedience from the population. Put crudely, charisma plus propaganda would ensure that the Conservative Party remained the embodiment of the nation and also a popular party. Thus, after having championed the Tories in their last-ditch stand to prevent the erosion of the landed interest by the repeal of the Corn Laws (1846) that protected British agriculture, Disraeli was able to slip out from Toryism into a refurbished Conservatism, made attractive to businessmen. Later in the century and with the development of competition abroad more businessmen were prompted to turn against the Liberal advocacy of free trade and competition and to the Conservatives. The specific lines of Disraeli's 'National Idea' remained blurred, and, judging from his acts when in power, meant little more than a colourful nationalism (spilling over into theatrical imperialism) with elements of domestic social reform. The institutions that formerly had embodied the severity of the *status quo*, the Monarchy and Houses of Parliament, became now the props for a stage show, the colourful decorative elements to play pageant, the circus that must amuse and so carry the loyalty of the mass of the population.

The problem which Disraeli solved – how to stabilize the new society, without the landed aristocracy that had ruled the *ancien régime* – was not uniquely a British problem. Perhaps it was unique that the British rulers were able to achieve a relatively slow transition, one social order imperceptibly merged into another just as one ethos gently smudged into its successor. France could make the same transition only through a series of more or less open clashes, and even then the transformation, begun in 1789, was not complete until very late in the following century, by which time the new order was already under threat from a new challenge, the industrial working class. In Germany, the smudging was similar but with the difference that the new order never properly defeated the old – rather did the Prussian monarchy and *junkers* become the agency for the new society.

However, in British Conservatism it is clear why Disraeli is such an important figure, and how far removed he is from the measured certainties of Burke, secure in the old social order, yet how close to the 'image-makers' and public relations men of modern Conservatism. Lord Randolph Churchill is a much less significant figure. An aristocrat by birth, he led the assault of middle-class men within the party on the older aristocratic oligarchs, and he precipitated the party's crisis in domestic 1832. He added the phrase 'Tory democracy' to the armoury of Conservatism, but in essence it merely repeated Disraelian positions. Tory Democracy, Churchill said, was a democracy which supported the Tory Party (1888). Churchill identified himself with the middle-class section of the Party, representing Conservatism's

assimilation of elements of Liberalism. The assimilation permitted, during the Liberal governments of 1906 and 1914, an
impassioned Conservative defence of the absolute rights of the
individual to do with his own as he wished, whatever the mere
majority might say, and the assertion that the market and its free
operation were above and beyond any ethically motivated interference. The Individual was now, however, far removed from the
social atom of earlier Liberal writing; he was rather an upper-
class gentleman, concerned solely with the infringement of prerogatives not by other 'Individuals', but by the 'masses', a name-
less sea that threatened to drown privilege. Beyond the
Individual, a Conservative gentleman, lay the Hero and finally
the Leader or *Herrenvolk*, distinguished again by magnetism, this
time deriving from ethnic origins (a theme Disraeli also favoured
in some of his writing), but that came only in conditions of social
collapse which, fortunately for Conservatives, did not occur in
Britain.

No sooner had the industrial classes triumphed both nationally
and within the Conservative Party, than specifically modern
problems began : the rise of the Labour movement domestically
and of intense foreign competition, both economic and political,
abroad. The two ended the charmed spell of Victorian Britain
and its ideology, Liberalism. The 1907 Conservative Party Conference (what we would call it now) voted for tariff reform, the
polite name for an end to free trade, namely protection. This, it
was said, should operate within the Empire (Empire Free Trade
was a later euphemism) so as to give the Empire economic form,
keep out all Britain's major competitors from secluded markets,
and provide revenue to finance social reform at home, which
would in turn damp down domestic agitation. Incidentally, it
would also permit an acceleration in the rate of cartelization or
combination among British firms in order to control output since
such moves were constantly threatened where foreign competition reduced the common interest of all domestic producers
within an industry. The issue divided the Conservatives as it did
businessmen, and particularly the first, since it seemed likely to
raise food prices, not an electoral asset. In the end the division

was not resolved until the events of 1929 made protection in any form an emergency for British industrialists.

Bonar Law, the first industrialist proper (he was a Scottish-Canadian iron-master) to become leader of the Conservative Party, was said to care about only two issues, Ulster and tariff reform, and this was probably true of many Conservatives at the time, provided other things remained equal. They did not, and the condition of England after the First World War and through to the Second was such that British public ideology could not but express the pessimism and confusion that existed in many minds over the way forward. Disraeli's prescriptions assumed things were going moderately well, but in inter-war Britain, for many, things were consistently disastrous. Conservative writings, more than at any other period in the party's history, frequently expressed a sense of almost apocalyptic doom. The essence of the old society had gone without a new one replacing it, and unless Conservatives could find some way forward even the ruins might be captured from them by ever-present Bolshevism, for revolution was the price of failure. It is perhaps because of that state of mind that Baldwin's era as leader seems often to present a picture of a holding operation, soothing the patient while the doctors confer.

The Conservative doctors were sharply divided into a number of conflicting groups. Some argued that things were much better than they seemed, and that nothing should be done except to give businessmen more financial help without imposing conditions for its expenditure. Some urged much more compulsion, a State that would inspire or coerce a hierarchy which would exclude class division and conflict, and be led by a National Coalition excluding the political divisions of class. Yet others – the most coherent and developed case being advanced by Harold Macmillan – lifted the Labour Party clothes (or perhaps the Labour leadership lifted Macmillan's, as was suggested by some Conservatives in 1945) and urged the State to reorganize industry so that one major operator, public or private was immaterial, held a monopoly position, the producers themselves being co-ordinated through a national plan. All the elements of the 1945

Labour government's plans were included in Macmillan's scheme, except that Macmillan's was more radical and was offered not so much as the transformation of the *status quo* but more as the only means to preserve it.

The spectrum of opinion, from those who favoured some form of Fascism to those whose opinions were indistinguishable from those of the Labour leadership, indicated how absent was a common perspective or disciplining tradition. The government for its part tacked between different currents, intervening to reorganize basic industries but being defeated when it sought to nationalize coalmine royalties, and offering few effective means to control the monopolistic or cartelized units created. Chamberlain as Prime Minister did go so far as to begin the formulation of some kind of planning agency (in essence, a statistical bureau) even though planning was the symbol of all that many of the party's followers hated.

A terminology is required to see the divergent trends, and a sociology to understand them. But again, it would be wrong to see the British response as peculiar, particularly at this time when the British problem was, in its extremity, a product of the conditions of the world economy. If the British Conservatives remained as they were, they accurately reflected most of the prescriptions that conservatives in other countries adopted. For the radical Conservatives the Roosevelt New Deal programme was one way out of the impasse and embodied, in admittedly a dilute form, some of the *étatiste* suggestions also advanced by them. In Italy and Germany, *étatisme* in the economy ensured some prosperity and growth at the expense of those countries' neighbours, but it was married to· so sharp a break with the preceding *status quo* that few Conservatives could imitate it without thereby jeopardizing many of their associates and much of their past. The legacy of historical continuity had its own ideological value in stabilizing the existing *status quo*. To break the continuity with violence was to invite others with different ends to break it again. France, hitherto the home of revolutionary and radical traditions, remained like Britain, snared in a balance of political power that inhibited most responses except passive acceptance. Yet beneath the surface the same intellectual ferment out of the same confusion of past perspectives promoted similar solutions and, in particular, the notion of corporatism.

For implicit in the view of many Conservatives was the assumption of a corporate society. The old market place with small competitive units had passed away in all except the rhetoric, and all were agreed that business was organizing and should organize its production along functional rather than competitive lines. But there were divisions in practice here. For some industries were small-scale producers, and as a group, such industrialists opposed their own forceful elimination in favour of one of their number. Their opposition was to the State's intervention, although they were not opposed to receiving subventions without strings from the State, even though those subventions would have severely 'distorted' the efficiency of the national economy. On the other hand, there were very large companies which already controlled a sufficiently large proportion of output to expect to benefit from the elimination of their rivals, and who were also large enough to benefit from systematic State intervention, including national planning which might divert resources to them from older declining industries. They were also large enough to be politically influential. And of the large companies, those involved in modern industrial techniques continued to expand through the inter-war period and therefore did not share to the same degree the pessimism of older industries (predicated on the contraction of those industries).

Thus, if we can characterize the two main trends of thought, we might do so by calling one pluralist corporatism (with strong opposition to State intervention, a pale distortion of what was once called *laissez faire*) and the other, *étatiste* corporatism. In neither did there seem to exist as forceful a justification for the new tendencies as there had been for the landed interest and the Liberal entrepreneur. If the first was justified by its relationship to the nation, the soil (and on that basis it could, in principle at least, have opposed its sense of the national interest to the middle-class (sectional) 'faction' that might temporarily command the government), the second laid claim to progress for all at progressively higher standards of efficiency through open competition and free trade internationally. But for the pluralist corporatist, what was left of Liberalism after the government had closed the borders to foreign competitors and the largest businessmen had organized their domestic rivals out of existence or into subordination, was little except the claim that those that hold should have, the right of the sitting tenant to continue in occupation whether it was good or bad, the hindmost getting what they could as best they were able. *Étatiste* corporatism, although it was some answer to this criticism – the State would embody the nation and watch over what business remained private, taking into its own operation that which was 'irresponsible' – was exposed on its other flank, for what defence was there now against a State tyranny? There were no checks to the operation of government power, just as in pluralism there were no checks against the operation of business power. The whole legitimacy of the *status quo*, social, economic and political, must come to rest on the suffrage, on half-decade elections to a House, itself progressively robbed of much of its earlier power by the permanent administration, precisely because the suffrage rendered it an unreliable source of decisions.

Thus, the tenuous mythology of parliamentary government, the overt public politics, must be the source of the justification for the whole of society, a most vulnerable situation for those in command. Of course, there were other palliatives to soften the picture – social welfare, the State's commitment to help the poor and provide common services for all, the ethics of a meritocratic educational system which could answer the grievances of the brightest, a promise to sustain high employment – but these were bribes, rather than specific means to justify the power of those that held it. As in Bismarck's 'State socialism' welfare was a substitute for effective political control by the majority.

Not that these questions worried most Conservatives: those in power can afford to be 'pragmatic' while things are reasonably successful. Nor were Conservatives probably aware of the powerful and, in the past, contradictory political trends that became synthesized in corporatism, or rather a refurbished corporatism impelled by slump. These trends were expressed more clearly in parts of continental Europe, and some of the themes will be suggested later.

The Second World War both ended the frustrations of those who criticized the government for being inadequate, and tended to erode the position of those who had prevented the government doing more. The emergenices of war permitted a scale and coherence of deliberate State intervention which mere unemployment could not. After the war the Conservatives were spared the dilemma of being brutal with their immediate past by the advent of a Labour government, committed to executing in practice the pre-war radical Conservative programme, although Labour rhetoric promised something supposed to be different.

However, although we cannot here go into the detail it is interesting to note that from about 1948 the British economy began the process of long-term growth which has been a characteristic of the post-war world since then, and that one of the by-products of that growth was the suggestion that the measures earlier advocated by Conservative radicals and the Labour leadership were rather more designed to combat slump than to create an entirely new kind of society. In terms of 'progressive' thought the period 1931 to 1948 is dominated by the same concerns, the same demand to extend the State and public ownership, to control and plan the economy, to create a stable hierarchic society in which all would know their duties and their rights (which included a commitment to popular welfare).

As in Europe and the United States after 1948, anti-slump measures appeared as a restriction on an expanding economy rather than a support to an ailing one, and a whole new phase of neo-Liberalism affected both Labour and Conservative together. Planning for the Labour government became little more than a statistical commentary on the immediate past with suggestions for the immediate future, welfare aspirations were successively curtailed, and the 'bonfire of controls' indicated that the instruments of planning were already redundant. Those that identified economic controls (in the main, wartime Coalition measures) and nationalization as the essence of socialism lost a creed, while on the other side what was to have been the Conservative Party's adjustment to the modern world of social democracy, the 1947 *Industrial Charter*, turned out to be rather the last statement of pre-war radicalism than the inauguration of a new era. On the other hand neo-Liberalism, ironically, rendered the Conservative programme which brought them to power in 1951 more 'diehard' (in the terminology of the time) than that which had lost them the election in 1945.

In practice, the Conservatives in office differed relatively little from the closing years of Labour government, even though the anti-planning rhetoric was used to suggest a more exaggerated differentiation. It could not last, for the two underlying problems that have consistently shaped Conservative doctrine since the 1870s, the domestic threat (expressed now as 'wage inflation' precipitated by the trade unions) and foreign competition (expressed as a declining share of world trade held by Britain), remained as before. From the mid fifties the Conservatives were driven back willy-nilly to recover some of the elements of inter-war radical thought which had been abandoned in the late forties. Planning (although now planning for economic growth rather than planning for equilibrium or high employment) plus attempts at wage control returned in the early sixties, and it is perhaps ironic that it was Harold Macmillan who should have been the Prime Minister to initiate these innovations, having conveniently forgotten them in the halcyon days of the early fifties.

The conjuncture was pronounced in Britain because it had formerly played so important a part in the world economy, and its currency, a relic of past importance, was so subject to threats from international fluctuations. But the British response to a relative decline in the rate of increase of world trade was not peculiar. The French government had long sought to coordinate the domestic economy in a national plan, supported by corporative business-State agencies. West Germany, under the impact of recession, moved away from neo-Liberalism and towards the State-managed economy. In the United States, which was pursuing both domestic expansion, and massive foreign military expenditure as well as expanding its economic activities abroad, a relatively weak dollar demanded close supervision of the economy to offset inflationary pressures; the supervision went so far as proposed 'guide lines' for wage negotiations, a proposal Conservatives had sought to execute in Britain in the fifties. The word 'planning' remained in both West Germany and the United States part of what the respective governments claimed to abhor, but the practices British Conservatives and French Gaullists subsumed under the title were increasingly copied.

This account has done no more than touch on some of the symptoms of the changes in Conservative thought, both as a way of seeing how these changes can be seen in relationship to the context of problems facing the party (thus continuing the discussion of earlier chapters) and how little continuity there is in doctrinal terms, how little could be reasonably expected in the circumstances. Of course, there are continuities in Conservatism, but, in terms of beliefs, at so high a level of generality, that they offer no guide at all to what Conservatives might do. In general this is inevitable for any group which takes the *status quo* as being the best capable of achievement in the circumstances available. The ideal is broadly the real, and therefore there is no need for separate ideals which contrast with reality and oblige one to act to change reality. From time to time the exigencies of electoral competition have prompted Conservatives to postulate forward ends as counters to radical demands – the 'property-owning democracy' is one such end in this century – but in office Conservatives do almost nothing at all directly to achieve such ends. The forward ends are inoperative, passive, marginal to a system which is intrinsically harmonious already and needs only honest 'non-political' administration to keep it going, not structural innovation or reform. Of course, the 'traces' of the past colour the party's rhetoric, but this should not mislead the observer – Conservatives may say they have always had a special feeling for agriculture and the soil, but between 1870 and 1914 this special feeling did not prompt Conservative governments to do anything very serious to remedy the decline of British agriculture in that period; nor, when efforts were made to restore agriculture after 1931 and particularly during the Second World War, could this be attributed to any 'special feeling' so much as to the need to cut down imports essential to a basically industrial urban society.

The continuity of the Conservative Party consists above all in the existence of the party itself, with common symbols and terminology, rather than a coherent ideational system. The party has, since Disraeli, tended to follow a common line, or has assumed a common sociological function, namely that of embodying the demands of the highest élites of British society, modified to accommodate an electoral following and, in particular, middle-class (bureaucratic, rather than entrepreneurial now) opinion. It has sought to recruit new élites – as it sought to recruit industrial managers after 1945 for fear that Labour might win their support – to homogenize them *vis-à-vis* the ruling mores, to offer them a coherent generalized defence and to assimilate their own new perspectives. The rationale and justification for a leadership class has occupied a central place in Conservative writings from before Disraeli. Finding the 'natural aristocracy' is a recurring problem as social change takes place, even if it is not so serious a problem as it was in the transition from an agrarian to an industrial society. If one looks at Conservative speeches and writings about industrial disputes, for example, one is struck by the almost consistent identification of the management case as, in principle, the correct one. In industry there is always one answer, and a dispute is never a clash between equally valid interests or innocent workers and tyrannical employers, nor is it a problem of the structure of society impelling equally innocent parties to clash despite the best intentions, it is rather between a correct management and irrational or ignorant workers. Of course, managers may 'make mistakes', inadequately inform or educate their workers, be insufficiently sympathetic to the 'personal' problems workers have and so on, but all of these formulations implicitly take it for granted that managers, as a group, in principle have the right answers, that they are or should be the sole active element, and that workers should be passive recipients of leadership. Without 'firm leadership' the masses become 'confused' or 'puzzled', for, in principle, society is just and harmonious. The idea that there is only one valid answer to any and every social problem, and that that answer is solely comprehended by the leadership can be found in Burke and almost all Conservative thinkers since then. For Burke, the aristocracy embodies reason and the Divine Will, so that revolt against the aristocracy is by definition 'ignorant' and 'irrational' and, in addition, blasphemy, sacrilege against the divine order. One reason is embodied in what exists, so that those who are oppressed by what exists must be evil or stupid, and probably the first, for the rebel leadership, the misaristocracy of radicals that play Satan to the leadership's God (and are often described in Conservative writings as fallen upper-class men, for leadership has, as in Right-wing thought generally, an ethnic connotation also) is seen as diabolically cunning. The rebel rank-and-file are stupid, 'confused' by smart talk that takes the name of the Lord in vain. The two-class system, one active and one passive, runs through Conservative thought in its most diverse concerns and provides a solid link of continuity that is not normally acknowledged, since it is an assumption profoundly inimical to the democratic principles supposed to constitute Western orthodoxy.

This account has taken as its point of reference British Conservatism, and at stages made some rudimentary comparison with political ideas on the Right in other Western countries. However, in the course of examining Conservative assumptions no attempt has been made to compare these with alternative views in the Labour Party, partly because there are few alternative views held by the leadership of Labour. The common orthodoxy of British parliamentary politics has here been described as 'Conservative' and related to specifically Conservative roots. This should not mislead one into thinking the Labour leadership would want to argue with many so-called Conservative assumptions.

The West

This somewhat simplified account of British Conservatism over a long period of time has been a means to suggest some of the essentials in the complex of beliefs which offer a justification for modern Western capitalism, and some of the problems that have given these essentials their character. The overlap in phases is much greater than implied here, so that old battles go on being fought long after it seems one side has won.

It is a mark of the lack of a sustained and substantial domestic challenge to modern capitalism that it is so difficult to detect its outlines and the dominant beliefs of its leaders. That difficulty is epitomized in the differing ways of identifying Western society – 'managerial capitalism', the Welfare State, the mixed economy, and so on. I have suggested that the most useful terms to describe the spectrum of ideology within such society lies between *étatiste* corporatism and plural corporatism, an ethos quite separate from the preceding era of Liberalism or Liberal-Conservatism. The precipitating elements in the evolution of corporatist forms of organization and therefore the kind of political thought discussed here were quite clearly bound up with the nature of slump and the need to restrict the volume of industrial output. The depression was too profound a crisis for the trends crystallized by it to be destroyed by the Second World War and the following phase of growth. Indeed, the nature of capitalism had been changed so far that it is inconceivable the clock should be put back. Corporatism came to be the common medium for all kinds of policy formation, variously described as 'socialist' (by the social democrats) or appropriate to 'free enterprise'. It established a pervasiveness, a centrality, comparable to the role of Liberalism in the nineteenth century – it became 'common sense'. Thus, the neo-Liberal trends of the fifties, important in Britain, the United States and West Germany (Erhardt's 'social market economy') did not seriously impinge on the system of industrial organization which it inherited. In Britain, successive waves of reform in the nationalized industries neither restored them as a whole to private ownership, nor disentangled their operations from the demands of government policy. There was no immediate campaign of 'trust-busting', of legislative and executive action to end trade associations (whether sustained under public guidance or wholly business controlled), to restrict mergers and offer substantial aid to small business – to begin the very radical task of restoring a market with effective competition. Such aims would have been Utopian, and even the strongest advocates of neo-Liberalism did not go so far, and, indeed, usually retained tariff exchange, and immigration controls to preserve elements of the autarchic economy from free international competition. As a result, the freedom of enterprise often meant no more than the freedom for the largest companies to continue doing what they had already been doing, accelerating the corporatist organization of the economy.

Of course, the terminology of politics remained trapped in the slightly sterile formulae of the past, and in the United States what Galbraith stigmatizes as 'the conventional wisdom' (*The Affluent Society*, 1958) persisted in a language that had only tangential validity. 'Freedom' was not freedom to compete so much as freedom from public obligations embodied in the State. However, in the international sphere the United States continued a commitment to Liberalism, to free trade, just as Britain had done when its international strength guaranteed supremacy in any open competition, and the context, dominated by a multiplicity of international companies and nation-firms unstructured by enforceable law, constituted some approximation to a free market. Business collusion, international cartels as in oil or airlines, existed, but rapid expansion constantly tended to make them unstable. Contraction in the rate of increase of world trade could generate the stability required, and the great disputes over trade liberalization in GATT and the 'Kennedy Round' indicated the continuing tensions.

In the United States, the size of industrial institutions and the continuity of expansion (even if the rate was modest and variable by international standards) made pluralist variants of corporatism more often the language of politics, in contrast to the rather more *étatiste* versions implicit in Roosevelt's New Deal. But, the impact of the Cold War, ideological rivalry for supremacy with the Soviet Union, did prompt some writers (unlike those of most other western countries) to formulate an overall rationale for the new kind of society. The inherited ideology of the Soviet Union, as I hope to suggest in the next chapter, permitted a dual appearance: conservative at home, and revolutionary abroad, and this was a threat to the increasingly conservative appearance of the United States abroad. Of course American Liberalism, like British Liberalism in the mid nineteenth century, had had a revolutionary message – at the time of the First World War Woodrow Wilson's advocacy of the rights of national self-determination and democracy against empires and the rule of monarchs had posed a major threat to some European states, and the anti-imperialist position continued to have occasional radical implications right up to the period immediately after the Second World War (in relationship to the foreign possessions of the British, French and Dutch).

But conservative nationalism increasingly overtook such elements, particularly when the United States was faced with Soviet rivalry, when other nationalisms became often indistinguishable from communism. Like all conservative forces the United States had little to offer in competition for 'hearts and minds' except the presumption that what existed was already the very best that could be hoped for, the real was the ideal in the short-term, and immense political, economic, and military power to 'prove it'. But to defend the real, it must at least be described coherently, so the attempt of some American writers to formulate a coherent and realistic rationale for the new United States society answered a genuine need externally. For reasons suggested above, the stress fell on pluralistic corporatism, a consensual union of giant industrial corporations with associated centres of activity, estates. Indeed, the term 'pluralism' itself became of major importance.

Much of the case was designed to prevent what Berle (1955) called 'statism' or 'statification', and, provocatively, he suggested substantial similarities between the Soviet Union and the United States, the one being a 'Statist collectivism', the other a 'non-Statist collectivism'. It was for this reason that he decided to characterize United States society as, indifferently, 'non-Statist socialism' or 'people's capitalism.'

Berle suggests that competition and the market no longer control the main block of American industry which is under the control of large monopolistic corporations, themselves detached from control through ownership, and thereby, it is argued, from a direct drive for profits. Ownership, Berle says, is spread very widely among the United States population (which is in fact not true, although ownership is spread more widely than before), and because of the dispersion of ownership, industrial control is vested in the hands of a self-selecting oligarchy of professional managers, without outside check on their behaviour. Borrowing from the capital markets is too small to ensure control through private finance, and all industries are regulated by the corporations to prevent the sanctions of competition. Cartels, collusion, agreements, trade associations, all constitute forms of industrial planning to damp down competition and are political means to control economic fluctuations. Thus, Berle argues, a small group, either nominees of credit institutions or professional managers through the agency of a few hundred major corporations, controls and shapes United States society, just as the Soviet Union is dominated by its large corporate industrial institutions under professional managers.

The 'managerial revolution' follows well-known lines, although it does not include the 'euthanasia of the *rentier*' so much as his retirement. The problem that arises is why anyone should accept such a system. Why is it just? Once competition is excised from the model, what assurance does anyone have that this is 'the best of all possible worlds'? A number of suggested replies have been made, of which some might be listed thus:

1. Berle himself suggests that although the managerial oligarchy is self-perpetuating it is controlled – or, at least, influenced – by public opinion, by a consensus. By 'consensus' Berle does not mean the vote, but rather the support of certain selected authoritative figures drawn from the intelligentsia and the professions. He suggests a medieval analogy – the king and barons, holders of secular power, were controlled – or influenced – by the bishops, the Lords Spiritual, and now the corporation barons must be subject to academic approval. Now there seems no obvious reason why people should accept academic opinion

(and selected, at that) any more than business views, and perhaps Berle also feels this, for he does suggest that the ultimate sanction for society is the intervention of the State. This is slightly ambiguous because at other points there is almost a suggestion that the State is, or should be, the corporations in union themselves, the assembly of corporations, so that the sanction is by all corporations against one; there are no sanctions against corporations as such. Nor is it clear why, in logic, democracy is so impossible a vehicle through which to achieve public approval, unless it is only that such approval is unlikely to be forthcoming. However, these matters do not affect Berle's immense optimism – order is being created out of anarchy at home and abroad, for the international corporations and cartels are bringing world government without the need for conscious political activity.

2. It has been proposed that the interest of the public would be secured by placing special trustees on the boards of directors of the corporations, either nominated by the State (as happens in the nationalized industries in Britain and the agencies of French planning) or the trade unions. If worker representation becomes fully effective, it is said, then the firm or corporation will become a fully representative political and social unit of society; on the other hand, State nominations will ensure the public interest is secured. Co-partnership schemes offer a variant on this.

3. Some people have merely denied the problem, saying, as did Harold Macmillan in *The Middle Way* (1938), that since the managers were not motivated by the pursuit of profit, they could be fully trusted to pursue the public interest. The theme also appears in C. A. R. Crosland's *The Future of Socialism* (1956), a basic work for the British Labour Party leadership's perspective, and, indeed, the 1957 Labour policy statement, *Industry and Society*, remarks that 'under increasingly professional managements, large firms are as a whole serving the nation well', so that nationalization, as an aim for the party, is unnecessary. Public ownership in general is not necessary for the reform of capitalism because capitalism itself is being 'socialized',

the domination of ownership and the profit motive is coming to an end. Reform concerns not legal ownership rights, but rather organizations, and such reforms can be secured through management training, the study of organization and decision-making, the extension of the use of computers and so on.

4. Galbraith, the American economist, has suggested a general theory from which a solution to the particular problem could be extracted. Much as in the theory of the 'invisible hand', constantly ensuring that private greed only enhanced the common good, the theory of countervailing power suggests that 'excessive power' always begets a check that prevents damage to society. Thus, the excessive power of capital generated the power of labour and trade unions which checked it. The 'theory' seems no more than a formalization of optimism, a rendering of virtue in the garb of necessity. It is not unlike the thesis put forward by some theorists of pressure groups: in their multiplicity, pressure groups check each other and so ensure no harm to the public interest; the old age pensioners and Imperial Chemical Industries balance each other in equilibrium harmony.

5. Yet others have suggested that the solution lies in giving the managers a strict education for responsibility. Like Plato's Guardians, they will learn to think 'in social terms', to be statesmen rather than businessmen, whose decisions are grounded in the neutrality of scientific expertise and the ethics appropriate to the national interest. Unfortunately, if businessmen do behave thus, little distinguishes the State and business except that the one is subject to a periodic vote, which might be an argument for wholesale nationalization.

6. Perhaps the corporations could be granted public charters which recognized their autonomous authority and assigned specific responsibilities and powers. Thus, society would constitute an 'association of free, self-governing nations'. In reviewing the charter from time to time, society would be able to check the corporations. Scott Buchanan (1959) objected to this view on the grounds that the corporation must be an independent, self-legislating, sovereign power, meeting its cor-

porate peers in a congress of corporations: no power can check
it.

7. Finally, some have dismissed the problem in a hard-headed
way, saying that those who enjoy the benefits of the system
have no right to attack it. Implicitly, a social contract balances
the reward of affluence against the price of obedience and conformity. The 'solution', however, suggests mass disloyalty would
be a reasonable response to a new economic crisis.

It might be noted, in passing, that pre-war corporatist theory
saw the integration of society in terms of corporations corresponding to social, occupational or professional strata, estates:
so that, for example, labour might be organized in one corporation, capital in another. The accounts briefly examined here,
by contrast, see all strata of society bound up in a series of ver-
tically organized corporations: the workers, managers, owners
and others employed in General Motors will be solely represented
by General Motors itself. In terms of the central aim of corporatism, to eliminate conflict and the possibility of vertical conflict,
in particular class conflict, the recent United States versions are
superior to pre-war suggestions. It is also interesting to note the
particular people involved in the debate, for there are many
drawn from very diverse backgrounds, although the *étatiste* corporatism of the inter-war period seems the most common. In
particular Berle was important in Roosevelt's New Deal administration, and others are drawn from right-wing Social Democracy.

The diversity of background is representative of the diverse
sources for the justification of the society created after the inter-
war slump. Historically, corporatism claimed to descend from
the medieval conception of estates, and those who advocated corporate organization in the nineteenth century did so explicitly
as part of a Right-wing (and originally aristocratic) opposition
to the world of bourgeois capitalism, to the society that emerged
from the French Revolution and the religious schism of the
Reformation. Corporatism was supposed to be the essence of the
lost *ancien régime*, and it was these forms that, for example,
Marshal Pétain tried to foster in his abortive Vichy France, and
Mussolini borrowed for the decorative façade of Italian Fascism.

However, this kind of corporatism, expressed most fully by certain Right-wing thinkers in France and in early Christian democrat thought, had only a tenuous relationship with *business* corporations as such, even though the same formulations proved appropriate when the time was ripe. Certainly corporatism did not imply personal dictatorship – on the contrary, its corporate aspect was supposed to make dictatorship impossible. Neumann (1942), however, argues that the corporatist harmony is a myth, only capable of realization through its contradiction, ruthless autocracy. Be this as it may, racialism is, on the history of Italian Fascism, not an inevitable concomitant of Fascism generally, and certainly not an essential part of corporatist doctrines, except in so far as corporatism stresses nationalism above other loyalties, and nationalism often includes ethnic identification. The original forms of corporatist theorization would, without the development of modern industry and a major slump, have died a natural death, a shadowy opposition to a society already too advanced to go back. The new lease of life is perhaps ironic, for middle-class entrepreneurs had bred a new kind of industrial aristocrat who adopted parts of the doctrines of the *ancien régime* aristocracy, all that the entrepreneurs had fought and hated.

More significant perhaps than the Right proper was the evolution of liberalism itself in the late nineteenth and early twentieth century. For both intellectuals and businessmen were moving away from the conception of freedom in society that had been the essence of liberalism. Pareto, economist and social theorist, is a representative figure in that he was both a liberal and an anti-democrat, someone who more vividly felt the threat to his freedom than the oppression of others his freedom might entail, and who saw in Mussolini a saviour of his freedom. Walther Rathenau, the German industrialist, from a quite different intellectual origin, came to argue that ownership had become depersonalized in industry, and that accordingly the enterprise had assumed a public status, one of the constituent units in a unified society rather one private competitor among many. J. M. Keynes, the distinguished liberal economist, spoke in 1926 of 'corporations as a mode of government' and 'medieval conceptions of separate autonomies' (1926); he was later, in *The General Theory*, to urge an accelerated process to secure the 'euthanasia of the rentier' and thereby the stabilization of managerial power. More formally, the Liberal Party in Britain under Lloyd George, and those liberals who sought to help F. D. Roosevelt in the New Deal in the United States, had little compunction in abandoning most of the heritage of liberalism, the idea of the market, competition and the free activity of individuals, in favour of the power of the State, unified with society, under the impact of inter-war unemployment and slump.

And on the other side, in the intellectual flux of the twenties, some socialists saw in corporative organization a means to end the class war without revolution, to create integrated plants in which the workers had formal status, to end the clash of the market and thereby the oppression of periodic unemployment. Henri Le Man, the Belgian socialist leader, was probably the most prominent leader on the Left to embrace corporatism, but no doubt there was a strong strain of similar feeling among those socialists who adhered to the Nazi cause in Germany, who believed sincerely in the socialist element of national socialism. With the addition of 'dynamic leadership', panache, corporatism in the hands of Mussolini could attract wider support, such as that of the Fabian, George Bernard Shaw. Indeed, one might speculate even further that it was the *étatiste* corporatist elements in the Soviet Union under Stalin which, ironically, attracted intellectual support during the thirties; the Webbs, for example, had no time for the Soviet Union when it still promised freedom for workers in 1918, but came to support it in the thirties when the brutal autocracy, the ruthlessness of its ruler, its complete denial of freedom, had become plain in the Moscow trials.

With such a broad span of possible support, corporative forms of organization could not fail to be greeted with at most, enthusiasm, at least optimistic tolerance. In addition, that breadth of support permitted many individuals to evolve between apparently contradictory political traditions while remaining consistent. An interesting example in this respect is Sir Oswald Mosley who began as a Tory radical, a backbencher in the 1918 Commons, crossed the floor of the House, ultimately to become a junior Labour Minister in 1929, and ultimately withdrew from Parliamentary politics in disgust to form his New Party, which finally became the British Union of Fascists. The guiding thread was the pursuit of authority, the pursuit of a new integrated order to unify Britain and eliminate conflict. That central thread – to make class conflict impossible by substituting as central focus of loyalty the nation-State (so transferring domestic conflict to the relations between States – international replaced class war) – linked Mosley with many others from very different backgrounds, and nowhere more powerfully than in Germany where nationalism and socialism had proved, in competition, the two most powerful forces in the country.

Thus, the evolution of British Conservatism had nothing unique about it in the inter-war period, except that it did not go nearly so far as other comparable political traditions in abandoning the past. The evolution of industry itself defined the location of the problems which Conservatives were required to solve, and their own adherence to the maintenance of the *status quo* severely limited the possible solutions open to them. Acquiescence in an on-going process provided it did not threaten their power was inevitably more characteristic of their response than conscious pursuit of certain ends. Acquiescence permitted the evolution to continue, despite implications it might have for liberal values in which Conservatives also claimed to believe. Of course, it might be said that Disraeli's prescription of charisma plus propaganda (with ethnic criteria made the basis for national identification, despite – or because of – Disraeli's Jewish origin) was just what both Hitler and Mussolini adopted, but to say this is no more than to say that certain problems produce similar solutions in different societies. It is not to identify all particular Fascist practices as those British Conservatives would have copied. For Britain was not Germany or Italy. Many Germans and Italians shared the same principles but were neither Nazis nor Fascists, and, indeed, opposed them so far as to lose their lives. The identity between the formal doctrines and certain specific acts is not established, for the doctrines are ambivalent and cover many different kinds of act. If it had not been so the British Fascists would not have formed a separate organization but merely joined the Conservatives.

However, whatever the immense differences between the régimes of different Western societies, the industrial structure had evolved in a similar way within the logic of the world economy, technology and domestic conflict. Slump, which affected all those régimes, precipitated certain kinds of solution to comparable problems, and those solutions were consistent with a certain range of political beliefs. It was thus inevitable that, although the word 'corporatism' was discredited by Mussolini's régime and died with his Fascism, in defeat, the structural conditions for corporatism did not end, nor did the generalized political ideas which attained coherence and significance within the framework of corporatism.

Expanding trade shifted the emphasis, and the birth of immense international companies, not tied securely to specific nation-States, tended to impose new strains on the dominant nationalist orientation of corporatism. Yet, nevertheless, the framework for political debate between Right and Left remained, for the moment at least, bounded by the same parameters. War and national planning clarified the trends. The distinction between public and private, between State and business, was slowly disappearing, and the State increasingly behaved as a single company with many subsidiaries.

This chapter has sought to show the range of problems to which British Conservatism was a response, and to delineate what British Conservatism is and has been by examining that response. Continuity of one kind contrasts with immense discontinuity of another. For it has been argued that Conservatism is not continuous in terms of its beliefs, but is continuous in terms of the role Conservatives seek to play within British society and the relationship they seek to sustain with the rest of society. The role and the relationship, however, subsist between changing things, for the social group that provides the specific detail of the Conservative position at any given moment of time changes as the nature of British society changes. This account has exaggerated the changes in order more sharply to portray the different Conservative positions historically. Conservative evolution is helped by the natural conservative tendency to avoid theoretical formulations which might snare one group in the position of another.

In the process of examining Conservatism some characteristic features of modern Right-wing thought have been noted. It should not be inferred, however, that these features are essentially Right-wing in general, only in the modern period. It may be that these features have a wider significance and are valid not only for modern times, but to establish this would require a much more substantial historical survey than has been attempted here. Rather has it been suggested here that the letter of formal Right-wing doctrine is always ambivalent in general. The same doctrine can be put to many different uses in different contexts. These features correspond to the social role of the Conservative Party – the assumption that there is one single correct answer to all social problems, and that answer is broadly what the leadership group says it is; that the ideal is the real, so that no separate theory or scheme of forward ends is necessary as a contrast to what already exists, for what already exists is the best that can be hoped for in the circumstances. This perhaps needs qualification, for modern Conservatives have accepted forward planning of the economy. However, this forward planning is explicitly minimized, and the stress falls on coordinating the on-going processes of the economy rather than determining what those processes shall be, for the real, even where it is at the moment inadequate, is necessarily generating the ideal. The Conservative notion of the 'property-owning democracy' is a useful example of this point, for it is not a clear contrast with what already exists, a contrast which demands Conservative action to realize; rather is it a partial description of what already exists and a comment on what is coming about autonomously.

It follows from this account that where Conservatives do put forward ideals that seem to differ from what exists, those ideals are passive or inoperative, they entail no specific action (this sort of ideal contrasts sharply with ideals in radical thought which entail specific action; they are active or operative ideals). Finally, we have noted that in Right-wing thought generally, at the crucial point of justifying what exists, a retreat into an unspecified and particular (rather than universal) mystery takes place – into the mystery of leadership, of the national idea, of pageantry (usually called 'history'), of blood. The particular is its own justification, justified by its own existence (it is the real), not by reference to any universal principles governing all men equally.

Right-wing thought is a system of beliefs which have evolved within similar parameters in relationship to specific problems. The problems generate tensions within the orthodoxy as different groups or subgroups offer conflicting prescriptions within the common inheritance. Where different subgroups survive over lengthy periods together then the perspective becomes blurred and inconsistent positions can be simultaneously advanced.

We have already noted some of these features in relationship to religious beliefs and Right-wing doctrines. The next chapter moves to a radically different context, Russia, where by nature of the inheritance, theoretical exposition was at a premium. The evolution of Russian society has been left largely on one side (the material is vast and the space limited) to focus much more narrowly on the actual evolution of theoretical formulations, to locate the transition from radical to conservative.

5

Conservatism and the East

Men fight and lose that battle, and the thing they fought for comes about in spite of their defeat, and when it comes, turns out to be not what they meant, and other men have to fight for what they meant under another name.

WILLIAM MORRIS

MARXISM-LENINISM is a body of beliefs said to be the guiding perspective of the dominant groups in Eastern Europe and the Soviet Union. It is currently in a process of rapid change or, at least, substantial parts of it are being relegated to unimportance, so that a current definition of Marxism-Leninism would be almost impossible. Historically, the subject is vast, and it is proposed here only to examine briefly some of the background to the work of Lenin, that work itself, that of Stalin, and a little of what followed Stalin's death. The account cannot, for reasons of space, be a history of modern Russia, nor even of the revolutionary movements in Russia. It is only one narrow segment, which omits the many perspectives of other groups in opposition, from the Mensheviks to the workers' and Left opposition. This is a severe weakness, since the few themes examined are separated from the historical context which gave them specific content. In particular, this is crucial for Bolshevism, for it is a very specific response to a relatively narrow range of problems, and a characteristic means of vilifying Bolshevism is to present its themes without mentioning the problems analysed by those themes, to treat it as an atemporal theology, generalizations on the nature of man and society in all times and places. The approach was mentioned in the second chapter in the 'I-must-wear-a-macintosh' example.

However, the justification for this account is that a discussion of the history of Marxism-Leninism most vividly illustrates a group of beliefs which began as radical, profoundly opposed to the existing *status quo* (and thus, inimical to the postulates of Russian – and by derivation, British – conservatism), but ended as conservatism, in defence of the Soviet *status quo*. The theoretical framework for the transition was supposed to remain the same, and it is important to see the transition from one posture to its opposite within one apparent orthodoxy. The similarities at the end between Western conservatism and Marxism-Leninism are marked, although the two groups of beliefs are not the same, since the immediate conclusions are derived from different postulates, heirs of different inheritances, but the practical impact is the same. The transition includes that from purposes inimical to conservatism, to those identical with it – the contrast between ideal and real narrows; operative aims become inoperative, 'Utopian'; the given national framework replaces the postulated international. Common problems facing a group standing in the same relationship to its society as British Conservatives stood to theirs generate, within an apparently contradictory framework, similar responses.

Bolshevism, the viewpoint of that section of the Russian Social Democrat Party which assumed revolutionary power in 1917, exists essentially in relationship to the needs of revolutionary practice. Lenin's writings were always rooted in some immediate context, and most of them cannot be interpreted in relationship to general problems without severe damage to their meaning. He wrote very little 'general theory', and even when he did it was written in relationship to some immediate political purpose. It is thus impossible to understand what he wrote without understanding the charges to which he is replying. For Lenin, his theoretical work was a prelude and guide to his practical activity, a means to identify the right actions at the right time, and something which itself evolved with the experience of trying to do things. A continuing purpose and context gave general coherence and continuity to his work, but each part of his work must be seen, given these factors, relative to a specific task.

Lenin's succcessors did not need the same theoretical framework, did not need to guide their actions in the same way, for they were already in power. Already, the purposes that had guided Lenin were changing into new purposes; something of the real became ideal. So tenuous did the relationship with Lenin's purposes become that his words were increasingly used as a ritual, a theology, generalized so that they were said to be applicable at all times and places. The association of a perspective and the maintenance of authority had once more come to dilute and finally destroy the perspective; similar occurrences in popular religion were cited in the third chapter. In Stalinism, Leninist theory was used as a means of justifying Stalin's practice, after the event. What Stalin chose to do, without clearly specifying his reasons (and so framing a theoretical context for his actions), was subsequently reconciled with an earlier tradition, so that the popularity of the second could conceal the unpopularity of the first.

The change did not occur because Lenin's successors were muddled, mistaken or intellectually his inferior, but because their perspective on the world, their purposes, had been transformed. In this transformation lies the metamorphosis of Marxism from a means of so analysing society that an obligation to change society is immediately incurred by all who accept the analysis, into the conservative ideology of a new class society, a body of formalized doctrine designed to justify the existing nature of society and so leave complete freedom of action to its leaders. Comparisons have been made between Soviet ideology and various forms of theology, and this is, perhaps, an interesting exercise although it overestimates the static quality of the doctrines and is most plausible only for the heyday of Stalinism. More interesting are the comparisons which can be drawn between Soviet thought and some elements of Western conservatism as outlined in the last chapter.

A continuing theme in this account will be the changing relationship of theory, held beliefs relative to immediate problems, to practice, what one does about the problems. The relationship was summarized by Marx for socialists in the term 'sensuous practice'. In seeking to change the world, 'practice', men learn new lessons and adjust their theory accordingly, this adjusted theory then is subjected to the tests of further attempts to achieve the same ends. Implicitly, Marx is rejecting the conservative notion that men can achieve their aims without simultaneously attempting to be fully conscious of what they are doing, without analysing the world and being 'theoretical'. Of course, where the ideal is the real, as it is for conservatives, what they wish to achieve, day-to-day administration, can be achieved without general analysis, without being 'theoretical'. Thus Marx's prescription applies only to radicals and, even more narrowly, to socialists. But Marx is also stating that no theory can constitute alone an adequate means to change; it must be subjected to practical tests, and if it secures success for those who make use of it in practice, then and then only is it valid. For conservatives, the general social structure is not problematic, so general theory is not required, and the social structure, whatever it is, can be taken for granted. Of course, when the social structure comes under serious radical challenge conservatives do have to frame more general positions to counteract radical theory, and in doing so they may pass beyond conservatism – either identifying with the radical challenge, or offering a more militant counter-challenge. However, the sole point of interest here is that Marx's prescriptions are only for radicals, not for general purposes.

The Background to Bolshevism

Marxism was initially defined and shaped on a mass political level by the German Social Democrat Party, and this definition in the 1890s provided a framework for the union of the purposes of German socialists and the nineteenth-century philosophic doctrine loosely described as positivism. Positivism, very roughly, can be described in this context as the contention that a deterministic knowledge of the world is possible, and is so independently of any activity in the world. Indeed, some positivists maintain that knowledge is *only* possible if completely isolated from practical concerns and problems confronting men in their daily lives.

By implication, knowledge is atemporal in emphasis – what constitutes knowledge is what concerns all men at all times and places, rather than what concerns a few here and now. The belief that Marxism was part of an atemporal and deterministic science was already emerging in the later writings of Engels, and Marx himself detected the same tendency among some of his followers when he declared that he was not a 'Marxist'; his work, he said, was only an 'historical sketch of the genesis of capitalism in Western Europe,' not 'an historico-philosophic theory of the *marche générale* imposed by fate upon every people, whatever the historic circumstances in which it finds itself' (Letter, November 1877, Marx and Engels, 1953, p. 354). The warning did not prevent Engels from generalizing some of the methodological principles Marx employed in the analysis of European history (where man was the sole creator) to the world of nature. Generalizations about man's activity came to be seen as merely particular applications of general 'laws of nature'. Man was therefore ruled by scientifically determinable laws which, Engels claimed, were embodied in a doctrine which came to be known as 'dialectical materialism'. The implications of the shift were immense for 'dialectical materialism' could easily become a kind of religious doctrine, without reference to particular time or place, a theory of the cosmology, not a method of analysis for quite clearly specified purposes.

It was thus possible for men to look at society as a kind of natural organism, the evolution of which was 'inevitable' and did not require the intervention of men. Within this determinist framework the achievement of a socialist revolution was not so much the work of men as the inevitable result of natural evolution, much the same as the evolution of men from anthropoids. This version of Marxism as a collection of universal scientific laws was further developed by the two major theorists of social democratic Marxism before the First World War, Karl Kautsky and Georgi Plekhanov. Marxism had become less a philosophy of revolutionary action, and rather more an atemporal ideological system based upon faith in certain doctrinal postulates, called necessary and natural laws. This peculiarly stark form of economic determinism virtually excluded the opportunity for revolutionary action – since the revolution was 'inevitable', nothing much need be done about it – and it also made theory redundant, since it was irrelevant to the day-to-day problems facing the social democrat movement. Marxism was restricted to the role of analysing society for no particular purpose; it was not a guide to action in the here-and-now; it was 'science': that is, it accepted reality as it was without seeking to examine that reality in relationship to the purposes involved in changing it. Inevitably it became conservative. In day-to-day practice, German social democracy was at one with the non-Marxist English Fabians, suggesting how little a different general theory mattered.

But even as Marxism, in the hands of Engels and Kautsky, reached the respectability of positivism, general European culture was itself reaching a state of almost explosive rejection of some elements of positivism. The era of the peaceful expansion of industry which had underpinned the complacent optimism of the Victorian in Britain, the assumption of society as a simple self-equilibrating machine, was giving way to open imperialist clashes abroad and to increasing class conflict at home. But the domestic conflict took a new form, producing almost a division of labour between revolutionary theory and revolutionary practice, between 'science' and activism.

There were a number of different responses to the schism. One philosophic response accepted the Engels and Kautsky version of Marxism at face value, saying that it was therefore a simple form of economic analysis which presented a scientific view of the world but did not suggest why the individual should also want what was inevitable. Edouard Bernstein, who became the best-known advocate of this view, argued that, 'No amount of historical materialism can get round the fact that history is made by men, that men have minds, and that mental dispositions are by no means so mechanical as to be entirely governed by the economic situation.' (*Die Neue Zeit*, XVI, p. 749, cited Welter, 1958.) Marx's economic analysis thus needed underpinning with a system of individual ethics, drawn in the main from the work of Kant. The movement became known as Revisionism, but neo-

Kantianism had wider implications throughout social democracy and occurred in the work of perhaps the most important group of social democrat theorists, the Austro-Marxists. On a non-theoretical level anarcho-syndicalism, important in France and Italy, can also be seen as a response to the central problem, an attempt to restore revolutionary practice in explicit isolation from what had formerly been revolutionary theory. Again, to some extent, Mussolini's evolution from orthodox social democratic Marxism through the phase of leading a Left-wing 'ginger group' to stimulate greater radicalism by the Italian Social Democrat leadership, to Fascism (even though Mussolini ended as profoundly anti-socialist), could be seen as also a response to the central problem (cf. Nolte, 1965, pp. 151 ff.). However, the most important attempt to reunify theory and practice within Marxism, although not the orthodox version, was undertaken by Rosa Luxemburg and Parvus, and in Russia by the Bolsheviks.

Marxist ideas began to circulate in Russia, mainly in academic circles, from the 1870s, hot on the heels of the Narodnik socialists who had themselves sought to rid Russia of Tsarism. Narodnik activity had shown how limited were the possibilities for any kind of radical politics – some of those who have criticized Lenin for not behaving as if he lived in Victorian England or even the Kaiser's Germany make too few allowances for the ruthlessness of Tsarist autocracy and the comprehensive influence of the Tsarist secret police. The conditions which allowed the development of a strong democratic labour movement in the West were not permitted in Russia, and special tactics had to be employed for any revolutionary even to survive. Similarly, the central problem for Russian radicals was not, as it was for west European socialists, how to create socialism, but rather how to permit capitalism, how to end Tsarism and create the conditions for a bourgeois republic which would simultaneously develop the economy and allow the growth of a free labour movement. When that was accomplished, socialism would become a feasible aim.

The first social democratic organization in St Petersburg dates from 1885, and the first, abortive, congress of the Russian Workers' Social Democrat Party from 1898. Georgi Plekhanov led the attack on the ruling Narodnik orthodoxy among socialists – that the peasantry could create socialism in Russia without the country developing capitalism – by asserting that the Russian proletariat was the sole agency for the achievement of socialism, and that capitalism was already well under way in Russia so that any thought that a peasant socialism was possible without an intervening capitalist phase was illusory. One of the earliest Marxists actually in Russia (Plekhanov was in exile), Struve, wrote the first manifesto of the RWSDP, and it is of interest that he there repeats an opinion common among European social democrats and one of some significance for Russian socialists who wished to precipitate a bourgeois revolution and thereby create a republic:

> The farther east one goes in Europe, the weaker, meaner and more cowardly in the political sense becomes the bourgeoisie, and the greater the cultural and political tasks which fall to the lot of the proletariat. On its strong shoulders, the Russian working class must and will carry the work of conquering political liberty. (1898, cited Carr, 1950, p. 4)

At least three main trends of Marxist thought emerged out of this initial activity:

1. A group of intellectuals, the best known being Struve, Berdyaev, and Tugan-Baranovsky, who, in conjunction with the Revisionists in Germany, saw Marxism as profoundly weak as a general philosophy, without any ethical code to justify its 'inevitability' for the individual. The group avoided activity which might cross the censor or the Tsarist police, and thus earned the nickname Legal Marxists. Some of them subsequently pursued the ethical strand of thought into religious mysticism.

2. A slightly overlapping group, nicknamed Economists, who argued that the entrepreneurial middle class in Russia could and would overthrow Tsarism in due course once capitalism was fully established. Thus, workers should not worry about political matters but concentrate on improving their economic positions – the bourgeois revolution was coming, whatever workers did. The Economists placed heavy stress on the spontaneous activity of

workers as superior to a consciously disciplined organization, despite the chaotic conditions of early industrialization in Russia and the pervasive watch of the secret police.

3. The Bolsheviks, who argued against the first that Marxism included its own ethical presuppositions, and that any revolutionary group must inevitably go beyond what was legal in the conditions of Tsarist Russia. The case against the second group will concern us below. Those subsequently called Mensheviks were members of all three groups at different times.

Lenin

Lenin was a man of great simplicity, severity and dedication, and he possessed that peculiar synthesis of the sense of freedom and of necessity, of practice and of theory, which characterizes the work of Marx: the economically 'inevitable' and the ethically desirable are, in Lenin's work, once more one and the same in the 'sensuous practice' of a revolutionary. Lenin's theoretical writings are not, by the standards of Marx and some of the other Marxist writers of his times, great, since they are not so comprehensive in scope nor fully worked out. However, they are essentially bound up with his activities.

Like most of his contemporaries Lenin was burdened with the inheritance of positivistic Marxism so that, despite his attempts to overcome that burden, his philosophic work as a whole is split between crude and philosophically indefensible materialism, his clumsy version of 'positivism' and his refurbished Hegelian dialectic. He used the analytical work done by other social democrats in Europe (for example, Hilferding's *Finanzkapital* for his popularization of the theory of imperialism), but with a crucial difference: 'science' for Lenin was not passive contemplation by one individual of a world separate and unchangeable, but the study of the world by men who sustained that world and who by their action could change it. His view of capitalism accordingly stressed its continuing contradictory nature, the way those contradictions were resolved turning upon the choices and decisions men made. Thus, advanced economies were marked not just by cartelization stabilizing markets, but cartelization making competition between cartels that much more explosive; not just world unification through imperial conquest, but increasingly aggressive conflicts between rival imperialisms. The framework thus provided was the context for the strategy he designed for the Bolsheviks in Russia, and that practice was in its turn related back to the general European and world scenes.

Lenin was active in politics from the 1890s. Like many other Russian Marxists he judged that the weakness of the middle class in Russia was the main barrier to the overthrow of Tsarism, without which a parliamentary republic, free political parties and the growth of the labour movement would be impossible, thus making a socialist revolution itself some time in the distant future also impossible. The State and foreign interests had developed capitalism in Russia, so that a proletariat proportionately larger that the native bourgeoisie had been created. The small bourgeoisie would be too frightened of the proletarian threat to risk overthrowing the Tsar, despite the restrictions Tsarism might place on the free growth of private industry. However, the proletariat itself was still very new and primitive, at that anarchic stage where its members could not analyse clearly their own position in society as the basis for realistic action, but wasted their collective strength in sporadic and hopeless battles. The intelligentsia which had sustained the fragmentary Narodnik assaults on Tsarism in the sixties and seventies was radical enough, but equally anarchic. It could not supply the proletariat with a rigorous and continuing theoretical framework which would channel labour's manifest hostility into realistic activity; metaphysical talk, endless and fruitless, was all it seemed spontaneously capable of.

Thus, two related problems faced revolutionaries in Russia :

1. If the bourgeoisie would not overthrow the Tsar could proletarian pressure or initiative prompt them to do so? And how could the proletariat, still a small minority in a country overwhelmingly peasant, act thus but avoid destroying itself in the process?

2. How could the proletariat, with its ignorance, but drive and strength, be welded to the intelligentsia, with its education but weakness?

Many of the Economists and Legal Marxists replied that these were pseudo-problems. Since the coming revolution would be bourgeois in both form and content, the proletariat should restrain itself to supporting the middle class, thus simultaneously lending the bourgeoisie the strength to overthrow the Tsar and not frightening it into his arms. At an extreme, of course, this position entailed restraining workers in their day-to-day pressures for wage increases or improvements lest such pressure alarm the capitalists too much – 'economic' and 'political' activity could only for short periods be plausibly separated.

Lenin accepted up to 1917 that 'the democratic revolution will not extend beyond the scope of bourgeois social economic relations' (1905), but he insisted that workers must remain independent of the bourgeoisie: it was not feasible for workers both to fight and support capital. However, the 1905 attempted revolution against the Tsar radically changed the picture, for it seemed both that the proletariat could take independent action to secure the bourgeois revolution, and also the peasantry could play an important revolutionary role at least in the early stages – until the peasants' demand for land was satisfied, when it would become conservative in defence of its new property. Lenin therefore argued that there must be an alliance between workers and peasants, and this could force the bourgeois revolution which the bourgeoisie itself would not initiate. If the proletariat did precipitate the bourgeois revolution it would be able to carry out the main historic tasks of that revolution: the creation of a democratic republic, the confiscation of the estates of the large landowners, the introduction of the eight-hour day. If the revolution did not take place then a hybrid régime would result from the alliance of the Tsar and the bourgeoisie, an *étatiste* capitalism on the model of the Prussia of his day. The choice, Lenin said, lay between a landowner-capitalist régime and a proletarian-peasant 'bourgeois' revolution, between the creation of a society modelled either on the militaristic despotism of Prussia or on the republicanism of the United States. However, if the second was achieved the peasantry would immediately become conservative in defence of its new land ownership, and it would then ally with the bourgeoisie to oust the proletariat from political power.

A third view on the situation might also be mentioned, since, although it was not particularly important at the time, it proved in 1917 more accurate than Lenin's. The Trotsky-Parvus position accepted Lenin's judgement that the Russian bourgeoisie would not do the job, but it also maintained the peasantry was a force too disunited between rich and poor to form a united party for long. Again, if the proletariat seized power, it would be impossible to make it execute demands solely in the interests of the bourgeoisie. Inevitably, it would meet problems for which it could frame only socialist answers; freeing industry from the constrictions of the Tsar would be superseded by nationalizing industry. Thus, there would be a 'permanent revolution'. The bourgeois would merge into the socialist revolution willy-nilly. The phrase 'permanent revolution' was taken from Marx's 1850 *Address to the Communist League*, outlining a strategy for a situation in Germany at that time not dissimilar to that in Russia. Trotsky argued – against straight economic determinism – that there was no direct correlation between the stage of development of a particular country, part of an international economic order, and the type of revolution which ensued. After all, the Paris Commune of 1871 had occurred in a country economically more backward than Britain and the United States which had experienced no such revolt. We might note, in passing, that Weber's observation that religious innovations are likely to occur not in the major centres of the religion but on the periphery might be seen as analogous to this point – the revolution could occur on the edges of capitalist civilization, rather than in its main centres.

However, Trotsky went on, if the *attempt* at a socialist revolution in Russia was inevitable it was impossible that the new order could survive long unless the revolution in Russia sparked off a general socialist revolution in the more advanced countries of Western Europe. Russia was underdeveloped, its proletariat small and relatively backward. The revolution would not survive against the combined opposition of the Russian industrialists and peasants, the overwhelming majority, unless both the numbers and the economic aid of Western Europe came to its assistance. A European revolution would save the Russian proletariat and permit it to sustain the socialist revolution, despite the immense strains of development that must follow (Trotsky, 1906).

Lenin, like most social democrats, rejected this view as going too far; such proposals would disillusion the peasantry before the alliance had ever begun. He reiterated firmly that:

The task of the Russian proletariat is to carry the bourgeois democratic régime in Russia to its conclusion, *in order* to kindle the socialist revolution in Europe. This task has today come very close to the first, but it nevertheless remains a separate and second task; for different classes are to co-operate with the Russian proletariat; for the first, our ally is the *petit-bourgeois* peasantry of Russia, for the second, the proletariat of other countries. (*Some Theses*, 1960, p. 357)

Lenin maintained this position through the substantial fluctuations of Bolshevik support up to 1917. Only after the installation of the provisional government following the overthrow of the Tsar in 1917, and in response to the very radical mood of the St Petersburg workers, did he acknowledge the unrealistic nature of the proposal that the proletariat, having seized power, should quietly relinquish it in conformity with some 'historical law', independent of the consciousness of men.

For the solution of the second problem – how to build a disciplined revolutionary group, intelligentsia and workers, capable of surviving in Tsarist conditions – Lenin's proposals were unoriginal. In 1902, he accepted the opinion common among social democrats, summarized in Kautsky's rather élitist statement that

... socialism and the class struggle arise side by side, and not one out of the other. Modern socialist consciousness can arise only on the basis of profound scientific knowledge. ... The vehicles of science are not the proletariat, but the bourgeois intelligentsia. ... The socialist consciousness is something introduced into the proleterian class struggle from without, and not something that arose within spontaneously. (cited Lenin, 1902)

Since, Lenin went on, a mass democratic party with open public discussions was impossible in Tsarist conditions (the members would be gaoled), the party must be a small secret organization, demanding absolute dedication from its members lest it be betrayed to the police. It would be, when it was small, inevitably overweighted by the 'vehicles of science', the intellectuals, and it would have to be relatively undemocratic since it would have to choose its members carefully to avoid infiltration by police spies. It would demand great internal discipline and organization to avoid suppression. It would have to be composed of professional revolutionaries, not dilettantes or amateurs, since the weakness of one could endanger all.

There were implicit dangers in these proposals, as critics within the Social Democratic Party were quick to point out. The élite, sustained by the nature of Tsarism, could become a substitute for the force it claimed merely to represent. In so far as the Bolsheviks did do this they courted political failure, and perhaps some of the criticisms of Bolshevik tactics during the 1905 revolution are just in this respect. But the mere enunciation of certain tactics in a minor document, *What is to be Done?*, does not on its own demonstrate very much about the Bolsheviks in practice. Many Western critics of Lenin have pounced upon this pamphlet as complete demonstration of all manner of evils. But the proposals are partly common sense in Tsarist conditions, partly unoriginal (some Narodniks had responded to Tsarism in a similar manner, inevitably so given their aims), and partly contradicted by Bolshevik practice. Lenin had no power to enforce his will upon his followers. He had only their voluntary adherence to the cause to ensure loyalty, and that feature meant that *What is to be Done?* could, at best, be an aspiration, not an accomplished fact. Instead of attacking the aims the Bolsheviks had, some anti-communists have pursued the side issue of Lenin's organizational proposals, seeing in them the founding constitution of Stalin's tyranny. Yet Stalin could have been a tyrant without Lenin, and no inexorable railways lines were laid down in 1902 from which the train of Soviet history could not escape.

Bolshevik practice confirms the very doubtful validity of placing so much stress on one early document. Lenin and his followers changed their minds from time to time relative to changes in Russian political conditions. For example, in the 1905 revolution, with Tsarist control weakened by internal revolt, the party was able to open itself to mass membership. It was able to sustain an open public existence until Tsarist strength was sufficient once more to impose control and drive the party back into secrecy. On the other hand, Lenin quite clearly rejected Kautsky's dictum when he proclaimed excitedly after the 1905 revolt that 'the working class is instinctively, spontaneously, Social Democrat'. Lenin learned, and changed, much as most people do, and unlearned things over the passage of time. In 1917, the party was broadly opposed to the seizure of power, despite Lenin, and in the first instance Lenin appealed directly to the St Petersburg workers *against* the party which had become relatively conservative and supported the new post-Tsarist provisional government. Thus, in this instance, his attempt to build a party which was more revolutionary than the ordinary workers of St Petersburg had failed – at the moment of crisis, the party was just like all the others. Within the party itself Lenin was occasionally outvoted, so that it cannot realistically be seen as a one-man dictatorship. Indeed, any such picture of it would be unable to explain how it survived and was popular in 1917, for one man, no matter how attractive (and Lenin was certainly not an 'attractive' man), cannot carry many supporters merely on his own personality, let alone a politically significant movement.

In his writings also he indicated both how important open discussion was, and what kinds of limitations were necessarily imposed by Tsarist conditions. 'Democratic centralism', 'free criticism plus unity of action' were not a mysterious and sinister doctrine until the time of Stalin, and the first element was vital for the party to achieve the best perspective possible – 'without debate, conflicts, without a war between opinion, no movement, including the workers' movement, is possible at all. But without a merciless fight against the degeneration of conflicts into quarrels and squabbles any organization is *impossible*'.

What was called in Chapter 2 'ideational determinism', the notion that once an idea is enunciated it must continue for ever-more to dominate men, has peculiarly afflicted Leninism. It is said that Lenin's assertions lead inexorably to Stalin's policies, as Plato's or Hegel's or Nietzsche's ideas 'lead' to Hitler. Yet as many of Lenin's assertions can be interpreted out of context as democratic as can be seen as authoritarian. Lenin's successors were not bound to any inexorable track, they *chose* what was useful for their purposes (simultaneously abandoning other elements which did not contribute). In that choice a critique should begin.

The same remarks might apply to that hoary old chestnut, *partiinost* (literally, 'party-ness', and meaning 'party spirit'), beloved of United States Sovietologists. Lenin argued against Struve that someone with political convictions should behave in intellectual controversy in consistency with those convictions, he should be 'committed' rather than sustaining perhaps contradictory positions – on the one hand, a Marxist, on the other, a conventional social scientist or historian. The point was one that others had made, even though it was applicable largely to radicals who opposed society and to conservatives in time of war. It was a demand for responsibility, for consistency, for dedication, not for the posture of an idle bystander, someone who was uncommitted. However, critics have argued that this position, explicitly a recommendation to party members opposing Tsarism, is really the practical source of Stalinist censorship, interference in all cultural and scientific activities in society as a whole; again, as if Stalin needed such a relatively modest notion to create so tyrannical a weapon.

All that has been described so far derives directly from the actual circumstances of the Bolshevik attempt to survive as a disciplined party active in Russia rather than exiled to Siberia or Switzerland. Lenin was a hard man without the gifts of circumlocution and diplomatic courtesy. Inevitably he made many enemies, and most of the subsequent criticisms of him were made at the time by his contemporaries. But his vindication came in 1917, as Trotsky, who campaigned with the greatest bitterness against Lenin's ruthlessness (and earned, in reply, equally savage denunciation from Lenin), acknowledged:

Only the highest concentration on the goal of revolution, free from everything pettily personal, can justify this kind of personal ruthlessness. . . . His behaviour seemed to me inadmissible, terrible, shocking. Yet at the same time it was politically correct and therefore indispensable from the point of view of organization. (1930, p. 188)

The most traumatic event in Lenin's political life was the failure of the European social democratic parties to prevent war in 1914. For so many years, these parties had declared that they would not fight each other, and that any war declared by their respective governments would be promptly turned into revolution by the social democrats, yet at the moment of testing, the overwhelming majority opted for nationalism rather than socialism, and marched off to slaughter each other. The whole precarious house of cards, the theoretical inheritance of social democracy, collapsed in the trenches. The hopes that the Second International would lead Europe into a new society could no longer be sustained. The event forced Lenin to re-examine his own beliefs and the Marxism he had accepted for so long to see why those whom, even in criticizing, he had respected as his seniors in Marxism, had failed before the decisive challenge. As a result of this re-examination, he revised much of what he had taken for granted from Kautsky and German social democracy, so that although, in intellectual terms, the revision remained incomplete, his life's work fits into two inconsistent parts, pre- and post-1914. Thus, in philosophy, his main pre-1914 work, *Materialism and Empirio-Criticism* (written in reply to neo-Kantian revisionism), merely repeats in clumsy and philosophically indefensible terms the crude materialism of Kautsky. But after 1914, Lenin's pursuit of the theoretical sources for the failure of the Second International led to his rediscovery of Hegel's dialectic and his assertion that no Marxist had understood *Capital* for a quarter of a century. For Lenin, the dialectic both restored the primacy of human activity and threw a new stress on the contradictory elements in the new capitalism, summarized in his popular pamphlet, *Imperialism: The Highest Stage of Capitalism*.

As the challenge of new problems had shifted the German

social democrat leaders towards new purposes, rendering their theoretical inheritance irrelevant, so new events compelled the Bolsheviks to rediscover the theories associated with their own purposes. Bernstein had challenged the divergence between German social democrat theory and practice by urging that the theory be revised to conform to the practice. Lenin identified the same divergence, but demanded that practice conform to the theory, the aims claimed in the rhetoric be systematically pursued rather than used as decorative elements on a basically conservative standpoint.

But if social democratic Marxism had extinguished the role of human activity and consciousness in its deterministic interpretation of Marx, it had also absorbed other matching elements from its environment, and, in particular, bureaucracy, a heavy reliance on the State, and an implicit nationalism. In restoring the primacy of human agency in history Lenin, in like form, passionately reaffirmed freedom as the essence of Marxism and socialism in *State and Revolution*. The 'withering-away of the State' was not, as it had been for German social democracy, to be relegated to some Utopian limbo; it should begin immediately power was won. Lenin also rejected the alliance of socialism and nationalism that had destroyed the Second International and was embodied in the social democratic acceptance of the State as a substitute for popular participation and initiative. He affirmed that the aim of all radical socialist movements should be to *abolish* the State, and he accused Kautsky of censoring the writings of Marx and Engels which asserted that the State was necessarily an instrument of tyranny. When class domination ended the administration of society must inevitably devolve so that all would participate and control society. Uncompromisingly, he concluded: 'So long as the State exists, there is no freedom; when freedom exists, there will be no State.'

Such an unequivocal affirmation of the necessity for freedom and the form it must take could only lead to great pessimism or great optimism. In 1917 and 1918 optimism was the dominant motif – men could control society, the majority could be self-governing. In May 1918 Lenin promised his audience that those who were not over thirty to thirty-five years old would see the dawn of communism. Immediately after the October Revolution, he warned Russian workers that:

Remember, *you yourselves* now adminster the State. Nobody will help you if you yourselves do not unite and take *all affairs* of State into *your own hands. Your* Soviets are henceforth the organs of State power, organs full of power, organs of decision. (cited Carr, 1950, p. 244)

In January 1918 he explained to the Congress of Soviets that 'In introducing workers' control, we knew it would take some time before it spread to the whole of Russia, but we wanted the workers themselves to draw up, from below, the new principle of economic conditions.' The affirmation of the necessity for freedom is too frequent and too passionate to be the cold calculation of a Machiavellian.

The revolution was the supreme moment of Lenin's career, both vindication of his work and test of his strategy. It was also, ironically, a critique of the flavour of élitism that sometimes appeared in his work and derived from the conditions for a revolutionary party in Russia (sanctioned by the authority of Marxism's 'Pope', Kautsky). For Lenin could not rely on his party to champion popular demands of the moment that brought power in 1917. Organization had not been able to ensure that the party was always slightly ahead of popular wishes, was more revolutionary than the workers. For when the decisive moment came the party had to be whipped into championing those demands – even to the extent of stealing its programme directly from them rather than advancing what the party had already decided (cf. Lenin, 1917, p. 30).

But the winter of 1917–18 saw the effects of the World War and the dissolution of the Tsarist armies, as well as the revolution, leaving the administrative machine in ruins, and food supplies exhausted. Once it had gained land the peasantry no longer sustained the revolution, and there was not, as yet, a European revolution to fill the sails of the new Soviet craft. Lenin began retracing his steps, not by revising his general theoretical work, but by becoming deeply immersed in day-to-day administration, in mere survival. His statements have a tone of rising pessimism, a refusal to speculate on what had been achieved and what could be achieved, an identification of some of the central problems but without solutions. The civil war dealt a further staggering blow to the economy and the new government was compelled to take back into employment thousands of former Tsarist officials, so transforming the nature of the administration at the same time as its own followers, urban workers, were dispatched to the army to fight the White forces. Force had now become increasingly important as the means to win some food from the obdurate countryside.

Plekhanov once taunted Lenin with a quotation from Engels, and it became increasingly relevant from 1918 as the claimed social basis of the party drained away and no European revolution occurred to shift the balance of forces:

The worst that can befall the leader of an extremist party is to be compelled to take over the government at a time when the movement is not yet ripe for the rule of the class he represents.... He finds himself necessarily in an insoluble political dilemma: what he *can* do is in conflict with his entire previous attitudes, his principles, and the immediate interests of his party; what he is *supposed* to do cannot be done ... he is compelled to represent not his party, his class, but the class for the rule of which the movement happens to be right. For the sake of that movement he must act for the interests of an alien class, and must feed his own class with phrases and promises along with the assertion that the interests of that alien class are really their own. He who gets himself in that false position is irredeemably lost. (Engels, 1850)

The great hopes disintegrated in increasing gloom, only heightened by the revolt of the Kronstadt sailors (an earlier generation of Kronstadt sailors had been foremost supporters of the Bolsheviks), a wave of strikes and peasant revolts. It was clear the Bolsheviks no longer represented a majority of even the industrial working class; indeed, they represented nothing except themselves. Yet what alternative existed? Were they quietly to acknowledge their mistake, abandon hope of a

European revolution and give up power? Yet the White armies which would have inherited that power would show no such respect for any principle; they would probably have instituted the first Fascist régime in Europe, with an accompanying wave of terror that would surpass the brutality of the Tsars.

Lenin did not make his peace with Marxist theory; he left it in suspension. He became preoccupied with how to develop Russia, how to drag it out of backwardness, ignorance and poverty in the face of international hostility. The day-to-day problems of the economy became the most important affairs of State, and any tactic to drive the economy along assumed major importance – 'it is our task to learn State capitalism [not socialism, N. H.] from the Germans, to adopt it with all our might, to shrink from no dictatorial methods to hasten this transfer of Western culture to barbaric Russia, without hesitating to use barbaric fighting methods against barbarism.'

But still no revolution in Germany appeared, so that there was no option but to relax the pace once the civil war and the phase of war communism permitted. Requisitioning from the peasant was replaced by a fixed tax, with free trade for surplus foodstuffs; a number of small and medium industrial units were denationalized. Bukharin went even further and argued that, since the world revolution had failed, then the Soviet State must pursue a policy which would retain the 'alliance' with the peasantry. The withdrawal was not simply a 'tactical retreat', for the whole focus of attention was taken away from the international scene, the possibility of an international revolution, and turned inwards towards the defence and development of Russia. Of course, the terminology did not change, but it was a fatal shift, for the territorial interests of the Soviet Union as a nation-State now superseded the interests of the wider international class – 'the fight for Soviet Russia', the Second Comintern Congress resolved, 'has merged with the struggle against world capitalism. The Soviet Russian question has become the acid test for all organizations of the working class' (1921). Thus, as German social democracy had concealed its nationalism in the terminology of socialism so also the door to the same concealment was opened in the Soviet Union.

For Lenin, the theoretical problem remained unresolved. He offered no explanation for Bolshevik power, a socialist seizure in an underdeveloped country in the absence of a European revolution. In such a forthright man, that is a significant omission – for no peace with integrity was possible. He made do with piecemeal, pragmatic responses, with attacks on 'bureaucracy' and Russian 'barbarism', but with increasing pessimism:

Can every worker know how to administer the State? Practical people know that this is a fairy tale.... The trade unions are a school of communism and administration. When they [the workers] have spent these years at school, they will learn, but it progresses slowly.... How many workers have been engaged in administration? A few thousands all over Russia, no more. (cited Carr, 1950, p. 247)

The great trade union debate of 1921–2 – where Trotsky's demand for the militarization of labour (that is, for an explicitly tyrannical régime) faced the demand of the workers' opposition for the abolition of the State and control of the economy by workers' Soviets – is significant as an exhibition of Lenin's purely pragmatic tacking between extremes, in which his reasoning becomes uncharacteristically tortuous – 'Ours is a workers' Government with a bureaucratic twist. Our present Government is such that the proletariat, organized to the last man, must protect itself against it. And we must use workers' organization for the protection of workers against their own Government.' (1937, ix, p. 9.) Lenin seems to have lost his moorings, the conceptual landscape no longer provides the relevant landmarks – he is aware of the problem, but sees no social force available to solve it:

If we take that huge bureaucratic machine (the State), that huge pile, we must ask: Who is leading whom? To tell the truth, it is not they [the Communists] who are leading, they are being led [by the ex-Tsarist civil servants]. [Or again] With the exception of the People's Commissariat for Foreign Affairs, our State apparatus is very largely a survival of the old one, and has least of all undergone serious change. It has only been slightly repainted on the surface, but in all other things, it is a typical relic of our old State apparatus. (ibid., ix)

As a whole, then, Lenin's theoretical work is incomplete, but it does constitute, in the conditions he faced, something of a brief renaissance of the spirit of Marx's work. He did not undertake a systematic or comprehensive critique of the religion Kautsky had distilled from Marx, but he did demonstrate in his own life a very considerable unity of theory and practice. From 1918 the validating conditions of his own position broke down in a way that offered no possibility of solution; the unity had been so powerful it could not be restored again with honesty and integrity. The tragedy of Lenin remained unrelieved. Around him he could see an entirely new and unenvisaged order beginning to emerge; he could not possibly envisage how terrible that order would be, but, in any case, he had no solutions to offer. The proletariat had gone, the European revolution had not occurred, and both together left the party alone and isolated as the substitute for both.

Stalin

An entirely different range of problems faced Joseph Stalin, finally to emerge as Lenin's successor, and it is obviously impossible here to trace the nature of his diverse responses to thirty years in office. This is particularly important since some of the canons of Stalinism are not much more than the accidental positions of an internal party faction fight, the sources of which have long since been forgotten. Stalinism is essentially deducible from the practice of the Soviet State, and Stalin's exiguous theoretical output is, unlike Lenin's work, no longer any sort of guide to understanding the practice, but is rather a rationale offered after the event to justify it. Theoretical analysis is not a guide to practice, is not operative, but is an historical commentary. For the practice was brutal, and, for those subject to it, irrational, a matter rather for concealment, disguise, than theoretical illumination. As a result, Stalinism has an opaque quality. We can no longer detect its direct connection with the acts of the Soviet State, and we are constantly aware of a background echo of real but unspoken purposes. Discussion within Stalinism retreats into ritual, text-quoting, semantic quibbles, terminological disputes and clear historical distortion. Trotsky put it polemically thus: 'Its "ideology" [Stalinism] is thoroughly permeated with police subjectivism, its practice is the empiricism of crude violence. In keeping with its essential interests, the caste of usurpers is hostile to any theory: it can give an account neither to itself nor to anyone else of its social role. Stalin revises Marx and Lenin not with the theoretician's pen but with the heel of the CPU [Secret Police, *N. H.*].' (1937)

As a system Stalinism is idealist, rather than materialist (in the philosophical sense). It begins not with the accomplished event, not with social reality, the facts of experience, but with ideas, the text and the axiom. Conformity with Leninist ideals is not achieved by action, but by redescribing what has been done. As with the British Conservatives, propaganda is the means to reconcile the popular ideal with the rulers' real. Thus, Lenin's writings came to be treated in a manner even more extreme than that in which the German social democrats treated Marx. Lenin's work became a corpus of theological doctrine, a ritual, a source of endless citations out of context, not theory as a guide to particular action by a particular group of people in a particular historical situation.

The texts of Stalinism itself are heavy with mechanical images of great clumsiness, with spurts of malevolence, with theoretical vacuity married to mindless militancy. Zhdanov's attack on Soviet philosophy in 1947 characterizes some of this empty militancy:

We have often used in our discussion the term 'philosophic front'. But where is this front? ... does our philosophy resemble a real front? It resembles rather a stagnant creek, or bivouac far from the battlefield. The field has not yet been entered for the most part, contact with the enemy has not been established, there is no reconnaissance, the weapons are rusting, the soldiers are fighting at their own risk and peril.... (1947, cited Wetter, 1958, p. 27)

The writing of Stalin is brief and poor in quality although of central importance for the history of the Soviet Union since it dominated the entire intellectual scene. Its most interesting tendency is a groping for the characteristic forms of conservative thought, and its most striking characteristic an immense unresolved contradiction. It has no dialectic in any important sense, but it did provide the maximum scope for any action at all that Stalin might have wished to take. Stalin stressed both:

1. A 'material base' to society, the economic functioning of society, as almost independent of men. Ideas merely 'reflected' material reality (a point from early Lenin), and political consciousness merely 'reflected' the state of technology – put crudely, gasometers produce poetry via men. The actual lumps of the economic base – steel plants, cranes, factories and so on – seemed to possess a life of their own and to compel society to transform itself in conformity with this life. E. P. Thompson describes the relationship thus: 'Ideas are no longer seen as the medium by which men apprehend the world, reason, argue, debate, and choose; they are like the evil and wholesome smells arising from the imperialist and proletarian cooking pots.' (1957, p. 105.)

There is little or no interaction between the base and the rest of society, the 'superstructure', only the base dragging the reluctant superstructure along behind: 'The superstructure is created by the base precisely to serve it, to actively help it to take shape and consolidate it, to actively fight for the elimination of the old moribund base, together with its superstructure.' (Stalin, 1950, pp. 9–10.)

2. A crucial role for theory, for 'the tremendous organizing, mobilizing and transforming value of new ideas, new theories, new political views and new political institutions'. The embodiment of the role of ideas was the party offering leadership to the otherwise unliberated, confused masses. Paradoxically, the position can be compared to that of Disraeli; for, with the decline in the natural acceptance of an hereditary aristocracy as the national political élite, Disraeli also stressed the crucial significance of 'great ideas', married to leadership 'charisma', as the

sole practical means to sustain a *status quo* which was now industrial and therefore in continuous change. The two Disraelian elements recur in Stalin's work although much less elegantly formulated. For Stalin, his stress on the role of theory embodied his demand that the party should reach a 'correct' view of the world since its role was supreme in transforming society; theory was the one weapon of the party that it could acknowledge publicly.

The party's monopoly of theory thus symbolized the party's monopoly of power – like most rulers Stalin implied that power was held solely because of the popular support for the ideas the party propagated. The monopoly of theory was heightened, stressed, by the contention that mass consciousness always lags behind correct theory; the proposal fulfils the same function as the Conservative contention that people need leadership, need to be inspired by great ideas or else they will be confused, anarchic, uncoordinated. For Stalin, the lag of mass consciousness reached extreme proportions, for in 1937, twenty years after the revolution, he argued that ideological errors, contracted from the hostility of the 'remnants of the old exploiting classes', would get *worse* the further Russia was from the time of the revolution:

We must destroy and cast aside the rotten theory that with every advance we make the class struggle here would of necessity die down more and more, and that in proportion as we achieve success, the class enemy would become more and more tractable. This is not only a rotten theory, but a dangerous one, for it ... makes it possible for the class enemy to rally for the struggle against the Soviet Government. On the contrary, the farther we advance, the greater will be the fury of the remnants of the exploiting classes, the sooner will they resort to sharper forms of struggle. (1937, pp. 29–30)

Thus, although the present superstructure (that is, the mass of the population) is totally subordinate to the base (that is, the party), the superstructure of the past (Tsarism) could still operate with increasing independence, could more and more play the scapegoat when Stalin needed scapegoats. Through it all, the narrow-eyed suspicion of the *muzhik* lurks behind the apparent framework of Marxism.

The central contradiction in Stalinism is then between determinism and party voluntarism: determinism for the masses, voluntarism for the leadership. The schism parallels one within British Conservatism, for there also, although much less clearly, the masses are trapped in determinism (in 'human nature' most often, but for an earlier generation, in 'original sin', Stalin's economic base) while the rulers enjoy almost complete freedom (in both cases, through their pseudo-magical qualities as leaders, expressed in their power of creativity in ideology). The division is a class division between the necessarily passive majority and the active ruling class, enjoying a monopoly of legitimate initiative.

The contradiction was of no great importance to the advocates of Stalinism, and was effectively resolved in practice through Stalin's monopoly (crucially backed by force) of the right to define at any given moment what the material base was or was becoming and therefore what correct theory was. Conservatives retain the right to define the practical implications of 'human nature'; both enunciate the 'lessons of history'. Thus, as a theoretical system Stalinism needed a Pope, needed the central defining role of one individual or group to reconcile the whole, and it was not a system which could be conceived as standing apart from the group that created and used it. In Stalin's person is the necessary synthesis. He is the substitute for the party as the party is for the Russian working class and the international proletariat, the substitute for the (voluntary) wishes of the majority.

A number of subsidiary elements are related within this framework, only a few of which can be cited here.

1. *The State.* If Lenin had doubts about the future of the Soviet Union, about identifying what had been achieved and therefore what was to come, Stalin had no such doubts. He asserted firmly that socialism was possible in one country – that it was possible to create and sustain a proletarian dictatorship in an underdeveloped country where the proletariat was a small

minority, not the great majority as in Western Europe, and possible to do so without the aid of a European revolution. The statement, which began as seeking to make a virtue of necessity in the faction fight with Trotsky who maintained that socialism was ultimately impossible without a world revolution, became for Stalin a general principle applicable to all countries. Whereas the bourgeois revolution occurred only where capitalism was already fully developed (as Marx had suggested), the task of the new socialist order was not so much to emancipate a highly developed majority proletariat, as to develop the economy, to 'build socialism', which would thereby create a majority proletariat – the agent of the revolution only created itself *after* the revolution and through a process of industrialization which had historically been notorious for its brutality, Marx's 'primitive capital accumulation'. As Stalin put it:

The main task of the bourgeois revolution consists of seizing power and making it conform to the already existing bourgeois economy, whereas the main task of the proletarian revolution consists in seizing power in order to build up a new socialist economy ... in the proletarian revolution, the seizure of power is only the *beginning*, and power is used as a lever for transforming the old economy and organizing a new one. (1926)

As for many arguments, some of Lenin's tentative and very qualified statements at the end of his life can be found to support a grain of this, but Stalin's version is unqualified, and plays upon the ambiguity of the terms 'socialist order', and 'socialist economy'. For on the one hand such phrases implied a society in which the proletariat were ruling; on the other a society where the State owned the means of production. Hitherto, in socialist writings the two were seen by and large as one and the same, but henceforth, after the experience of Stalin, increasingly the two diverged: democracy, the rule of a majority proletariat, was not a necessary precondition for the expropriation of capital. Stalin detached the agent of the revolution, the proletariat, from the society which created a proletariat, so that there was no meaning left for the phrase 'socialist order' except 'an economic order owned by the State'. The class content of the phrase is extinguished, and socialism becomes no longer concerned with the emancipation of the industrial working class, but a tactic for forced economic development under State control; 'socialist' means 'State', regardless of who runs the State in whose interest.

The statement also portrays a political 'superstructure' that has the power to shape and expand the economic 'base', and which is 'classless'. The Short Course (*History of the CPSU(B)*, 1938), said to have been largely written by Stalin himself and used for many years as the standard textbook of Stalinism, describes the collectivization of agriculture in a similar vein; it was

a profound revolution, a leap . . . equivalent in its consequences to the revolution of October 1917. The distinguishing feature of this revolution is that it was accomplished *from above*, on the initiative of the State, and directly supported *from below* by the millions of peasants who were fighting to overthrow *kulak* bondage and to live in freedom in the collective farms.

No doubt the Ukranian peasants would have been pleased to know how they supported a process which destroyed so many of them, and which was for them quite clearly an external oppression.

For Stalin then, in contrast to both Marx and Lenin, the State in the Soviet Union was neither the embodiment of class tyranny nor the temporary feature of a transitional phase, but a classless and creative element. Both Marx (in *The Eighteenth Brumaire*) and Engels (in *The Origin of the Family, Private Property and the State*) had suggested that the State need not always embody the rule of a dominant class, for it could act as a mediating, initiating agency, where classes were locked in balanced equilibrium. This was a point Stalinism consistently rejected, since it could have constituted grounds for saying the Soviet State was not necessarily the agency of proletarian class rule.

2. *Nation*. The 'classless' State implied also a change in the notion of class, a concept which is possibly the most important one of all in the work of Marx and Lenin. Stalin slowly replaced

the idea with that of nation, for if the 'proletarian class' was identical with the Soviet State, the Soviet State embodied historically the Russian nation, so that the role of the State corresponds to the stress on nationalism, a conjecture Lenin had bitterly criticized in German social democracy.

The stress on *national* (not class) solidarity, embodying the necessary harmony of Soviet society, was slowly increased to reach its maximum during the Second World War. The change was extrapolated backwards in Soviet versions of Russian history also to iron out the class cleavages of Tsarist society that had been the central concern of Lenin's work. A decree of May 1934 condemned all previous accounts of Russian history and rehabilitated words like 'homeland', 'patriotism' and so on. From 1940, the Russian people's role in history was increasingly glorified, its origins were traced back to the civilizations of the Chaldeans and Assyrians of the second and third millennia before Christ (in similar fashion, the families of even minor gentry in England and France 'go back to' Charlemagne), and to its historical ingenuity all major inventions were attributed. Inevitably, since the basic historic unit was now identified not by its role in the social structure but by its ethnic descent, racialism appeared, for only 'the blood' could identify who was part of the heroic people.

As Stalin was the sole active agent in the party, and the party in the Russian people, so the Russian people became the sole active agency in the historical population of the world – a pyramid or hierarchy of values that reflected the creation of a clear hierarchy in Soviet society. The Soviet Union remained the nation 'for whom history has prepared the great mission of the liberation of mankind' (*Pravda*, 6 June 1949, cited Barghoorn, 1956, pp. 248–9). Even the intermediate layer, non-Russian subjects of the Soviet Union, received a special intermediate stratum in the hierarchy. The Russian people were superior to all non-Russian people in the Soviet Union, and should be acknowledged as such even by foreigners: 'Love for the Russian people ... is not only one of the most important aspects of Soviet patriotism; it is a characteristic feature of every genuine proletarian movement, even in capitalist countries'. (*Problems of Philosophy*, 1948, cited Wetter, 1958, p. 271.)

3. *Class*. The Soviet Union was a 'classless society', or rather a society in which the term 'class' referred only to units which were functionally complementary, peasants and workers in harmonious interaction within an obvious division of labour, not competitive units locked in rivalry (as Lenin suggested peasants and workers would be after the revolution). Ossowski (1963, p. 115) notes that this conception is rather Adam Smith's than Marx's, and that Stalin comes close here to the gradualism favoured in, say, the United States, rather than any revolutionary perspective: 'When the future of their own society is concerned, the ruling groups in both capitalist and socialist countries always take an evolutionary attitude.' Of course, 'remnants of the old exploiting classes' were kept on hand to offer some explanation of any domestic conflict that occurred, useful scapegoats perpetually in league with foreign powers (as they had to be to validate 'basic national unity') and periodically infiltrating the party, even at its highest levels, as revealed in the Moscow trials of the 1930s. If the 'remnants' were inadequate, spies were lacking, then scapegoats could be found in ethnic minorities, Jews and so on. In each case the rebels, if such they ever were in any real sense, played the same part for Stalinists that the 'misaristocracy', the 'faction' of a merely sectional interest, played for Conservatives. The 'mis-leaders' plotted, apparently with motiveless malignity, anarchy and disaster. The role of scapegoats was discussed in an earlier chapter. They help to secure solidarity, and thereby safeguard the orthodoxy, thus securing more firmly the rule of the existing leadership.

But the main elements of conflict, the fragments of the notion of class struggle, were reserved not for domestic but for external use. Some basic national harmony stood in sharp contrast to the real cleavages that lay abroad: indigenous strain was exported to the international scene where no basic loyalties were accepted except the national. Class was liberally attributed to groups or individuals according to the attitude they were thought to have towards the Soviet Union – thus, there could be a whole series of unlikely proletarians, or, if that term was really implausible, then 'patriotic' would stand instead as in 'patriotic African tribal chiefs', meaning chiefs who had perhaps been enthusiastic at a Nairobi Russian Embassy cocktail party.

Ultimately, the struggle was said to be between 'proletarian nations' and 'bourgeois nations', a formulation also favoured by, for example, right-wing nationalists in Italy after the First World War, operating in a context where Marxist terminology was important. The internationalism of Marx and Lenin dissolved into nationalism, the character of which was unimportant provided it included a favourable attitude towards the Soviet Union, for the 'proletarian nations' were not proletarian at all. The phrase signified nothing about their domestic class structures. They were distinguished usually by their poverty and the overwhelmingly peasant character of their societies. And 'bourgeois nations' were merely anti-Soviet rich industrialized countries. Of course, in fact, the first were usually involved in a nationalistic revulsion against imperialism, and the second were, to a greater or less degree, imperialist powers, but this factor should not conceal how little Stalin was seriously interested in the real social structure of the countries concerned. His interests were in international relations, between sovereign nation-States, not in international class struggle where national boundaries were of little significance. The most appropriate weapons for Stalin were primarily diplomatic, or professional warfare, for which agitation, cast in the language of class struggle, was occasionally an appropriate adjunct – much as it was for the Tsarist *agents provocateurs* or is for the American Central Intelligence Agency. Again, the loophole can be seen in some of Lenin's later formulations, heavily qualified and tentative in context, but no less a major shift. From a Russian revolution snapping the 'weakest link in the capitalist chain', so precipitating a European revolution, focus shifted to China or India as the 'weakest links in the imperialist chain'. The end of the evolution arrived when the Comintern became not the leader of an international working-class movement, of which the Soviet Union was merely one small part, but a subsidiary agency of Russian foreign policy, of which the international working-class movement was merely one small part. Foreign communist parties became the rearguard of the Soviet Union, not the vanguard of world revolution, agencies, at least in their leadership, for the subversion of their local *status quo* in the interests of a foreign State rather than in the interests of the proletariat. The transition cost the lives of most of the old Bolsheviks, not 'flexible' or 'pragmatic' enough to convert themselves into all they had opposed for so long. Occasionally, the transition did pose problems for Stalin; consider the following nimble hair-splitting: bourgeois nationalism is rightly condemned by Marxists since it has

the object of doping the masses with the poison of nationalism and strengthening the role of the bourgeoisie. What is national culture under the dictatorship of the proletariat? It is culture that is *socialist* in content and national in form, having the object of educating the masses in the spirit of socialism and internationalism. It would be foolish to suppose that Lenin regarded socialist culture as *non-national*, as not having a particular national form. ... The period of the dictatorship of the proletariat and of the building of socialism in the U.S.S.R. is a period of the *flowering* of national cultures that are socialist in content and national in form. [Stalin goes on] It may be said that such a presentation of the question is contradictory, but is there not the same contradictoriness in our presentation of the question of the State? We stand for the withering away of the State. At the same time, we stand for the strengthening of the dictatorship of the proletariat, which is the mightiest and strongest State power that has ever existed. ... Is this contradictory? Yes, it is contradictory. But this contradiction is bound up with life, and it fully reflects Marx's dialectic. ... (1930, *Collected Works* 12, pp. 278–81)

The General Secretary could rest assured that none in his audience were brave enough to shout 'Gibberish!', no child innocent enough to say the emperor was naked.

After the great traumatic experience of collectivization, industrialization and world war, after the immense sacrifices demanded of the Soviet people were no longer needed, Stalinism mellowed somewhat, permitting the more orthodox conservative tone of tranquillity to emerge from the earlier harsh ritual. Stalin tied together some of the ends of his practice in his two last works, *Concerning Marxism in Linguistics* and *Economic Problems of Socialism in the U.S.S.R.* The first, ostensibly designed to answer certain problems in the narrow field of linguistics, in fact goes much further by stressing the common elements of a nation (pre-eminently its language) rather than its temporary class elements which, in Marxist terms, underpin internationalism. The second lays down the economic conditions for the prelude to communism; its tone is cautious, conservative, and suggests almost indefinite postponement of what has clearly become a Utopian aim.

What Stalin left of the terminology of Marxism was relatively useless for any specific purposes his successors might have, but this did not inhibit them in any way, any more than Stalin was inhibited by the pronouncements of his predecessors. Stalin's practice was not a series of pragmatic adjustments to new circumstances, the 'logic of power' much favoured by conservative commentators, but rather the pursuit of purposes quite incompatible with those of Marx and Lenin – against their class internationalism he posed Russian nationalism. One cannot use 'pragmatically' a general theory directed at destroying a certain kind of society for the purposes of *Blitzkrieg* economic development, any more than one can use an explosives manual for building a factory. Naturally, the terminology of freedom continued, but now to conceal a tyrannical reality, not to raise men's sights to the immense possibilities open to them. The terminology was decoration, not guide to practice, the sophistical arguments designed to make slaves not merely accept their slavery but rather kiss their chains as the symbol of their freedom. The régime never felt confident enough to dispense with police and army, any more than do Western régimes. The reality was such that the terminology, although it concealed much, also became debased coin, the butt of cynics. 'After 1929', Joravsky argues (1966)

the ideology actually at work in the minds of the chiefs is to be found much more in their intuitive judgements of practical matters than in the largely irrelevant texts of theoretical ideology. ... Much of what passes for theoretical ideology in the Soviet Union is a traditional survival. It performs the same functions as Corinthian columns on modern public buildings, or the invocation of Jesus' name at the launching of a nuclear submarine.

In similar fashion, Western prime ministers and presidents summon to their support God's aid on important occasions.

Thus, it would be a mistake to see Stalin's successors as having made difficult and daring ideological innovations since his death. What has happened is that they have permitted certain formulations to lapse (Stalin himself let some points of doctrine lapse in the later years of his life). Stalinism did retain some elements of radicalism. They were not of the Leninist variety – concerned with the emancipation of the industrial working class – but rather the radicalism required to industrialize a backward society, to explain and justify the ruthlessness of the process and the sacrifices required from the mass of the population. When that process was nearing completion the Second World War and the following Cold War kept alive certain elements of militancy.

But the logic of modern industrial society inevitably made itself felt in the organization of the Soviet Union once these three factors declined in importance. Indeed, the decline of the Cold War is part cause and part effect of that logic, in conjunction with the purposes of United States foreign policy. Stalin's death was rather the pretext for, than the cause of, the domestic relaxation in Russia. Narrowed wage differentials, raising the lowest day rates, shifting slightly the industrial structure from heavy to light industry, from industry to services, placing a much greater stress on the consumption patterns appropriate to 'affluence', these were all part of that logic of modern industrial society, and not held back by either curious ideological beliefs or the petulance of a bad-tempered old man.

The changes in modern Soviet leadership beliefs are, then, no more than a mellowing of the conservative features implicit in Stalinism. The last chapter sought to suggest that conservatism, in conditions of reasonable stability, needs no general theoretical formulations. Immediate administration is the centre of attention, not the necessity for structural change. For this reason Soviet ideology is not a powerful and irrational constraint on the actions of the Soviet leadership. Ideology does not clash with the 'facts', 'reality'. The recent adjustments – for example, polycentrism in foreign policy, the Libermann plan to charge interest on capital employed – are not belated recognitions of reality, except if one believes that a conservative perspective is 'reality': what the West says is real is the ideal.

What inhibits doctrinal innovation in the Soviet Union, as in the West, is not some preceding doctrinal position, but other people, people who feel rightly or wrongly that they stand to lose by the innovation or gain by opposing it, since in their estimation the innovation summarizes some changed state of affairs, some new purpose or intention. The conflict is between people, not ideas or ideas and facts. Stalin's successors have had no need to make substantial changes in an on-going process – despite Krushchev's Twentieth Congress speech in 1956, where Stalin was used as a convenient scapegoat for the errors of the past, errors in which the current Soviet leadership might also be implicated – and this is so because they share a basic tenet of Stalinist ideology, namely that the existing distribution of power in Russia should remain as it is. Existing ideology meets no great obstacles. The ideology, judged from a Western conservative position, merely seems to fade or is trivialized, since it no longer reasonably mediates between the purpose of the leaders and the desires of the led.

When the old soldiers of Stalinist ideology have faded away then the 'liberalization' of the Soviet Union can be seen for what it is. The adjustments are part of the adjustments of Soviet society, perhaps part of the transfer of increasing power from the old party to a new managerial élite, the new party. If this is so – and the evidence permits only speculative formulation – then the parallel with British Conservatism becomes even closer. Whereas in Britain the transition was from individualistic and entrepreneurial liberalism to *étatiste* and pluralist corporatism, in the Soviet Union the transition has been from collectivist and developmental *étatisme* to *étatiste* corporatism. Certainly, the external appearance is not dissimilar. The Russian *status quo* appears as equally a fully-formed class society, even though based upon

State property, not mixed private-public property under State guidance. The beliefs of both the leaderships lay heavy stress on nationalism, class harmony, the common interest of all in the existing *status quo*, modified by a meritocracy and welfare services but embodying considerable social inequality. The State, *étatisme*, and bureaucracy go together in similar ways, along with nationalism. The key ideals in both cases are broadly inoperative, the ideal is the real.

This comparison cannot be taken too far, for the different historical roots of both groups of beliefs mean that although the implication is much the same, the prior formulations are different. Marxist-Leninists do not retreat into a mystery, and have no use for the idea of basic human nature. British Conservatism still cherishes fragments linked both to the landed gentry and to 'free enterprise', and electoral considerations compel it to appeal to the middle classes, including many small private businessmen, in a way Marxist-Leninists do not.

This chapter has been burdened with, perhaps, relatively boring detail and a narrow focus of attention, but it has been necessary to pursue the limited themes properly. The aim has been to show the transformation of a group of radical beliefs into their opposite, how this was achieved in doctrinal terms, and the implications involved. Lenin has been described as an heir to Marx in a way German social democracy was not. He broke out of the constricting conservatism-in-practice of social democracy, rejected its failure to match behaviour and theory, and sought to restore the idea of the active agency of the industrial working class in the phase of history in which he lived. He defended the aim of freedom as the essence of Marxism against the bureaucratic, *étatiste*, and nationalist revisions implicit in German social democracy. Ironically, it was just this revision which Stalin revived in the new alliance of the Russian State and Russian nationalism.

The next chapter pursues the theme of Marxism, now transferred to a properly underdeveloped country under foreign domination (Russia was underdeveloped relative only to the European context). The legacy of Stalinism was important here, but again new purposes created doctrines which are not strictly Stalinist.

6

Nationalism and the South

Bismarck's 'State socialism' was 'the renaissance of the Mercantilism of the seventeenth century, adapted to the benevolent and illuminated despotism of the eighteenth century and the conditions of a militarist State, remoulded by the phenomena of modern industrialism.'

G. C. ROBERTSON, cited in Issawi,
Egypt in Revolution, an Economic Analysis

THE South, the underdeveloped (or 'developing' or 'backward', the alternative usages, like those for the poor, are many), includes the majority of the world's population and a far wider cultural diversity than exists among the developed. Many are neither in the South proper, nor 'underdeveloped' to anything like the same degree. As a result, what can be said in general is bound to be superficial or false for at least some of the countries concerned. This account deals in the main with modern China, and touches briefly on a few other countries in Asia which I know best. Initially, the account seeks to examine what happened to Marxism when it arrived in China, and then what happened to it in the hands of Mao Tse-tung. This provides a means to extrapolate some of the important features of underdevelopment for our purposes here, and thereby the impact of underdevelopment on some important – hitherto – Western assumptions, Marxist or not. The ambiguity of purpose in some movements in underdeveloped countries permitted those movements to participate in groups of political ideas that in their original context would seem inimical to the immediate aims of those movements. However, elements of orthodoxies remained intact, despite the transformed content. Yet events also changed the operative significance of well-known beliefs so far that they no longer seemed to be the same beliefs at all. The adjustment of meaning – typified in the transition from Marxism to 'Chinese Marxism' – illustrates how far beliefs formulated in one context can be utilized in an entirely different one, how far contradictory purposes can lie behind similar terminology.

Marxism's Journey East

It would be wrong to see some of the characteristic forms of Stalinism as solely precipitated by Stalin or the peculiar conditions existing in Russia in the 1930s, just as it would be wrong to pin the word 'Stalinist' over all beliefs that seemed similar in some way to Stalinist doctrines. Because Stalinism was an authentic response to some problems of development, a response by a ruthless development élite meeting an obdurate environment, one would expect to find similar ideas in countries which claimed to participate in the Marxist tradition and were underdeveloped, sometimes formulated before it was possible for the formulator to have contact with Stalinism, or, indeed, before Stalinism existed. The underdeveloped countries do not, by definition, have the class structure Marx described as appropriate to industrialized countries, so one would expect 'class' to be a difficult issue. On the other hand, the oppression of foreign imperial powers would be a prime datum for all radicals in backward countries, and that oppression could easily be seen in racial terms, given the racial predilections of some of the imperial powers. Thus, the substitution of 'nation' for 'class' is implicit (if not by any means inevitable) in the situation, and perhaps of 'race' for 'nation', without the influence of Stalin at all. One might reasonably expect that the social content of Marxist categories would be blurred, the political implications stressed – anti-imperialism becomes very much more significant than anti-capitalism; proletarian movements become much less important than 'popular' movements, where the constituent elements of the 'people' remain unclear.

But there are deeper implications than this, for the underdeveloped countries are largely peasant, so that any significant popular movement must include or have significant appeal for a large number of peasants. Now Marxists identified the industrial proletariat as the sole agency for achieving socialism (and there-fore, socialism was only an appropriate aim in developed coun-tries where the proletariat was a majority), not just because it was poor, but because of its role within the economy, because it sus-tained and developed the industrial economy by its own efforts, because it was concentrated and organized in the major cultural centres, because it learned discipline and the advantages of inter-dependence, because by its experience it had the ability to run the economy. By contrast, the peasantry tended to be isolated in particular localities, its horizon bounded by the district, self-dependent on its land rather than interdependent in a complex division of labour and advanced skills; the target of its hostility was the local landlord, moneylender or policeman, not a ruling class governing the whole of society, of which it could have no conception; its most radical aim was a just sharing of the com-mon poverty, not the generation of wealth by and for all; finally, it did not have the skill or the awareness to conceive of running the whole of society.

However, this is not to say that Marxists did not incorporate peasant revolt in their strategy for proletarian revolution. For example, Marx in *The Eighteenth Brumaire* (1852 edition) esti-mated that a possible revolt by the French peasantry against Louis Napoleon might precipitate a proletarian uprising. But he also judged that peasant revolt would ultimately have to be led by urban forces, by industrial workers also in revolt. In societies where the peasants constituted a majority of the population a proletarian revolt could not succeed without a simultaneous up-rising of the peasants, so that Marxist strategy in such countries must ensure a synchronized movement, or both would fail sep-arately. But the peasant revolt, of its nature, could not be a sub-stitute for the proletarian revolution, and could not alone secure socialism as it was understood by Marxists.

Lenin, acting in a country the majority of the population of which was peasant, inferred from the Tsarist land distribution that the Russian peasantry would be revolutionary in order to secure land. Once secured, they would however become conserva-tive in defence of their new land holdings and turn against the proletariat. However, at no stage did he conceive of the peasantry as acting on a socially significant scale except under the 'leadership' of the urban proletariat, and even that was not for a 'socialist revolution'. One might reasonably infer that in countries where the urban proletariat was, proportionate to the peasantry, even smaller than in Russia, and where the Marxist tradition was relatively weak, radicals calling themselves Marxists might seek to use the peasantry as a substitute revolutionary force, making themselves – outside intellectuals – the crucial coordinating link between the otherwise isolated revolts in particular peasant localities. The dangers we noted in the last chapter as implicit in Lenin's early organization proposals might become accomplished fact in this context.

But the implication of this change is crucial for Marxism because it means that, even theoretically, 'self-emancipation' is impossible – the intellectuals emancipate the peasantry, for the peasants cannot emancipate themselves. To summarize, then, one would expect a 'regression' from Marxism to Populism, even if this Populism was expressed in Marxist terminology, a return to some of the themes Lenin and Plekhanov attacked when advanced by their Narodnik predecessors. It is of interest in this respect to note a recent comment on Li Ta-chao, one of the two main founders of the Chinese Communist Party: 'In Li Ta-chao's conception of the peasant revolution there was that characteristically Populist contradiction between a passionate faith in the spontaneous energies of the people and a conviction that the revolutionary intellectual must bring enlightenment and leadership to the mass movement'. (Meisner, 1967, p. 251.)

What would this 'regression' entail? A belief that the intelligentsia plus peasants could produce a revolution; that that revolution could create socialism; that 'nationalism' completely encompassed socialism, that the 'people' encompassed the proletariat; that the local national struggle was the key to the progress of mankind, that the country concerned could industrialize without undergoing capitalism, that socialism was a peasant way of life rather than an emancipated developed society. Li Ta-chao is of particular significance here, since he advanced many notions which in the last chapter were identified as Stalinist, but long before Stalinism existed, many ideas which had occurred in Russia in Narodnik writings and which subsequently became identified with the name of Mao Tse-tung.

Li tended to see the main revolutionary elements as students and intellectuals, and urged them to go to the villages to enlighten the peasants, to strip back the corruption and reveal the inner goodness which would recreate a great China (apart from parallels with Narodnik thought, one can see traces of the same ideas in the work of such diverse thinkers as Rousseau, Gandhi and even Che Guevara). Li accepted the need for struggle but did not identify very clearly *class* struggle, and for him 'struggle' was not something generated necessarily by the class structure, but was rather a campaign to change hearts and minds, to raise moral consciousness. Above all, he was a nationalist – Meisner says that it was ironic that 'the first Chinese supporter of this profoundly internationalistic creed [Marxism] was a young intellectual who, even within a highly nationalistic milieu, was noted for his frankly nationalistic and even chauvinistic inclinations' (ibid., p. 177). The identification of class struggle and national struggle against foreign domination produced, in 1930, the conception of China as the 'proletarian nation' (a phrase noted in the last chapter in Stalinism and Italian nationalism in 1920), so that the national view became, by definition, a proletarian view, and national independence the signal for the emancipation of mankind.

No longer was the struggle to break the weakest link in the imperialist chain, so precipitating a revolution in the advanced countries (without which socialism was impossible). Socialism could be won in China by the Chinese themselves. Meisner (p. 145) and Brandt (1958, p. 57) mention in this connection also Tai Chi-t'ao, a prominent Kuomintang ideologist on the Right, who identified the class struggle as a struggle between nations, although he used this idea to deny the possibility of class struggle *within* China. Rather inconsistently, Li always excluded from the 'nation' the largest landowners and those Chinese who acted as intermediaries for foreign capital. This dual purpose to one conception illustrates the ambivalence of doctrines generally – most ideas can be used for contradictory purposes in different hands or different situations, and merely knowing the doctrine is no guarantee that one knows what it means in practice.

Ethnic identification has historically tended to follow intense national identification. Domestic ethnic diversity is conveniently forgotten in order to suggest a basic biological unity to the nation, to point up the contrast to the single enemy, the foreigner. In 1924 we find Li arguing that 'the race question has become the class question and the races, on a world scale, have come to confront each other as classes' (Meisner, 1967, p. 191).

Li's general views cannot be said to have been copied from Lenin's work, for Li seems, on Meisner's account, to have been imperfectly acquainted with this work. His Marxism came reasonably directly from some of the work of Marx and Engels. Ironically, although Li seems to have been a kindly and courteous man, the flavour of some of his work seems closest to Fascism, even if the social content of what he had to say was sharply different. The Russian Bolshevik leaders detected the same divergence on occasions in other revolutionaries and criticized it. Trotsky once warned against 'that national revolutionary Messianic mood which prompts one to see one's own nation-State as destined to lead mankind to socialism' (cited Deutscher, 1954, p. 238). But society is not changed by admonitions, and even though Li's intellectual evolution was not inevitable (Ch'en Tu'hsiu, the other main founder of the Chinese Communist Party, remained an internationalist and committed to the industrail proletariat), one can understand how that evolution came about, and see how effective the same ideas were in the hands of Mao Tse-tung.

The Marxism of Mao Tse-tung

Stalinism, it was suggested in the last chapter, recreated the dogmatisms which excluded popular revolutionary action and which Lenin had been so concerned to criticize in German social democracy, and it has been necessary for *any* revolutionary movement to revise Stalinism and make some break with the Soviet leadership or operate independently in order to achieve a revolution. The Soviet perspective of stability, stable Cold War frontiers and peaceful co-existence between East and West, has meant in the post-war world that any revolutionary movement has had to act *in spite of* the Soviet Union, whether the movement was led by Tito, Mao or Castro. At best, a tacit agreement operated whereby the Soviet Union was formally accepted as leader but its suggestions largely ignored, as in China. In Cuba, the Communist Party only became a supporter of Fidel Castro when his victory seemed virtually certain.

Thus, there has developed again almost a division of labour. Before 1914, it was suggested, that division separated ostensibly revolutionary theory in the hands of the social democrat leaders and revolutionary practice by the anarcho-syndicalists. In the post-war world, revolutionary theory is supposed to find its home in Moscow, and practice, with scarcely any coherent and guiding general theoretical framework, in the 'Third World'. Of course, in fact, Moscow's revolutionary theory was revolutionary only in rhetoric: in reality, the Soviet Union relied on orthodox political relationships, aid and trade, to achieve its foreign policy ends. On the other hand, the restoration of 'activism' in the underdeveloped countries had theoretical implications, although the more important of these were not specified – for example, what kind of revolution had been or was to be achieved, what the class content of such revolutions was, and so on.

The contribution of Mao Tse-tung to formal Marxist theory was relatively small and, by earlier standards, rather primitive; at most the loosening of a few themes, the omission of some major Stalinist points. However, Mao's practice does show substantial divergences from what Stalin suggested as appropriate for a revolutionary. The loose combination of agrarian populism and radical nationalism which constitutes Maoism in practice has its closest parallels not with ideology in the Soviet Union so much as with those doctrines advanced by non-communist leaders in other underdeveloped countries.

Unlike the Soviet Union, China had neither a proletarian

nor a liberal heritage to overcome. Consistent with the absence
of the class structure postulated in Marx's writings, and with
the role of the intelligentsia, free from loyalty to a particular class
which is tied necessarily to a particular role in the social structure, Maoism is essentially 'voluntarist': that is, the aims of the
leadership are seen as feasible provided they work hard, rather
than provided the objective situation permits. The role of theory
is thus changed from that suggested in Marx; for Mao, theory is
a somewhat eclectically selected element in public relations work,
in the propaganda necessary to change consciousness, rather than
itself a more or less accurate analysis of reality to guide practice.
Of course the role changed: it was not always – as it became after
1948 – a doctrine with mystical-magical qualities, formulae to be
manipulated by the leadership to achieve miraculous results (the
current *Thoughts of Mao Tse-tung*). In Mao's 1942 speech,
Reform in Learning, the Party, and Literature (cited Schram,
1963, p. 120), he specifically warns his audience against the
danger of seeing theory as magic – 'It seems that right up to the
present quite a few have regarded Marxism-Leninism as a ready-
made panacea: once you have it, you can cure all your ills with
little effort'; Schram notes that in the latest edition of this speech
the text has been changed so that it is only 'isolated formulae
drawn from Marxist-Leninist literature' which are dangerous,
the implication being that Marxism-Leninism as a whole *is* a
'ready-made panacea'. Certainly, the sensible aphorisms of the
'little red book' are not seen as anything but charms to ward off
disaster or conjure success.

However, the implication of this attitude in general theoretical
terms is that Mao has renounced Stalin's heavy stress on historical necessity and the autonomous economic base, leaving
alone and unhampered the complete voluntarism of the 'people',
the party and its leadership; activism in the nation has eliminated the need for theory at all. The 'freedom' is freedom from
association with any particular class, freedom for the leadership
to do as it wishes. For Mao, unlike Stalin, retains no residual
identification with the industrial working class. After the Kuomintang's shattering blow to the Chinese Communist Party (CCP) in

1927, 'proletariat' in communist writings came to mean little more than the party itself. The CCP scarcely involved urban classes at all after 1927, and the actual proletarian membership was less than one per cent in Mao's period of leadership before 1948. The cities in general became the rearguard of the revolution, not its vanguard.

More than this, for the actual vanguard was largely a *military* force, not a class embedded in the on-going social structure, and an army composed of heterogeneous elements – the remnants of the 1927 party (leaving their work-places for exile with the party), dispossessed peasants and labourers, professional soldiers, mutinous units of the Kuomintang or warlord armies, even bandits (cf. Isaacs, 1961, Appendix) – all moulded into an effective fighting force by members of the intelligentsia. The role of the army, separated from its disparate class origins necessarily over the long period in which it was not in power, constituted a separate force rather than the representative of a class, proletarian or peasant. So much was this so that Schwartz has argued that 'the experience of Chinese Communism . . . casts a doubt on the whole organic conception of the relation of party to class' (1958, p. 191), for it became clear that the voluntarist intelligentsia could in the conditions of inter-war chaos impose its will upon its followers, reshaping or even creating what the leadership called 'proletarian class attitudes' regardless of what actual 'class attitudes' existed. This approach was possible precisely because consciousness was the key element, moral attitudes, rather than the objective situation, the attitudes men imbibed from the particular role they played in the social structure. Thus, where 'non-proletarian' attitudes persisted, phrased more accurately as opposition to the leadership, the cure lay less in changing the sociological composition of the army, but more in intensified education and exhortation; for deserters from the other side, 'The Red Army is like a furnace in which all captured soldiers are melted down and transformed the moment they come over'. (Mao, 1, p. 83.) (The phrase 'melted down and transformed' in the 1954 New York edition of Mao's *Selected Works*, is translated as 'transmuted' in the Pekin edition.)

Nor did the actual experience of the party lead it to locate itself more securely in the class structure. The party had to adjust itself to a multitude of different administrative circumstances, not to one dominant social conflict. The productive and cultural level of the areas commanded by this kind of new warlord force permitted little radical transformation of the social structure – the party had to tack continuously between different social groups, including landlords, rich peasants and merchants, and had to do so in order to survive, for the primitiveness of the areas allowed little scope for anything except reliance on the existing *status quo*. Thus, in 1934, after four years of party control, Mao complained that rich peasants controlled eighty per cent of the central district of the Hunan-Kiangsi Soviet Republic (Mao, 1933, cited Isaacs, 1961, p. 344).

The resulting picture of the party before the Second World War is, then, of a fluctuating political force, rather detached from the Chinese social structure, ruling in the areas where it operated rather than embodying the aspirations of the ruled. Its power lay not in how far it embodied popular feeling in its own areas, but in its command of military force, and thus its political behaviour was not so central to its general position – policy could and did vary very widely, depending on local circumstances, and encompassing at different times the spectrum from radical land confiscation to the mildest amelioration of conditions. Since the army was the vanguard it became the essence of the revolution, and the dominant ideal after it, the substitute for a proletariat proper. This is very far from earlier conceptions of the class struggle – indeed, it cannot plausibly be seen as '*class* struggle' at all. It was struggle between different territorial political entities rather than struggle arising necessarily out of the nature of the social structure, a struggle which was military, not social.

Wherever possible, the party sought to bind the peasantry to itself by appropriate agrarian reform proposals directed at the larger landowners, and since the Kuomintang was reasonably consistently devoted to the interests of, among others, the landowners, political differentiation remained fairly clear. But land reform for the party remained less its *raison d'être* as a peasant party, rather it was a useful means to win support as an outside body. If land reform lost important support the party could temper its programme to the central aim.

The proletariat proper had little part to play except in an agitational role as a minor adjunct to the main military effort (the analogy in the relationship between Moscow and foreign communist parties will be clear). Indeed, in the actual process of revolution the proletariat always remained a potential danger, liable to diverge from the aims of the party and impede the military impetus, requiring constant discipline and supervision once the party had achieved power. It is interesting to note that, although communists proper would not be so cavalier with their claimed traditions as to say that the proletariat was something of a nuisance in achieving revolution, others – less traditional – might. Che Guevara, for example, did see the proletariat as an inhibiting factor, and argued that 'It is more difficult to prepare guerrilla bands in those countries that have undergone a concentration of population in great centres and have a more developed light and medium industry, even though not anything like effective industrialization. The ideological influence of the cities inhibits guerrilla struggle'. (1961, pp. 65–6.)

In China, the controls were carefully spelt out: workers were ordered not to take over their own factories as the revolution progressed, but to support their managers and await the party's consolidation of power; factory committees of workers – created to represent the work-force – were always rendered subordinate to the head of the factory. After the revolution, the new State trade unions were designed not as defensive representative organizations but as essentially disciplinary and propaganda agencies of management; the trade unions exist 'to strengthen the unity of the working class, to consolidate the alliance of workers and peasants, to educate workers to observe consciously the laws and decrees of the State, and labour discipline, to strive for the development of production, for the constant increase in labour productivity, for the fulfilment and overfulfilment of the production plans of the State.' (Constitution, 1953, in *Labour Laws*, p. 17.) Special tribunals ensured that stringent sanctions were imposed on those who might diverge from the letter of law in being negligent in behaviour or with materials or tools.

The implications of abandoning the conception of the proletariat in practice are decisive for Marxism. In abandoning the conflict within a particular social structure, a communist party abandons the only (Marxist) theoretical justification for its existence and embraces the élitism of the Narodniks. In addition, internationalism is jettisoned for nationalism. For Mao, as for Li Ta-chao, the first enemy was a foreign occupier, and he argued from the common interest of the Chinese nation against that foreigner, not from the common interest of the Chinese working class and foreign working classes against their own and each other's ruling classes. The nation becomes the most important operating concept in pursuit of a *national* revolution (class nature unspecified), and class merely a derogatory or commendatory term to apply to one's friends or enemies. Like Stalin's hair-splitting with form and content, Mao argues:

> A Communist is a Marxist internationalist but Marxism must take on a national form before it can be applied. There is no such thing as abstract Marxism but only concrete Marxism. What we call Marxism is Marxism that has taken on a national form, that is, Marxism applied to the concrete struggle in the concrete conditions prevailing in China. (1938, p. 209)

Effective class internationalism does not arise out of the organization of international capitalism, but is relegated to the realm of sympathy, without any operational value in a peasant and noncapitalist China. Each ruling class is the problem solely of its own ruled; the historical accident of the borders of each nation-State provides the perimeters of operational consciousness.

Of course, in a national struggle there is no crucial class to be emancipated. The prime tasks of the revolution become 'classless': anti-imperialism abroad and industrialization at home, the two aims being, in a nationalist framework, distinguished in no crucial respect from those of any other nationalist movement in an underdeveloped country. As in Stalinism, 'proletarian' refers to friends at home, so abroad it tends to identify whatever force opposes imperialism, and, in the nature of the case, those forces exist primarily in imperial or ex-imperial territories, in the under-developed countries. As a result, Mao has no role to offer to the people of the developed countries. They can merely support the Third World. The scheme is a direct repetition of the lack of role for urban people in China during the revolution, and indeed the analogy has been explicitly made by Mao himself – as if it was an original thought – although it occurs much earlier; the 1928 Comintern Programme included the observation that 'Colonies and semi-colonies ... represent the *world rural district* in rela-tionship to the industrial countries, which represent the *world city*.'

If the tasks are 'classless' because the agency for the revolution is 'classless', then any social forces willing to accept CCP leader-ship are equally relevant. Mao revived the strategy of a 'Four Class Bloc', originally formulated by Stalin as the national coali-tion of forces required to achieve a *bourgeois* revolution in China (the agent of the revolution to be the bourgeois nationalist force, the Kuomintang, supported by the CCP). This had had disastrous results in 1926–7 when the Kuomintang nearly destroyed its ally, the CCP, but the strategy was appropriate for Mao's own perspective, provided the CCP rather than the Kuomintang could lead the coalition and it would achieve a 'non-bourgeois national' revolution. More than this, Mao sought also to recreate the alliance with the Kuomintang itself before the Comintern made the pursuit of a united front mandatory on all its member organ-izations, again despite the terrible massacre of communists in 1927. Mao showed no compunction about pursuing this aim, and, indeed, went out of his way to flatter the Kuomintang and Chiang Kai-shek personally as one of the two national forces (Report, 1938).

Capitalism itself as a social system was not the primary target and, indeed, Mao's 1945 *On Coalition Government* proposed that the 'task of our New Democratic system is ... to promote the free development of a private capitalist economy that benefits instead of controlling the people's livelihood, and to protect all honestly acquired private property' (p. 281). One is reminded of social democratic attempts to escape an 'anti-capitalist' position in favour of national unity. In the 1949 Constitution of the 'People's Democratic Dictatorship' (class content unspecified), the 'national bourgeoisie' is part of the 'people', but the 'bureaucratic capitalists' are not, since they are in league with imperialism. The means of identifying the 'bureaucratic capitalists' is not, however, their role in the structure of the economy or society, but merely whether or not they support the CCP. In practice, the 'national bourgeoisie' came to include many of the very largest capitalists (fully as much in league with imperialists when it suited their purpose), including the 'four families' of the Kuomintang period. Nor was the subsequent gradual infringement of the prerogatives of private industry pursued as a central political commitment, sustained by the anti-capitalist feeling of a genuine proletariat, but rather was it a subordinate element in the State's planning activities, much as the extension of the public sector has been in other non-communist underdeveloped countries: the CCP did not oppose the profit motive *per se*, but rather opposed the State's deprivation of funds for capital accumulation.

Mao's thought, then, places almost sole effective stress on common national elements, rejecting the idea of a necessarily divisive class system within China; China is effectively a 'proletarian nation'. Of course, the emphasis changes before and after the revolution, and also after the revolution in relationship to different kinds of crisis, but by and large the residue of class terminology still utilized is a function of nationalist aims, describing those who are non-Chinese or linked to foreigners as opposed to 'true Chinese' people, a particular ethnic stock with a particular attitude to the CCP. By implication, like Stalinism, Maoism inherits, uses and identifies with a common national heritage, with the pre-1911 achievements of the emperors. It is implied that a common national culture links past and present and is more significant than temporary divisions. The marriage of this cultural tradition and the 'alien' Marxism comes in the claim that Mao has created a 'Sinification of Marxism', a Chinese or Asiatic Marxism. Of course, defining what constitutes true 'Chinese culture' or Sinification is the prerogative of the party, and at different times different elements become appropriate according to short-term political requirements.

It is the nationalist emphasis which prompts the CCP to generalize its experience as the *only* model for future revolutions (and since the basic preconditions for this experience are lacking in developed countries, they cannot have a revolution) and as a profound 'discovery', as if revolution were a matter of technique. 'The tactics we have derived from the struggle in the past three years', Mao argued in 1930, 'are indeed different from any other tactics, ancient or modern, Chinese or foreign' (p. 124), and Li Li-san, much more firmly, asserted in 1949 that 'The working class definitely cannot fundamentally better its status and livelihood, not to speak of winning the revolutionary victory like that of today, without building a revolutionary army under its own leadership and waging a revolutionary war against the rule of imperialism and its lackeys, with the broad support of the broad masses of the people.' (1949, p. 19.)

It is unlikely that the CCP's conception of guerrilla warfare was so new, since guerrilla warfare has been, historically, not uncommon, ranging from pure banditry to peasant revolt or terrorist campaigns for political ends. In any case, to put the stress on technique alone prevents one examining the CCP victory in a realistic light, seeing the accidents and good luck which contributed substantially to that victory and without which no amount of technique would have proved successful. The claim is the product of nationalist egoism, and is repeated wherever unorthodox conditions have, against prior predictions, produced success. The Vietnamese guerrillas today make similar claims (and firmly repudiate the idea that they are merely copying the Chinese, as if copying would work for guerrilla warfare which depends so crucially on unique conjunctures of events), and the correspondence between the Yugoslav and Soviet Central Committees in 1948 shows the Russians ridiculing the Yugoslav claim to have invented the peculiar form of partisan warfare which, Belgrade claimed, had made a major contribution to the 1945 Allied victory in Europe. Of course, in China, the demand for national revolutionary autonomy embodied in the claim to have created a 'Chinese Marxism' (as opposed to Moscow's presumably 'Russian Marxism') tends to conflict with the claim that other countries have to follow China's pattern of revolution; the difference is between a party, out of power, seeking to establish its independence from Russian hegemony, and the party in power, commanding a position equal to the Russian and loyalty from other less successful communist parties.

However, even if classes proper do not exist for the CCP in China (although Stalin's 'remnants of the old exploiting classes' are kept in the wings for use in particular campaigns, as in the early phases of the current Cultural Revolution), disagreements do arise. The means to overcome disagreements, or rather to subordinate objections to the leadership, lies in party propaganda and education. In practice, the party can also adjust its own position; it is susceptible to a large range of social pressures. No domestic divisions (as opposed to divisions linked directly to imperialism) cannot be overcome provided the will is there, for society has no structure necessarily engendering certain sorts of conflicts. Conflicts depend on the *moral* nature of the opponent of the party, and that nature is as it is because the party has not educated (or indoctrinated) him. Thus, in principle, it is not a specific material reality which shapes certain forms of consciousness, but rather moral illiteracy, ignorance, and, in more traditional religious terms, backsliding.

In a country as disastrously poor as China, material reality cannot be changed in the short term, so that changing consciousness might seem a short-cut to security, for doctrine can be changed by the leadership. British Conservatives agreed in this stress on manipulating 'ideas'. Fidel Castro, being less snared than the CCP in the orthodoxies of Marxism-Leninism, has expressed this viewpoint more boldly in claiming that there is no ideology in a revolutionary struggle, only a road to power which 'acquires' different ideological beliefs on that road (choosing them and abandoning them according to the immediate needs of the struggle for power). Theory has no role at all. Che Guevara acknowledged this when he described the Cuban revolutionary leaders as 'only a group of fighters with high ideals and little preparation' (*Hoy*, 16 July 1963). The concern should be to find the road to power, not to pursue the right political aims (for which power is to be used) or to locate those aims in an appropriate analysis of the situation. The assurance of success lies not in appraising the objective situation but in the group's spirit, morale, will, drive. The echoes of Sorel and pre First World War anarcho-syndicalist activism without theory are here very loud.

In the Marxist position proper, by contrast, the analysis of objective conditions should indicate how the struggle should be undertaken. 'Armed struggle' is only one of many possible means, not the 'highest' or 'real' one. Indeed, it was implied that the use of open or military (formal or guerrilla) force was likely to be only the very last stage when most of the issues had already been settled, not the first – guerrilla warfare takes us straight back to Narodnik thought, to the revolutionary minority seizing power in the name of the people – despite the people – to the traditional *coup d'état* rather than social revolution. Continuous guerrilla warfare means that military tactics replace revolutionary theory, that professional soldiers in battle replace a class struggle rooted in a real social structure, and that power is inevitably concentrated in the hands of generals, with mass consciousness merely being a subsidiary factor in morale rather than the dynamic of the whole. Soldiers need to obey orders, not appraise their daily experience in work relationships. It is necessary to stress the magic of guerrilla warfare where a popular mass movement does not exist, since the minority only can undertake action of this kind. With even smaller support, some Narodniks were reduced to individual terrorism for the same reasons. The emphasis does not explain the large number of failures – why the CCP took such an enormously long time to win power; why the Malayan, Philippine and Burma communists failed to win; why the Telengana peasants, the Nagas and Mizos failed to win in India; why indeed the Khampa rebels against China in Tibet do not win. And if the CCP replies to this question that 'ideology' is the distinguishing feature of successful movements, how was it that Castro won in Cuba as, broadly, a liberal, certainly not a Marxist-Leninist?

Armed struggle is supposed to create the objective conditions for winning power, and, in Castro's words, those conditions can be created in the 'immense majority of Latin American countries' if between four and five dedicated men can be found to undertake it (Speech, 16 January 1963, and cf. Guevara's *Guerrilla Warfare*, p. 11). The CCP is not quite so cavalier about the role of theory as the Cubans but still it is seen as little more than a weapon to achieve obedience and thereby the free initiative of the leadership. 'Socialist ideology becomes a weapon in mobilizing and organizing the masses and becomes a material force in society ... it becomes instrumental in establishing a socialist economic base by acquiring political power and by destroying the capitalist economic base with that power.' (Hsu I-jang and Lin Ching-Yao, 1959, cited Meisner, 1965, p. 168.) Another writer puts the point more sharply: 'men are not the slaves of objective reality. Provided only that man's consciousness be in conformity with the objective laws of the development of things, the subjective activity of the popular masses can manifest itself in full measure, overcome all difficulties, create the necessary conditions, and carry forward the revolution. In this sense, the subjective creates the objective.' (Wu Chiang, cited Schram, 1963, p. 80.) Allied with peasant superstition and belief in the power of magic, the magic of the formula, the text and the aphorism, it is hardly surprising that the works of Mao become elements of a popular religion, prescribed as a cure for any problem at all, from treating burns, selling water melons or winning table tennis (some of the few examples reported recently). We are here clearly in a world closer to that of medieval Christianity than of Marxism.

The elimination of specific class content, the stress on voluntarism and the role of an élite, automatically blurs distinctions earlier Marxists stressed, and makes it impossible to distinguish different countries in social terms – to distinguish, for example, between Egypt, based upon a *coup d'état* by radical army officers, Algeria, with a military and guerrilla but non-communist movement, and China itself. The classification of such countries is read off from the country's foreign policy stance, not its domestic class structure, even though that foreign policy might be based upon quite accidental or opportunist factors. For the CCP, the test of revolutionary politics turns on one's attitude to the United States, and any sort of critical stance, even in a conservative authoritarian and private-enterprise country like Pakistan (a member of United States alliances and recipient of United States aid) evokes fraternal warmth.

If the revolution abroad means opposition to the United States and little more, building the national economy at home for the purposes of national power makes the necessity of poverty a virtue. The siege economy dictates that tomorrow's abundance is forgotten and communism converted into meaning common abstinence. Hobsbawm notes in another context that 'The pre-industrial poor always conceive of the good society as a just sharing of austerity rather than a dream of riches for all' (1959, p. 82), and this seems to be the most prominent feature in the following reprimand by *China Youth* (31 October 1964): 'The kind of life advocated by Comrade Feng Ting, which would provide good things to eat and wear, good places to live in, and cordial relations between husband and wife and between parents and children, does not conform with the Communist ideal.' Of course, in the early phases of industrialization in all societies, the same flavour of Puritanism seems to be repeated. Production becomes an end in itself. In China the apotheosis of Marxism as the instrument of primitive accumulation reaches its ironic conclusion. The modest affluence of the Soviet Union is a continuous threat to the need for common poverty, and periodic campaigns are one way of reviving the spirit of self-flagellation. Perhaps Mao might feel some sympathy for John Wesley when he complained:

I fear, wherever riches have increased, the essence of religion has decreased in the same proportion ... For religion must necessarily produce both industry and frugality, and these cannot but produce riches. But as riches increase, so will pride, anger and love of the world in all its branches. (cited Weber, 1930, p. 175)

In conclusion, then, Mao has revised Marxism to such a degree that it cannot really be considered to be merely a local 'application': the essence has disappeared. What constitutes revolution is not the most advanced urban masses securing their own emancipation by their own efforts, but guerrilla warfare by the least advanced rural groups, operating outside the ordinary social structure over many years, in order to seize power and begin industrialization. A would-be ruling élite, dispossessed and alienated from the *status quo*, within a decaying agrarian social structure, fits naturally into Maoism, although even more naturally into Castroism which was not part of Marxism-Leninism in its revolutionary phase in Cuba. Activism and populism provide the dominant themes. Outside the underdeveloped world, radicals may borrow the important activism of Maoism (particularly against the conservatism of Moscow), but its substantive principles can have little relevance, or rather, what relevance they have leads to inactivity, to waiting for emancipation at the hands of Third World peasant armies.

The closest parallels to the 'national revolution' in Marx's terms would be the bourgeois revolution, but this does not really fit, for the bourgeois revolution presupposes an established capitalism, a private economy the businessmen of which merely complete their power by appropriating the political sphere. By contrast, the national revolution does not take place in a predominantly private industrialized economy, and the political power gained is directly used to *develop* a backward economy. The issue of property has concealed the significance of the national revolution. Since public property is seen as one of the dominant expressions of the new régimes, then it is described as socialist, whatever its specific content, whatever the diverse reasons for which different States may nationalize.

This section has, then, sought to illustrate the continuing transition of basic Marxist themes – class, internationalism, proletarian revolution – in the Chinese context. The terms lost their original significance, and other, contradictory, concepts became much more important – nation, nationalism, and a peasant revolution. After the seizure of power the imperatives of development, exacerbated most recently by continuous foreign threat from the most powerful nation in the world, the United States, have even further reshaped the dominant beliefs of the Chinese leadership. Both the internal and the external conditions are such that the

CCP cannot pursue the same process of development in terms of beliefs that the post-Stalinist leadership took. China will remain underdeveloped for a very long period and, indeed, there is nothing inevitable about its development. Its situation forces its leadership to pursue radical policies at home and abroad, and in pursuing those policies the residual Marxism is even further lost in nationalism.

The conditions of China shaped the transformation of Marxism which the CCP undertook. But it was a transformation characteristic of most doctrines in the context of underdevelopment. Nationalism was the key focus for all anti-imperialist struggles, and domestic class issues were subordinated to this struggle. It could only have been otherwise if events had occurred in accordance with the Leninist perspective, if the industrial proletariats of the West had pursued a socialist revolution in the West, and thereby brought to the aid of the underdeveloped countries their strength and the accumulated knowledge and wealth of their societies. Thus, from many diverse backgrounds, some located in a specific Western political tradition, some not, the common logic of anti-imperialism and development reshaped the beliefs of the Third World in specific ways, even though each national leadership claimed to be as original as – many of them, indeed, even more original than – the Chinese Communist Party. The uniqueness was perhaps true in their own societies, but on the world plane it seemed less so.

The Nature of Underdevelopment

A significant number of underdeveloped countries have, in recent years, made a shift from their post-independence régimes to a new sort of politics. The new politics seem to be marked by an irresistible compulsion towards centralized State autocracy, embodied in a national dictator or one party which monopolizes all political initiative (military, nationalist or communist), and advocates national planning, a steady expansion of the public sector and substantial State intervention in the economy. The general ideology is ultranationalist, anti-imperialist, and we might provisionally describe it as '*étatiste* nationalism'. Even those countries which do not undergo a radical social change find it useful to imitate aspects of *étatiste* nationalism and on occasions even execute it under the auspices of traditional rulers – Nepal, Bhutan, Afghanistan, are all monarchies, but all have national plans which involve expanding public initiative and a public sector. Even relatively conservative régimes follow suit, as for example Pakistan or Diem's South Vietnam.

Historically, some aspects of a similar process have been visible during the development of European countries. A mild autarchic nationalism was seen in Britain, and a rather more radical version, involving extensive positive State initiative, occurred in the France of Louis XIII and XIV. Bismarck's 'State socialism' is well known, and one historian's comment is put at the head of this chapter.

The work of Mehmet Ali (1804–42) is interesting in this respect, for – with the same pre-eminently military motives that inspired the European era of 'Enlightened Despots' – he sought to shift Egypt from a subsistence to a modern economy ('modern' by the standards of the time). He revolutionized land tenure, expanded communications, established State monopolies to handle crops and begin industrial projects, all behind a wall of protection and operated by an expanded bureaucracy. The process was checked by outside intervention in 1841, and Egypt did not gain sufficient political autonomy to undertake another exercise in *étatiste* nationalism until after the Second World War. Military purposes, the aims of foreign policy, provided the main incentive to modern Egypt's second attempt, particularly after the Suez affair of 1956, but now the nature of modern industrialization itself exercised a powerful compulsion towards State direction – the concentration of resources and skills now required is much greater than ever before (cf. Issawi, 1963, p. 21).

Unlike the numerous earlier attempts (Bismarck's exercise apart), modern efforts usually acquire the label 'socialist', and those efforts usually include a more explicit commitment to popular welfare. The 'socialisms' present a luxuriant variety, apart from Chinese Marxism which we have already examined –

NATIONALISM AND THE SOUTH   189

Egyptian or Arab socialism, Burmese, Indonesian, Ugandan, and even Cambodia's 'Buddhist socialism within a nationalist framework'. Sometimes explicit European influences are involved – Stalinism and Fabianism to mention only two – but important sources of the creeds are local, even if offered in 'foreign' terminology. This does not mean that they are proper expressions of an indigenous culture that predates development, but rather that there are common problems of development and independence which particular groups of beliefs seem to 'fit'. Some elements of Stalinism 'fitted' the problems of China.

However, much the most fruitful parallels with political ideas in modern underdeveloped countries can be found in Narodnik thought in the 1860s and 1870s. The Narodnik terrorist tradition influenced both Chinese intellectuals immediately prior to the 1911 fall of the Ch'ing dynasty and Bengali aristocratic youth in the early part of the century. Gandhi found a major source of inspiration in the work of Tolstoy, and Li Ta-chao in Kropotkin. The Narodnik 'Back to the People' movement of urban intellectuals had its parallels in Li Ta-chao's appeal for Chinese students to go to the villages and enlighten the peasants, in Gandhi's similar appeal to urban Indians, and in the Japanese *atarashika mura* (New Village) movement to promote village communities to practice rural communism (Kropotkin's work was a direct influence here). All, in some measure, felt cities to be corrupt and corrupting – much as Guevara viewed urban influence – and sought the pure Rousseauite man beneath the rough exterior of the 'simple' peasant.

One can also see close parallels in the condition of the intelligentsia itself at some stages, its proneness to 'withdraw' from the troubled world when faced with major political obstacles (Li Ta-chao considered withdrawal to a Buddhist monastic sect for a time in 1913). Fröhlich (1940, p. 20) cited Rosa Luxemburg's account of the Russian intelligentsia in the 1880s when major Tsarist reforms were withdrawn:

In this atmosphere of apathy and despondency, metaphysical and mystical tendencies began to make headway amongst the Russian intelligentsia. ... The propaganda of 'non-resistance to evil', the condemnation of all violence in the struggle against the dominant reaction (which was to be opposed only by 'the inner purification' of the individual), and the general theory of social passivity developed.

It was an anarchic quality in the Narodniks which Lenin sought to discipline by his organizational proposals, and which others in modern underdeveloped countries also seek to discipline through direct military discipline, through a one-party State, through successive limitations on individual rights, Preventive Detention Acts and executions. Those who pursue such courses of 'discipline' for their opponents are not 'copying' Lenin (any more than Stalin needed Lenin to imprison or execute his opponents), nor are they probably even influenced by him. But common problems tend to generate solutions which are similar in form – with the difference that Lenin did not, when he framed his organizational proposals, have the power of the State behind him.

It is very much more difficult for an underdeveloped country to develop today than it was in the past, for a large number of reasons related to the relative gap between advanced and backward countries (technological and material), the pressure on existing resources in densely populated poor countries, the shortage of capital in relation to the need, and the occupation of the world, the domination of its markets, by the advanced countries (who decreasingly need products of the kind that the backward produce). The implications for growth are sombre, and there seems to be very little hard evidence to support the kind of general optimism about development – it is an inevitable process given enough time – which is often current in the developed countries.

Poverty plus relatively meagre prospects alongside the urgency for development shape inherited traces in certain ways. For example, that wide range of social conflict, the issues of which do not permit compromise, grows as the alternatives become fewer. One cannot compromise between standing on a cliff and falling off it, and when the margins of survival are narrow, all decisions assume the form of either survival or death. Compromise which even in other societies is often more limited than people think, depends upon the existence of choices other than the two mentioned. Where such alternatives are absent, it is not peculiar psychology or lack of education or an unfamiliarity with the preconditions for parliamentary rule which prompts men to fight, but the sheer need to survive. The climate of insecurity is such that it affects all – it is not just the poor who are less compromising, but also those who have further to fall in the social hierarchy. The truncheon is one way of silencing the struggle for survival.

We tend to forget the crucial conditions for liberalism in Europe (as well as the degree to which liberalism was more or less qualified in practice). Its popular validity turned upon reasonably continuous prospects for expansion, and slumps and recessions were a constant source of anti-liberal doctrines. Present sacrifice was sugared with hope for the future, and compromise became that much more possible. But without much hope, against a long history of poverty, despair and insecurity, of a ruthless struggle for survival, then it is impossible to 'sink the differences'; for the differences mean the livelihood of oneself and one's family.

The immensely expanded role of the State in underdeveloped societies needs some explanation. Under imperial rule it was the military State which wielded the truncheon, not the 'logic of the market' or the electoral contest; and it wielded the truncheon with little regard to the substantive axioms of liberalism. It was this State against which any independence movement measured itself and which it inherited in victory – a State which was a conjuncture of political, economic and military power overshadowing the rest of the society. It is hardly surprising that there were no social classes capable of resisting the State, as entrepreneurs were able to resist the British State in the early nineteenth century. The newly independent government became both business (to develop rapidly) and the regulator of business (both to underpin its own economic activities and to ensure some measure of protection for its supporters real or potential); sometimes it was and is both employer and trade union and arbitrates between its two selves.

The drive to develop – itself partly mandatory as a means to survive in the modern world – combined with the needs of defence and the logic of modern industry, produces a powerful compulsion towards *étatisme* in the absence of counteracting factors. Indigenous capital is far too weak to resist this process and, where foreign capital continues to operate in the independent economy, it needs the State to protect it. That need is sometimes met at a high price for the line between 'Indianization' (or Ceylonization, Egyptianization and so on) of business and its nationalization can become very fine.

The independence struggle has been, with some notable exceptions, a largely urban phenomenon, or at least under mainly urban leadership. Where the urban population has succeeded in overthrowing the old régime the new State must take particular care to retain its loyalty. A higher proportion of national production must be devoted to urban working-class consumption, or at least to the consumption of particularly crucial sectors of workers, which limits the surplus available for investment. The cities are, by and large, the bearers of national feeling. It was suggested in the discussion on China why the peasants were unlikely to be nationalist, and Meisner argues that in China ' "Mass nationalism" was not something that welled up from the elemental forces of the countryside and eventually reached Mao Tse-tung and his associates. It is more historically accurate to say that nationalism was brought to the peasants from without by an ardently nationalistic *élite* intent upon shaping history in accordance with its ideals.' (1967, p. 266.) For India, Bailey suggests that in Orissa the Congress independence movement made relatively little progress among the peasants until it was pointed out that since many landowners supported the British, land reform would be one result of expelling the British: at which, a very large number of peasants became 'nationalist' (Bailey, 1963, pp. 172–3). The cities delineate the boundaries of the 'nation', for they are aware of the geography between themselves, of the complex transactions that take place between themselves, of the need to control and administer the area in between the cities. 'Accidental' geographical areas are centralized not just by military conquest, and much less by the concept of 'ethnic identity', but by the interaction of merchants and traders who supply an entire market, by bankers and moneylenders who supply the requisite credit for merchandising, and finally, by the great industries which are needed to supply the market. But if the economy is relatively backward or controlled by foreign business, then in reaction to that backwardness (and thus weakness) or foreign control, a substitute nationalistic agent must be found in the urban middle class, the intelligentsia, the clerks employed in the bureaucracy that make imperialism possible.

In newly independent countries, then, the State is the largest single institution, against which no other organized national group can stand. The State and nationalism are the creation of the cities, but the cities are a threat to the State once it is independent, and it has happened in a number of underdeveloped countries that the political party which controls the government has sought to shift its support away from the cities to the countryside, in order to render its own power less subject to urban opposition. If the CCP began as urban intellectuals using peasant power to capture the cities, the Indian Congress has steadily tended to lose control of the cities since independence. However, the articulate public political arena remains urban and remains largely dominated by the educated national middle class, still by and large clustered round the State as employer or potential employer – a powerful attraction where higher educational facilities have been expanded under middle-class pressure faster than jobs for the educated are available. The middle class embodies both the most developed sense of nationalism and the greatest interest in the expansion of the State: State and nation are one.

The need for intense national loyalty seems all the greater where countries are mere amalgams of different tribes and peoples that have not historically had any unifying feature except a common foreign invader. But schismatic trends are powerful even in countries with a relatively high degree of cultural or ethnic homogeneity and a common unified history. Schisms borrow on what Geertz calls 'primordial' sentiments, 'the "givens" ... of social existence: immediate contiguity and kin connection mainly, but beyond them the givenness that stems from being born into a particular religious community, speaking a particular language, or even a dialect of a language, and following particular social practices.' (1963, p. 109.) Groups can identify a common interest in multiple ways and some of the 'primordial' loyalties are invented, or at least newly 'discovered', by the new political situation. Invented or not, the climate of great insecurity generates immense tensions, 'reduced' in the final analysis by the blunt and arbitrary intervention of the State. Since the trends to disintegration are so great, an accordingly heavier burden of compelling an unwanted nationality falls on the State and the national middle class.

So great is the need, so widespread and low the cultural level, that elements of 'modernism' (of which nationalism is one constituent) towards which the national middle class is striving, tend to attain magical forms, to become fetishized – education, nationalism or Marxism can take on the character of an intense religion, a cure for all ills. This tendency is only one aspect of the continuity in an urbanized context of a number of elements of rural life – the values of the peasantry, still the majority class and the source of the new urban sector, pervade the atmosphere. Traditional peasant society often includes very strong kinship groups, and these provide the immediate context for all the activities of the constituent family unit. In the cities, by contrast, a multiplicity of alternative associations can exist, and loyalties to any one of them can be very mild and limited. There are many people to depend upon lightly, and relationships are likely to be more strictly functional. The new rural immigrant, accustomed to intense and intimate personal relationships that spread out over all he does, is likely to feel lonely and alienated.

When large numbers of people move away from village to city it is likely that the 'modern' elements in the city will become reformulated in rural terms, and not just for the rural immigrant. The romanticism, the nostalgia for a past golden age, for the medieval village in Europe, has already been mentioned. More concretely, workers tend to identify less with their fellow workers in the same occupational stratum or factory, more with their kinship group, caste or district. New urban immigrants tend to inhabit urban areas already populated by some from their village, to take jobs where other villagers are employed, to form friends and marry within the same group. Thus, the *class* alignment is muted, and loyalty goes to a group which may include a number of members of different classes, or merely to authority.

With the middle-class dependence upon public authority, this context inhibits the appearance of a clear and popular liberal critique of authority, without which individual rights, civil liberties, become merely so much paper, a deferential gesture to foreign political traditions. Opposition oscillates between deference, often sustained by bribes or relatively vague promises, and outright opposition, ending perhaps in civil war. Among workers, when the hard conflict with an employer comes, fragmentation, the lack of solid organization, makes it sporadic, violent, anarchic – a sudden outburst of fury and frustration rather than part of a rationally disciplined campaign to achieve specific ends. In passing, Hobsbawm's interpretation of Luddism, machine-breaking by workers, in Britain, might be noted, for he calls it a 'primitive form of collective bargaining'. In the underdeveloped countries, sometimes even in the act of opposing, the basic feeling of dependence is reaffirmed – strikers demand not so much their rights as the satisfaction of their needs. Implicitly, the plea assumes powerful but kindly authority, a *deus ex machina* who will shoulder responsibility and permit workers to evade the responsibility for achieving their demands through their own efforts. This is one element in the absurd inflation of the role of particular leaders. Whether it be Stalin, Mao, Gandhi or Nasser, in a religious peasant-dominated society such men come to play the role of gods, intervening charitably in their omnipotence on behalf of the oppressed; to *give* them independence or economic development. We have already noted in an earlier chapter the role of the Messiah in giving coordination and collective consciousness to an otherwise isolated hostility, and it should not be surprising that the same feature appears in this secular context. However, the appearance of the god-like figure should not mislead one into thinking popular commitment necessarily implies readiness to act for that person: the transformation in the fortunes of Sukarno or Nkrumah indicates just how shallow this 'charisma' can be in practice when challenged.

For some among the educated urban middle class, identification with the State (as part of nationalist feeling) constitutes an incipient authoritarianism and can be part of a wider romantic reconstruction of rural society that serves both to compensate for the loss of presumed security and integration within the village group, and provides an effective justification for their own position. With the State as the pivot, society must be integrated like a village (naturally, real villages are quite unlike the romantic picture, and may be sharply differentiated into factions or kinship groups, locked in almost perpetual battle). Identification with the kinship group at the village level becomes identification with an ethnic group at the national, and is embodied in particular leaders upon whom one is dependent. What is at stake is not the detail of what the leader does or says he proposes to do, so much as his mere existence as a symbol of unity.

Just as the village (or the village faction) depends for its unity upon a shared hostility to outsiders which enforces common sacrifices on all members, the new nationalism depends upon sharp differentiation between in-group and out-group.

We noted earlier that the solidarity enforced by common hostility safeguards the positions of the existing leadership (although to say this is not to imply the common hostility is invented by the leadership for the sole purpose of safeguarding its position). The former imperial power provides one target, and a target with more historical justification for hatred than many, but the target loses significance over time and needs replacement by more easily identified enemies: Israelis for Arabs, Indians for Pakistanis, Ethiopians for Somalis, Chinese for Indonesians, and vice versa. A sense of group honour is one symptom of group existence in the village, and the 'honour of the nation' now becomes a practical political term. Men react with violent sensitivity to imagined slights on their national integrity, and personalized international relations portray the United States as an evil old man scheming with almost motiveless malignity the disaster of the pure virgin, the nation.

The presumed nature of armies conforms to some of the aspired ethics: order, security, hierarchy (where all accept their given place naturally and unquestioningly), each place in society carrying incumbent duties and rights that demand neither debate nor change, the whole coherently directed at one central purpose. In China, Egypt, Pakistan, Algeria and so on, the role of the army in providing the civil population with certain kinds of ideals has similarities which overshadow some of the enormous differences between them. Actual armies, of course, are as likely to be riven with the same divisions as society at large, and soldiers will seek to maximize their returns and minimize their contribution as much as anyone else, with the difference that their activities are curbed to a greater degree by a system of pure force. The army embodies in its internal organization the coercion it is designed to exercise on others outside the army. The rural myth implies that unanimity and harmony spontaneously arise among villagers, but armies are straightforwardly commanded by generals at the top. The appearance of spontaneity is carefully created to hide the use of force. Armies themselves (or rather their officers) foster the illusion of complete unity, for this is an element in the fear they seek to strike in those they oppose, and like to appear as outside the petty squabbles of mere politicians. They have no market interest (with some exceptions, as in Thailand), for their life depends on taxation, not sales, so that they seem honest and unselfish. In their natural attempts to control their own paymaster, and thereby their own existence, seizure or at least control of the State can answer a diversity of different needs.

This account has sought to suggest some of the features common to the nature of underdevelopment, or rather early phases of development in modern terms. It is a dangerous exercise since one can quite mistakenly generalize a local peculiarity as a standard feature, and because it takes the discussion away from the hard reality which is its essential discipline. However, space does not allow more than a general account, designed to suggest that

Western and Soviet accounts which separate communist and non-communist, or communist, non-aligned and Western-aligned, conceal some basic similarities which are problems ideology has to explain. Many of the features solemnly identified as essentially socialist in both communist and non-communist countries are no more than the historical concomitants of development, the conversion of harsh and unpleasant necessities into slightly more attractive virtues.

Nationalism, the belief in the population of a given politically defined area as the basic operating unit of consciousness, the source of all virtue and legitimacy, is the guiding thread, and inevitably the nationalism of the underdeveloped countries has very close similarities with nationalism in Europe – 'And there has arisen . . . blood against formal reason; race against purpose-ful rationality; honour against profit; unity against individualistic disintegration; marital virtue against bourgeois security; the people against the individual and the mass.' (Ernst Krieck, leading National Socialist philosopher at Heidelberg). National socialism can be a coherent doctrine for some of the population, even if its appearance in inter-war Germany and Italy makes it seem no more than an elaborate make-believe to conceal a personal dictatorship. Of course, it would be quite wrong to see such diverse beliefs as 'Fascist', but intense insecurity for the urban middle class in a hostile international environment can recreate eerie echoes. Similarly the combination of the notion of struggle from socialist or Marxist sources and nationalism occasionally awakens old memories. Inevitably, nationalism is a minority cult, and as a result it is misleading to infer a popular response from the behaviour of either a member of the urban middle class or one of the major leaders of society. Geertz comments on the nationalism of an Indonesian newspaper as a 'sort of intensely felt but curiously abstract kind of ideological expression, part of a symbolic masking of real value conflicts within the society, a kind of cultural protesting too much, by means of which conflicts which threaten to upset the social equilibrium can to a degree be kept out of conscious awareness or at least from open expression.' (1960, p. 370.)

The sociological shallowness of the feeling engenders a similar kind of ideological shallowness (which is not to imply that the feelings expressed are shallow). The doctrines are loosely defined and relatively incoherent, drawn from apparently contradictory sources that are only united in the passionate faith of the believer. The examples of what is known as syncretism are diverse: the description of Burma as a 'nation built upon a combination of Burmese national identity, Buddhist philosophy, British political organization and socialist economic theories – both Marxist and non-Marxist'; Nasser's suggestion that 'Islam in its early days was the first socialist State'; Ben Bella's 'Islamic socialism'; Nkrumah's remark that 'I am a non-denominational Christian and a Marxist socialist, and I have not found any contradiction between the two'; Sukarno's Indonesian socialism, and the Indonesian Communist Party's Indonesian Marxism-Leninism; the Indian Praja Socialist's marriage of Marxist historical analysis and the Vedantist ethic. Nor is this just play with words, for, as Lewis Feuer has pointed out, when Burma's U Nu and China's Chou En-lai signed a treaty on behalf of their countries they did so at 5.50 p.m. on 1 October 1960, since that was the exact time which astrologers had indicated was the most propitious. Stark (1966, p. 175) cites a somewhat tragic example of the synthesizing of past and present in the catechism of some Italian republican peasants:

Question: What are the three distinct persons in Garibaldi?
Answer: The father of the nation, the son of the people, and the spirit of liberty.
Question: How did he make himself man?
Answer: He took on a body and soul just like ourselves in the blessed womb of a woman of the people.

Yoking together apparently quite inconsistent threads of argument is a characteristic feature of the use of a doctrine in a place other than that in which it was formulated. The examples here repeat some of those noted in the earlier discussion of religious beliefs. Economic development is a 'Western process', and the cultural forms hitherto associated with development are derived from Western sources. There is nothing intrinsic in this, but as a matter of historical fact the Western development process, including in this the experience of the Soviet Union, has dominated the field. For the moment, at least, efforts at development borrow from this cultural inheritance and Third World leaders try to marry it to carefully selected elements of indigenous culture, inherited 'traces'. The marriage is imperfectly consummated by Western standards since the doctrines derive from incompatible sources – to achieve any conjuncture at all involves small or large redefinitions of both elements, so that in the end one is sometimes left with no more than a play on words. Thus, if 'democracy' is to mean anything distinctive it must carry certain connotations, and not merely be used to describe any form of organization in which, to an outsider, it seems a consensus is created. Putting together traditional practices and 'foreign' doctrines is part of the attempt to carry contradictory audiences, the local peasant and the Westernized élite.

It is also a form of special pleading, for in the 'foreign' doctrines there are often criteria publicly available for appraising whether or not the words are being used reasonably correctly. 'Ruritanian socialism', however, is carefully concealed from such inspection, for any criticism is dismissed as being made by a person who does not 'really' know the peculiarities of the local situation. Sometimes this is true, sometimes it is merely an evasion of an embarrassing criticism. For in the examination of the new orthodoxy one must also ask the opinion of those members of the indigenous society who are in prison.

Syncretism is a major and important feature of political ideas in underdeveloped countries. Very few people are actually involved in political debate of the kind which borrows 'foreign' doctrines, so that the political implications of syncretism are possibly not as great as one might imagine. Often the syncretist formulations are framed deliberately for foreign consumption, or are no more than part of the discussion between members of the small élite. For the average peasant, Marxism is, quite reasonably, as remote as the society in which it was originally formulated. Indeed, in the larger Third World countries the peasant's own State is almost as remote. Thus, one must keep a strict sense of proportion in appraising the new orthodoxies, for probably they do not go very deep, and even where they do go deeper, they are almost certainly reformulated in entirely traditional terms. Mao to an average Chinese peasant probably seems less like a champion of Marxist-Leninism, and more like an emperor-cum-prophet.

Nor should one underestimate the groping pragmatism which the new orthodoxies are merely late attempts to rationalize. We have already noted how Fidel Castro did not become a 'Marxist-Leninist' until after he came to power; his Marxism-Leninism was not a revolutionary aid so much as the indication of a certain foreign policy alignment. Indeed, the Cuban Marxist-Leninists did not support Castro until his success was almost accomplished. In Egypt, the army officers who seized power in 1952 had no clear philosophy, no clear programme of what they intended to do beyond 'clean up'. They were initially rather conservative, and it was really only with the events of 1956 that they moved towards a much more radical transformation of the economy and society of Egypt. Thus, 'Egyptian socialism' evolved relative to a series of determinate challenges, rather than from any inner force of its own. The combination of elements we have called '*étatiste* nationalism' are not the simple expressions of national souls, but rather the contingent adjustments of peoples striving to survive in a world dominated and, indeed, exploited by the most advanced countries.

This chapter has sought to continue some of the themes discussed earlier. Common problems in the Third World shape a similar response, although the differences that also exist in both the problems and the responses have here been ignored in order to emphasize some of the common elements. The terminology has been borrowed from many different sources, so that, in terms of language alone, the differences seem very great – between 'free enterprise' in those countries directly subject to American domination, through the Fabian 'mixed economy' of India, to the Marxist-Leninism of China, North Vietnam and North Korea. Yet, beneath these labels, similar processes are concealed, a common combination (to different degrees) of *étatisme*, nationalism and voluntarism. The closest actual parallels in European history come from populist and nationalist régimes, rather than from Fabian or Marxist traditions themselves. The countries of the Third World have to fight for survival in conditions far harsher than those that governed the development of the Western countries – indeed, the Western countries are the major obstacle to the development of the underdeveloped. The struggle for survival lends a radicalism to their orthodoxies which contrasts with the conservatism of the West, both capitalist and 'socialist'.

We might ask at the end of this chapter whether in fact doctrines can ever be transferred between societies without fundamental transformation – where does the line come between the particular and the universal? As we have noted in the second chapter, the word 'society' is a difficulty here. For the answer to the question turns very much on what we mean by 'society'. If we mean by the concept, nation-State, then doctrines can certainly be transferred intact. The reshaping of Marxism which took place in different countries in Europe in the hands of the member-organizations of the Second International was not a transformation of Marxism, but merely filling the given categories with local content. The 'industrial working class' was not filled with peasants or professional revolutionaries, but, according to the case, with real German or French workers. However, if by 'society' we mean broad cultural zones, characterized by fundamental conditions, for example 'Western society', then the idea of transfer becomes more difficult, according to the conditions specified. Let us say we identify 'advanced industrial society' as characterized by the fact that industrial activity plays the dominant role, by an industrial working class which is a majority or very nearly a majority of the population. Then it is obvious that political beliefs which suggest the possible rule of society by that industrial working class are inappropriate in a society where the majority occupation is cultivating the land, where industrial pursuits are marginal. Almost all modern Western political ideas presuppose Western society, presuppose basic structural conditions which are present to the full only in Western society, so that transfer can only take place to societies where those conditions do not exist at the cost of the ideas themselves – they are redefined to mean something else.

What inevitably happens where transfer takes place between two quite different contexts is that the doctrine both needs ancillary aid from other doctrines (Marxism and Islam in Indonesia), but also, in losing its specific validating conditions, it becomes an atemporal doctrine. It comes to refer to 'the nature of man' (as the only solidly atemporal concept we have, even if it means almost nothing) rather than the nature of a specific society. It is interesting to note how this process has emerged most clearly in China, for Marxism in China is less about how society should be organized and more about the salvation of souls. A 'socialist' becomes a person of particular ethical persuasion (used by the socialists to mean kindly and susceptible to popular wishes; by their enemies to mean evil and élitist), rather than one committed to a particular analysis of a particular society or a particular view of the future organization of society. The analysis of society becomes less and less important, and the voluntarism of the socialist more important. But, the voluntarism of the political leaders is bounded by the conditions of their office, by the forces at home and abroad compelling actions of a certain kind (unless the politician has his own separate source of overwhelming and dedicated support). It is the way the liberated are forced to go which constitutes the main lines of '*étatiste* nationalism'.

7

The Logic of Dichotomies

Defenders of the *status quo* are 'inclined to present the structure of their own society in terms of a functional scheme or one of non-egalitarian classlessness. Revolutionaries, on the other hand, tend to view the world in terms of a dichotomy with opposed attributes. It can also happen, however, that the same scheme lends itself for application by two opposing social tendencies.'

OSSOWSKI, *Class Structure and Social Consciousness*, p. 174

THROUGHOUT this account so far a series of related dichotomies has recurred. It is worth looking at some of the dichotomies separately and in general terms, even though to do so might muddle what is an essential part of the structure of a particular view of the world with what is merely an historical or circumstantial accident. One can be misled in thinking that particular views necessarily 'hang together'. Merton (1957, pp. 501–2) notes that it might have been possible to think that anti-slavery was necessarily associated with pacifism up until the time when war, in which the abolition of slavery was one of the demands of one of the belligerents, divided those that favoured both issues into 'anti-slavery non-pacifists' and simple pacifists who favoured the abolition of slavery only under certain specified conditions. In a similar way, one can say either that the Russian leaders are not Marxists or that a Marxist is not necessarily opposed to making profits if made by the State in the form of Libermann's proposals for the charging of interest on capital employed in Soviet enterprises.

One of the inferences to be made from the preceding chapters is that one cannot discover the implication of given doctrines, the direction of the perspective, if one knows only the formal statement of the doctrines. One needs also to know the context in which the doctrine was enunciated or in which it is assumed to be significant, and what the people who adhered to it meant by it, what they did, what purposes they pursued. In the evolution of British Conservatism, 'leadership' in practice covered an inconsistent range of different things over a period of time; in Marxism-Leninism, the 'proletariat' similarly covered contradictory elements. In the unification of Italy, nationalism was included in a certain range of other radical proposals, among them republicanism. But in the unification of Germany under Bismarck, nationalism accompanied a series of conservative positions. Nationalism in Japan was one of the attributes of a military élite seeking both to preserve Japan's *ancien régime* and expand abroad. Nationalism in China was initially a radical force, republican and liberal, before it divided into pro-Soviet and pro-Western factions.

One of the threads running through this account has been the dichotomy, ruler and ruled, and it has been seen as corresponding to the ideological dichotomy, conservative and radical. Historically, this is not a strictly accurate alignment since it is certainly not self-contradictory to speak of conservative ruled and radical rulers. But the correspondence does help us to organize beliefs in a provisional manner, and it derives from the trivial point that it is difficult to be radical unless there are some obstacles to change, and these obstacles are often what constitute the *status quo*. Now what the '*status quo*' is, varies in relation to the context and the purpose one has in mind in identifying it. Not merely is the dichotomy useful within society as a whole, but also between societies and within sub-sections of society. Thus, we have earlier used the dichotomy to refer to different groups *within* the British Conservative Party, the *status quo* in that context being the party leadership and organization. At the other end of the spectrum, the opposition of the countries of the Third World to the world *status quo*, to the domination of the advanced countries, qualifies them also for the term 'radical'. The terms, like the beliefs and doctrines we have discussed, are only clearly defined in a definite context.

Perception of the world and of society varies between rulers and ruled, for perception is related in part to different purposes and different standpoints. People both see the world in relationship to their own purposes, and learn to understand what these are or should be by observing the world, by gaining experience in trying to do things, by separating what they feel is essential from what is less essential. This difference in perception is not a difference in the world perceived, but a difference in the priorities with which the same objects are perceived. For example, it is the lower classes who perceive the existence of class most sharply and vividly, for they are subject to its discrimination. It is the black who perceive clearly the discrimination of the white. While the upper classes or the whites either do not perceive their own discriminatory behaviour at all or take it for granted as part of the natural order of things. The allegation that class exists may then be treated as no more than the product of private resentments, and solutions suggested as remote from the problem as Marie Antoinette's invitation to the *sans culottes* to eat cake if there was no bread. Taking the existing class order for granted helps to sustain it, helps to inhibit the dangerous idea that things could be different. However, if the idea that class exists is enunciated, then it can be described as something positively beneficial. Ossowski cites the delightful observation made by Theodoret of Cyrrhus, a summation of benevolent self-congratulation : 'One must admire God for having organized things so wisely in giving the wealth to the one, the industry to the other.' (1963, p. 91, author's translation).

The mutual interaction of rulers and ruled, of conservative and radical beliefs, has been only incidentally implied in what has been discussed earlier. In many cases the target has not been described, although its main form in terms of ideas could be extrapolated. The successive and differing challenges to British Conservatism identified different *status quo*, and these evoked different responses from Conservatives. The attack on the aristocracy and the monarchy gave way to an attack on 'established institutions' (the monarchy and the House of Lords, in particular), which in turn overlapped with an attack on private property. Even earlier, Nonconformists had challenged the monopolistic position of the Church of England. Each challenge added some new element to the body of Conservatism, even if in subsequent time the defence of *all* the elements was not required. It was, after all, a Conservative government in recent times which began to erode the hereditary basis of the House of Lords, and made an application for British membership of the European Common Market (thus, in the long term, jeopardizing 'established institutions' in Britain by merging British sovereignty in a supranational authority).

However, in employing the dichotomy one must not thereby infer some false symmetry of beliefs between rulers and ruled, for the tactics of defence are different from those of attack, particularly where the defence takes place within the context of an established society, associated with given institutions, the symbolism of which is deeply woven into the texture of the culture men inherit. Converse notes in this context the asymmetry of parties of the Right and of the Left. The upper strata of society is more consistent in its support of the Right than the lower strata is in support of the Left; the Left has a 'natural' majority but one that is less dependable and loyal. As a result, asymmetrical strategies are necessary, and there is an increasing stress on group loyalty as one moves leftward across the political spectrum. The Right stresses non-political independence of individual judgement, but for the Left the 'transmission of gross, simple, group-oriented cues is a functional imperative. For rightist parties, there is much to lose and nothing to gain in such publicity, for the basic clientele can be counted on for fair support without blatant cues, and the tactical needs are to avoid the alienation of potentially large-scale "haphazard" support from the lower-status clientele.' (1964, p. 249.)

The distinction between passive or 'non-operative' and operative beliefs partly relates to conservative and radical. In practice, there are at least three levels of personal beliefs – things we say we believe but are unlikely to do anything about; things we believe and are committed to doing something about; and things we believe, are committed to doing something about, and are shared by a large number of other people so that social or political action is possible. There are also things we in fact will do something about although we are not aware beforehand that we have a belief about them. The first two categories broadly correspond to passive and operational beliefs, but, in the context of ideologies which presuppose beliefs shared by a social group, the third is the more important.

In practice, it is impossible to separate passive and operational very clearly simply because people do not themselves know with any certainty what they will do in unspecified circumstances. However, we can see certain paradigms. For example, if in a survey we ask people, 'Do you believe in God?' and find someone who says 'Yes,' we do need to discover what this entails – murdering the man next door who replied 'No,' to the same question? refusing to speak to him, not speaking to him on particular days, not lending him the lawnmower or borrowing a packet of tea from him? withdrawing his child from a school which his neighbour's child attends or which has an agnostic headmaster? or behaving in a perfectly conventional manner so that his belief in God seems to affect his behaviour in no perceptible respect? In the last case, it might be reasonable to say his belief is passive, it entails nothing in terms of action at all, it is merely a 'trace' from the past, like celebrating Christmas for many of us, after the validating conditions for its being an operational belief have disappeared. Of course, we might be wrong, and under certain circumstances the man's belief in God might begin to provide a compass for his action but, on the evidence available, we have no way of determining this.

The distinction between non-operative and operative beliefs is relevant to the present discussion precisely because conservative doctrines have a peculiarly high proportion of non-operative beliefs, traces from the past that have little or no relevance for immediate practice. Radical theories, on the other hand, have a high proportion of operative beliefs, beliefs which entail some action in the world to achieve given ends. Radicals must have some conception of a society which is, in principle at least, different from that in which they currently live, some view of the possible. But conservatives have no such need, for they take for granted the society in which they live, the real which faces them is, by and large, the ideal. Indeed, conservatives have a positive interest in preventing a general consideration of society, since this then demands a general response by them, a response which forces them not to consider each issue as a separate and isolated one. However, if radicals do present such theories, conservatives must answer them with general theories also, so that a conservative general social theory is possible, even if not an essential part of conservatism. More ordinarily, 'theory', the coherent exposition of specific purposes in relationship to the general analysis of society, is spurned as an irritating diversion from the real job of day-to-day administration. The down-to-earth practical man of affairs stands contrasted to the speculative intellectual, the dogmatist and theoretician, trapped in the foolishness of an ivory tower. The place of theory is filled by odd 'traces' from the past, names and phrases, not related to each other in a general way but to what immediately faces the conservative, unanalysed reality.

The 'traces' are embodied in ritual, in lovingly conserved detail detached from the context where it was originally created, in pageant and ceremony, detached from the meaning of the objects ostensibly symbolized. The conservative defends the historic mythology of institutions, without necessarily being able to say in general why people should be loyal to institutions. If conservatives, in conditions of reasonable stability (that is, the *status quo* is not under threat), see only the form of institutions, radicals see only the content, the meaning of institutions in practice. If the institutions meet no need – or meet needs which cannot clearly be specified – then the institution, the ritual, the trace, should be removed. The conservative stress on the importance of the particular, the peculiar, meets the radical emphasis on the universal, the needs of all men equally. This division between a stress on form and content, on particular existence and universal meaning, was noted in the discussion of religion, where the association between authority, the role of the ruler, and a doctrine was suggested as a process whereby the doctrine is robbed of meaning in popular opinion, reduced to ritual.

Again, under challenge, conservatives can adopt the universalistic approach of their challengers, even if in a much diluted form. For example, Lord Randolph Churchill, identified earlier as a radical figure within British Conservatism (but a conservative figure in British society as a whole), argued that a utilitarian justification could be offered and ought to be offered for the British monarchy – the monarchy was useful. It was a dangerous position, for it implicitly admitted the radical methodological principle and made the monarchy a matter for argument, rather than acceptance. Burke, much earlier and faced with a less immediate and less coherent challenge, contented himself by saying that what existed must be useful since it existed; whatever had survived the ravages of time, must serve a function, and was therefore justified. However, he refrained from saying what function might be served, or to whose advantage the serving of that function might be, for to have done this was once more to have exposed the argument to rational and universalistic critique. Rather he chose to assume that existing society was basically good, so that all existing 'functions' were likewise good; the real was the ideal, even if men could not always see how this was so.

The division between form and content concerned us in the discussion of Stalinism, for many of the forms remained intact while the content changed, the meaning shifted. Freedom was defined as what existed in the Soviet Union, in its 'established institutions'; it was not a universal criterion by which the institutions of the Soviet Union might be critically appraised. The same shift has occurred in the West, for 'democracy' is identified as existing parliamentary or constitutional institutions, rather than being used to appraise those institutions. The change in Stalinism was more generalized. Ossowski observes that 'In the same way as the French revolutionary ideology of the threefold rights of man or the medieval teaching of the Gospels had done, so Marxism, in the period which was to be called the Stalinist period, split into a revolutionary ideology and an official doctrine, petrified in its intellectual content but flexible in its use as an apologetic shield for current policy.' (1963, p. 189.)

The conservative focus on immediate reality, immediate problems of day-to-day administration, rather than on appraising the general picture of society so that reality may be changed into something better (the real is different from the ideal, and therefore needs changing), severely limits the range of possible political argument, to the immense advantage of conservatives. This limited focus is often called 'pragmatism', although this is a misleading word for it implies that the conservative will choose *any* means appropriate to a given isolated problem. On the contrary, conservatives have implicit priorities which severely limit the range of possible alternatives. The priorities cannot be specified (indeed, conservatives may not even know what the priorities are until they actually grapple with a given problem), for to specify them would be to indicate that there were other choices besides the actual course chosen, would be to invite discussion, debate, controversy, would set out a series of purposes which could be construed within a general theoretical framework. Rather do conservatives seek to imply that whatever course they took was 'inevitable', dictated by events, merely 'practical'. But the priorities are there none the less. For example, a number of different courses of action were open to the British (Labour) government in the economic crises of the sixties, but nevertheless the government sought to suggest (and did so with remarkable success) that there was one and only one course of action open to it. Or again, one cannot imagine the pragmatism of a British government which would lead it to nationalize all private enterprise in one swoop, even though a pragmatic case could be made out in relationship to one or a range of problems. No amount of evidence will produce this result, because it conflicts with an implicit priority. The actions called 'pragmatic' by conservatives are defined by the unspoken priorities of preserving the *status quo*; what conflicts with those priorities is called 'doctrinaire', 'dogmatic' and so on. Of course, in a different sense Lenin was quite pragmatic in his behaviour; what this means is that, having made his essential purposes quite clear, he could afford to change or abandon less important priorities.

Administration means, for conservatives, breaking down problems into units which can be dealt with in isolation, rather than synthesizing problems so that they can be seen as coherently related to each other and open to a single solution. The point is not merely relevant to politics, for it constitutes a general methodological principle – the particular is all, the universal unreal. A conservative might argue that every problem should be reduced to what he identifies as its basic elements and handled in isolation. For example, this man's neurosis is his own problem, or, at most, a problem created by his family or immediate locality. By contrast, the radical moves outwards, generalizes rapidly, so that this man's problem can become merely one symptom of a general crisis in society, the solution to which is only to be found in a general solution. It is not enough to say the conservative is 'realistic' because he can frame solutions immediately applicable to the problem, for his solutions may not solve anything; the radical may indeed be right. Whether or not you believe he is right turns in part on your general estimate of society as a whole. Thus, if you believe society is basically harmonious (or at least, not problematic), then problems can be isolated in the way the conservative suggests; and if his first solution does not work, then others can be formulated in the same way for an indefinite period of time. Most societies treat their poor in this way, for the poor are identified as a marginal problem, isolated and suitable for direct solution, rather than the inevitable product of the constitution of society. In Britain, different governments have seen as one obstacle to the poor improving their position the stigma associated with the name of different forms of welfare payment made to them. So the names are changed – most recently, from National Assistance to Social Security – each revised name rapidly acquiring the stigma of the old. Here, isolating the problem as one of a name clearly makes almost no difference at all, because the problem is part of the social structure as a whole; nominalistic disguises do not conceal the problem for very long. Lower secondary education has at times been treated in a similar mannner. A radical might hazard that the welfare system for the poor and the educational system are designed to fit and perpetuate a certain kind of class system; name changing is then no substitute for changing the class system, nor is it a means to this end.

We have already noted in Burke and British Conservatism the conception that in society there is always one and only one correct answer to a given social problem. Stalinism repeats the same methodological principle, and the same assumption operates within the established authorities of major religious orthodoxies. The one truth is the collective judgement of the dominant group, the ruler, and what the ruler says, is what defines what truth is. But for the ruled, the social relativity of 'truths' is more apparent. There are inevitably many answers, depending on who one is at what time and what place. For the truth of the led, its experience, contrasts with the truth of the leadership, the administering authority. If the conservative, from the pinnacle of the social pyramid, looks down and sees an integrated and harmonious whole, the radical looks around him at the flat plain of his society, covered with warring tribes. For the radical, society is not integrated; it is disharmonious. The subordinate groups are seen as existing on a par with the ruling group, as equally entitled to a valid perspective on the world. Classes are, for the radical, equally competing collectivites. For the conservative, classes either do not exist or they are merely functional organs of a common body, harmoniously related parts of a mutually beneficial division of labour. Both British Conservatism and Stalinism employ both forms of escape from the concept of class. Of course, where there is disharmony there must be some social source for it, but that source cannot be a class, cannot be part of the basic nation. The Conservatives identify the threat as coming from a disgruntled and selfish faction, usually of alienated upper-class men (the legend of Satan's ejection from Heaven is peculiarly illustrative of this feeling). Revolt is thus not a basic and integral part of society, it is a noxious excrescence. The same feeling was expressed by Stalin in his phrase 'remnants of the old exploiting classes', and it was within the party leadership, the Soviet version of the Conservative's upper-class men, that he found the prime target for his successive heresy hunts.

Thus, the conservative's assumption of a basically harmonious society confronts the radical's affirmation of a disharmonious society or, rather, the universal and common interest of mankind as a whole. The conservative may certainly admit that there are marginal problems, but these do not affect the basic harmony. But what is the 'society' which the conservative identifies? It is the territory which the dominant group controls and administers, the area held by the élite, aristocracy, king or communist party, of which the conservative is spokesman. Thus the nation-State is 'society', and it is conservative control of the State which is the precondition for the conservative's feeling that society is harmonious. When a new group secures the State the conservative retreats either into indignant exile, into apathy, or into militant counter-revolutionary activity.

By contrast, the radical, not being a member of the governing élite, has no vested interest in the existing territorial area, and is likely to see a multiplicity of groups and associations which are not national. The lower classes are not bounded by the interest of their own control in the nation-State, a concept corresponding to the power of the ruler. The relationship of ruled to ruler can give the lower classes either an indifference to an operative national loyalty or a positive internationalism, regarding the institutions of the nation-State as only outmoded 'traces' of the past, ritual without universal meaning. Once again, the emphasis on the particular by the conservative contrasts with the radical emphasis on the universal. Thus, it is particularly significant to detect the transition in Stalinism from an emphasis on a particular lower class, the working class, with internationalist implications, to either the Russian nation or the classless notion of 'all producers', infelicitously translated from the Russian as 'toiling masses'.

If conservatives start from what already exists and radicals from what could exist, conservatives do not need to argue their case except under severe threat. But radicals must always argue their case, must present a coherent theory or programme based upon universal rather than particular grounds. Inevitably, under threat, conservatives do get forced into offering some justification for what exists. However, as noted in earlier chapters this justification frequently retreats into an assertion of mystery; the final justification is unknowable. Beneath the appearance of reality lurks divine mystery, original sin and divine grace, heredity or blood, ethnic or family charisma, national spirit or fate. Perhaps the text from Lenin plays the same role in Stalinism. Radicals, however, must argue from first principles, relying on logic and accurate analysis of the environment as a whole, submitting themselves to universal criteria of judgement. For the radical, the conservative's mystery is illusion, or myth designed to conceal conservative power. For 'human nature', which the conservative offers as the great obstacle to progress, is, for the radical, just one of the elements which changes historically. The radical is optimistic, for history is an ascending plane, a saga of progress and man's self-improvement. The conservative claims to have been soured by life's experience, so that ideals are no more than the phantoms that plague the untutored imagination of youth. No progress beyond that already achieved or being achieved is possible, for the ruler is as progressive as 'reality' permits and the attempt at a more rapid rate of progress may jeopardize what is already being attempted. History is a cycle, not a rising plane, and even if, on the upswing of the cycle, material progress sometimes occurs, it is inevitably destroyed by the lack of moral progress in man, for human nature is its own unchanging law and barbarous at base. The past shows the conservative the barbarity of which human nature is capable, and therefore what is inevitable in the future.

These different viewpoints are not portrayed as a way of suggesting that the division is one of autonomous personality differences, psychological attitudes. For the individual psychology is also a variable, shaped in part by the perspective adopted. Reducing political divisions to attitudinal divisions is one means conservatives sometimes employ to isolate radicalism and dismiss it – radicalism is, they might say, the posture of inexperienced youth, or 'mere intellectualism'. Rather are these attitudes appropriate to different social groups, groups standing in different relationships to the rest of society, the one constituting the *status quo*, the other controlled by it. Each group's view of the other clarifies its perspective. The conservative sees the desirable attributes of the ruled as humility, obedience, acknowledged dependence, acceptance of things as they are, respect and affection for the ruler, social passivity; and he sees himself as burdened with duty, with heavy responsibility and obligation, with an unwanted monopoly of what little initiative is available to men. The radical demands of the ruled their anger, action, initiative, systematic thought, self-dependence, rejection of things as they are in favour of how they could be; and he sees only that the rulers enjoy immense privileges which constantly tend to increase unless checked; that with that privilege, still they are the last to sacrifice when sacrifice is needed and they sacrifice least. The conservative argues that people *need* leadership (as the world 'needs' British leadership), for otherwise the ruled are confused, muddled, anarchic and incompetent; the main priority for the conservative is order (that is, stability of the *status quo*) and discipline, each firmly in his place, and although this may not always be pleasant, it is vital if civilization – that is, things as they are under conservative rule – is to survive. The radical argues that the rulers themselves are the cause of present problems, for they are an unwanted imposition that deprives men of both livelihood and liberty; men *need* freedom, as mankind needs freedom, for otherwise, tyranny merely compounds the problems of survival and progress. The dichotomy, order and freedom, is a social companion of the philosophic division between necessity and freedom. In Vietnam, the United States are compelled to preserve the *status quo*, order, against the challenge of radicalism, freedom, and if the first is identified with the cause of peace, the second reflects the cause of justice. Thus peace, represented in that eminently conservative aim, 'peaceful coexistence', confronts justice, for which the conservative has less concern.

The conservative's necessity for leadership is ultimately concealed in mystery and, in practice, only properly identified as what already exists, the existing hierarchy. The radical replies that the mere existence of power does not justify it, and justification can only be secured by measuring power in relationship to the needs of all men equally. Thus, the final universalism emerges, democracy. It is not the rights of established interests that should determine politics, but what is in accordance with the needs of the majority, the collectivity, the community. The conservative identifies in existing society different entities, different qualities; the radical argues that the power of numbers, majority rule, should determine society – justice, not peace, should be the main aim.

This discussion has pressed to an extreme what are only tendencies, half-formed or tentative. It has exaggerated in order to draw a sharp contrast even though, in practice, our imaginary conservative and radical do not exist. It would be wrong to see any beliefs as uniquely defined, and, as preceding chapters have suggested, doctrines can be used in contradictory ways. The discussion has, in addition, omitted to discuss reformists, those groups which seek to straddle the gap between the two. British Conservatives today tend to see history as embodying some progress and the future as promising, as holding the prospect of a progress which can be secured by efforts here and now. In practice, the British Conservatives have absorbed some radical positions, even though this absorption has often entailed the dilution of the position. Yet still the dichotomy helps to define the area of debate, and the connections which hold between different parts of each side in the controversy. The viability of reformism depends on short-run factors historically, whereas the two extremes are both more reasonably constant and define the area within which reformism makes sense. Also omitted are attempts, such as that of Marx, to supersede some of these related dichotomies – for example, freedom and order, freedom and necessity, the universal and the particular – in order to enunciate a final radical vision.

With considerable qualification, then, exploring the related dichotomies does help to show the kinds of purposes which may be detected in different emphases, and the ways in which different ideologies are related to those purposes. In origin, beliefs are related to determinate problems; they are not merely random occurrences, nor the products of an arbitrary psychology. That men forget the origins of their beliefs does not affect the issue, for men still select which of a multitude of 'traces' they will use. In the conjuncture of problem and active purposeful consciousness the 'traces' are sorted in particular ways, the relevant is chosen, the ambiguous is defined. Where we do not know the origins of our beliefs our ignorance is an invitation to locate what purposes we embody in them now so that the essential and inessential can be separated.

8

What is to be Done?

To him who looks upon the world rationally, the
world in its turn presents a rational aspect.

HEGEL

Hitherto philosophers have *interpreted* the world
in various ways; the point, however, is to *change*
it.

MARX

IT might be asked: if all opinions are purely relative to a particular social position, embody the partial perspective of one
group of people only, how are we ever to make reliable judgements ourselves, to believe we are right to such a degree that we
can form opinions and act accordingly? If everybody is 'on the
make', surely the only defence is a purely negative cynicism, the
derisive superiority of the uninvolved bystander. Or, if the corrupting influences of the world are so indiscriminate and so
comprehensive, then the preservation of one's soul demands that
one withdraws, to hermitage or monastery.

Yet, even this is not enough, for we thereby make ourselves
irresponsible – if men die unjustly and we ignore it we are thereby
implicated. The logic of our morality demands, quite unreason-
ably, that we accept responsibility for all men, and even if we
plead ignorance we feel we should have cared enough to find
out, to overcome our ignorance: each man's suffering should be
our own. Thus, on this logic the villagers who lived near German
concentration camps are morally implicated in what took place
in those camps, even though they could do nothing except destroy
themselves by openly opposing them; so unreasonable is our
morality, which includes accounts of heroes who walked knowingly into fatal disaster for what they believed. Thus, to withdraw
is not to guarantee our virtue at all, nor is the cynic unimplicated.

Rather can both be seen as examples of moral cowardice, of the evasion of that responsibility which is implicit in the moral tradition which alone makes meaningful both withdrawal and cynicism.

Yet, ideological analysis cannot fail in some measure to debunk, to devalue, the validity of all judgements, much as popular psychoanalysis debunks what we feel – I only love my daughter because I secretly long to sleep with her. If 'freedom' is what the small shopkeeper says it is when he opposes the abolition of Resale Price Maintenance, or what the white South African says it is as he enforces apartheid, then perhaps, unless we happen to be small shopkeepers or white South Africans, the word is meaningless, a purely 'emotive' term to summon up warm feelings but essentially indefinable and unusable? But this counsel of despair or nihilism need not be inevitable. MacIntyre (1967, p. 204) suggests the analytical solution that Hegel and subsequently Marx suggested:

> What freedom is in each time and place is defined by the specific limitations of that time and place and by the characteristic goals of that time and place. So it is correct to say in the Hegelian sense that the Levellers, the American colonists, John Brown at Harpers Ferry, and the South African Bantu today are all claiming freedom, even though what they claim is substantially different in each case. To put it in another way, when we speak of men as being unfree, what we mean is always relative to an implicit normative picture of human life, by means of which we identify what human bondage is.

Thus, what we mean by 'freedom' depends on how we are unfree. But if this helps us to understand others, it does not necessarily establish our own rightness, what we are to mean by 'freedom' here and now. Nor does it necessarily help us to know who is right in a particular debate, and how to pursue the truth through the complexities of an argument.

Consider the argument that a higher rate of growth in the British economy would result if top managers were paid more, if the State took less in taxation. The argument at its simplest suggests that higher pay means 'higher incentives' for those who direct British industry – they will work harder if promised more cash. A more elaborate version might suggest, in addition, that more income for the richer would, since they tend to save a higher proportion of their income than other people, lead to increased national savings available for investment; on the other hand, more money would also lead to higher consumption, so that businessmen would thereby have a higher incentive to build new plant to supply the increased demand for goods. As a result, the economy would grow more rapidly, more would be available for export, more would be available for income of the 'less rich'. It is not a valid reply to assert simply that the person arguing the case is, knowingly or not, putting forward a case for the rich (although he is doing that as well) for the validity of the case needs answering in its own terms. A marginal note on the sociology of the argument does not, in logic, refute it. Another man might disagree with the argument, and assert, instead, that rich men will work harder if they get *less* pay, or rather, if they have to run faster to stay in the same place. Further, he might go on, economic growth will follow if the rich are taxed more heavily, if the increased public revenue is then distributed to the needy so raising general consumption and thereby stimulating businessmen to an even greater degree to expand their output, to invest in new plant and so raise the growth rate. Again, to reply that the second man is 'just' advancing the interests of the poor does not offer a critique, for, like the first man, if both are reasonably honest, he too will infer that you are accusing him of personal corruption. The fact that each gains (if they do indeed gain) if his argument is adopted by the government is not *logically* related to the validity of the arguments involved. Nor does it follow with this brutal simplicity that social position and prescriptions for action match, for there are always some people who, for one reason or another, transcend the opinions of their social group and attach themselves to opinions normally appropriate to a different group. We have seen in earlier chapters that some of the foremost representatives of the ideology of a group are in fact 'outsiders' – the Jew Disraeli, the Jew Marx; Phillipe Égalité of Revolutionary France, who had been the duc d'Orléans of the *ancien régime*; Edmund Burke was not of the aristocracy, nor Lenin a Russian industrial worker.

It is clear that we must try to keep reasonably separate logical and sociological or historical questions, but it is also clear that the historical point of reference is an important determinant of how far we can regard things as true. From the passage of time emerge such odd questions as: was the world round before men decided it was? is it possible for something to be true when nobody knows it? Now, in terms of logic, it is of course obvious that the world was round before men began to think it was, but in terms of history, we are left with the tautology: the world was thought by men not to be round before they decided it was round. In terms of logic, the truths of natural phenomena have always been valid, even though for men at different points of time, they were not truths.

But in relationship to historical judgements we have the benefit of hindsight, or restrospection – we know that the roundness of the world is considered generally to be true (although the Flat Earth Society upholds that it is false). We do not know, from among the things we believe to be true, what men in the future will consider false, and, indeed, so false that almost no one will bother to question its falseness. We do not know how many astrologies lurk among our sciences, how many witches and fairies there are inhabiting our common sense. Yet most of us act nevertheless. We act in good faith, since our lives are too short to wait for perfection, and, indeed, the whole idea of 'perfection' is probably fallacious. In a similar kind of way, within society here and now, the different loci on which hang different beliefs stop being a relativistic whirligig when we choose, and having chosen, act in good faith.

But is there some perspective which will inform our choice so that when we judge we may be reasonably assured of being right? The problem, the relativity of what we regard as the truth, has been a central concern of almost all theorists who have written about the sociology of knowledge. For if we say, with Wirth (introduction to Mannheim, 1936), 'there is no value apart from interest and no objectivity apart from agreement', do we not thereby damn what we ourselves say, are we not trapped in the philosopher's favourite example of an infinite regression: the Cretan who says 'All Cretans are liars'? Mannheim's paradox (as it is known) seems insurmountable and not overcome by Mannheim's own solution; for he argues that:

... each ideology, though claiming absolute validity, has been shown to be related to a particular position and to be adequate only to that one. Not until he has assimilated all the crucial motivations and viewpoints, whose internal contradictions account for our present social-political tension, will the investigator be in a position to arrive at a solution adequate to our present life-situation. (cf. full case, 1936, p. 130 *passim*)

The socially unattached intellectual has, in principle, the best opportunity to formulate the synthesis, according to Mannheim. The thesis has been advanced for a very long time by intellectuals – one can perhaps see traces of the idea in Coleridge's Clerisy or Plato's Guardians (who combine power with knowledge of the truth); in the 'community of scholars', popular as the alleged validating authority for 'consensus' in the United States, Berle's Lords Spiritual; and Marxist intellectuals have not been averse to suggesting something not altogether dissimilar, from the explicit intellectual élitism of Kautsky (copied by the early Lenin in *What is to be Done?*), to the flavour of the same thing in Gramsci, and the explicit concern for 'the role of the intellectual' of the British *New Left Review*.

However, the argument is problematic because 'intellectuals' do not, by and large, constitute a coherent social group. Being an 'intellectual' suggests something about the kinds of topics in which you are interested, the way you are interested in them, but it does not denote a single perspective. As was suggested earlier in relationship to the work of social scientists, intellectuals are to be found in a large number of different social groups, presenting the viewpoints of different classes within society. Now, some intellectuals have offered themselves as a class above other classes, but this does not seem to me to be a viable long-term proposition. More often than not the offer turns out to be a slightly dilute version of some other case – for conservatism or for social democracy. Other intellectuals offer education as the means to emancipation, and demand that the social structure be open to all with talents, for the intellectual is a person pre-eminently with talents. But the meritocrat's argument for a meritocracy is, in principle, not superior to the capitalist's argument for capitalism or the aristocrat's argument for an aristocratic society. Certainly, it could be suggested that, for example, if the social scientists of a given society have worked well on the problems central to that society, the information and suggestions they will have should inform discussion and take it to a higher level, focusing more clearly on the genuine points of disagreement. But the opinions of such social scientists on the central political decisions that should be taken do not fit into the same category for they are not problems of that kind. A social scientist is in no superior position to say who should gain and who should lose, and what theories he might have on this are often no more than reformulations of general opinion.

The example cited earlier – whether or not the British government should decrease its taxation revenue from higher income groups – illustrates this, for the theory, the relationship between the given concepts employed, can be worked from both ends to produce contradictory conclusions. The rich will work harder if they can earn more money by doing so; the rich will work harder if they are taxed more heavily, for then they will have to do so in order to stay where they are. Historically, evidence can be cited to support both arguments. This does not mean that the social sciences have nothing to offer, but it does mean that people cannot evade the responsibility for political decisions by inventing the omnipotent godhead of science, the pure 'facts', the answers of which are 'right'. What the right answer is depends on who you are, whether you are rich or poor or something else.

In practice, of course, it is scarcely conceivable that scholarly orthodoxy could diverge very far from ordinary social orthodoxy. An embryonic ideology does tend to develop, as in most occupational groups, but fortunately does not go very far, for it is the rest of society which pays for the community of scholars, and it is ultimately in the interests of scholars as a group (whatever particular individual scholars may do) to retain a sense of identification with the society in which they live, with the dominant orthodoxy within society.

One of the major difficulties in the whole question – a central concern of both political theory and social science – is the nature of the 'right' answer. The word 'right' is suggestively ambiguous, for it can mean 'correct', 'appropriate', 'honest' or 'straight'. We know that the correct answer to the sum: two plus two, is four, and anyone who asserts 'four' is 'right'. We know that if someone asserts 'The cat is on the mat,' and, when we look, we can also see that a cat is indeed on a mat, the person is 'right'. In both examples, we could, without loss of meaning, use the word 'correct' instead of 'right', and we could put both statements in the form, 'It is true that . . .'.

However, these primitive examples are of almost no help at all when we come to consider general social and political questions, for there is not just one observer, idly observing, but vast numbers of people whose livelihood is at stake, whose prospect for a comfortable old age or a decent life for their children is intimately related to the casual stroke of a politician's pen. That pen disposes of millions of pounds, and those pounds are extracted from the sweat (or simulated sweat) of us all, and can go to purchase the means to destroy thousands of people or to raise the poorest towards some minimum level of basic survival. These are not idle calculations that should be taken in the privacy of solitude by 'disinterested' parties, for the disinterested parties are just those who do not pay the cost. The division of labour becomes some who decide who should pay, and others who pay; some who decide to go to war, and others who die in battle. The decisions cannot be in the form of a simple mathematical equation, except if the real battle takes place beforehand on how the variables are to be defined (are you the variable to which things are added, or from which things are subtracted?), nor can they be questions of simple perception, because the perception will vary according to who you are. Objectivity in social questions can mean no more than a certain openmindedness; a willingness to acknowledge that one is oneself a party, or at least has priorities; a willingness to examine all the information available, all the arguments, and a willingness to answer them. It cannot mean presenting an answer over and above the answers of the existing parties to a dispute, adopting the posture of God who sees all things as they 'really are'. Of course, in practice mediation or arbitration is sometimes useful, but this is an *ad hoc* procedure either to split the difference or strengthen one side; it is not revealing the true nature of reality which has been obscured by fractional prejudice, for we are all prejudiced.

Thus, the question with which we began, 'How can I know that I am right?' is more easily reformulated as, 'What purposes shall I pursue?' The reformulation indicates the fault in the argument about the relativity of all judgements : all judgements are relative, and there is no alternative to their being so, for what is wrong is the simple notion of a judgement absolutely true at all times and places. We do have rules, but they are rather rules of thumb, guide lines, than absolute obligations wherever we are. It is for this reason that, in our society, we all believe broadly that it is absolutely wrong to kill other people, and yet, every few years, a large number of us, supported by the rest, go out with the sole aim of systematically killing a large number of other people, a mass murder called war. Of course, everyone also agrees that it is, 'in principle', wrong to do this, and suggests that the whole blame for doing it rests on the other people. Yet, it happens too often to be plausible that there is a solely virtuous and passive people, our own, and a large number of nasty and active people who threaten us. Yet, very few are interested in time of peace in trying to make the rule of thumb into a proper absolute; that would be 'pacifism', and that is to be deplored, or so the argument goes.

Just as the notion of absolutes can be a pitfall in discussing how we can reach the 'right' philosophy, so the idea of a general philosophy which we choose is also suspect. Men say, or at least some of them do, that they are looking for a 'philosophy of life' even though, in practice, such a philosophy is not something one chooses at all, but is rather something which grows out of one's life, which is a summation of many piecemeal experiences and *ad hoc* decisions, each perhaps taken without reference to the others. Retrospectively one weaves the whole into a fabric of consistency and coherence, or one detects the underlying themes that have continually reasserted themselves.

An ideology can be slightly different, for there one does sometimes have an opportunity to decide beforehand. If a social group has enunciated its perspective and one can see what it is by asking members of that group or reading the works of its foremost writers or publicists, and it is different from common sense (that is, there are several ideologies), then one can choose some of the elements. But even so, one may not be able to choose an ideology as a general scheme – or if one does, it will be reshaped into little more than a peg on which to hang one's personal predilections. Rather must one be convinced about the aims and purposes of the social group concerned, so that its ideology does really offer a perspective on the world which is meaningful in relationship to those aims and purposes.

It is for this reason that attacks on other people's ideologies are so often tangential, for they attack the general scheme, what they think it is, rather than the aims and purposes of the group concerned. The argument must be, not about what men believe, but what they should do, and only in relationship to what they do will what they believe become relevant. The discussion about systems of ideas is often no more than evasion, an attempt to escape facing up to the existence of contradictory purposes – much as conservatives like to ignore the issues at stake in, say, an industrial dispute (issues which demand that one decides which side is closer in its demands to one's own position), and talk solely about the 'failure of communication' which has taken place, the 'lack of understanding' which both sides display. This is an evasion of the issue, no less so because it is often wrapped in the pretensions of pseudo-scientific language – for example, Leninism was really a psychological ailment. The analogy of the medical practitioner becomes explicit, for the doctor does not argue with the man about his insanity, he merely locks him up. The issues at stake are ignored in favour of force. In the

treatment of other people's ideologies this approach is a sur-
reptitious attempt to define out of court the rationality of one's
opponents because one does not like their purposes – what is
'rational' is what the speaker believes and the speaker is mankind's
universal doctor.

The debate then should be about purposes, not ideologies, and
in being about purposes it must be about the real situations in
which people act, the reality of events – the problems people face
and have to overcome. Without this base, examination of ideas
tends to look like the portrayal of a quite separate universe of
ideas, a sort of parallel line to real experience. One then has the
impossible problem of saying what is the relationship between
the two sets of parallel lines, ideas and events: does one influence
the other, is one logically or practically prior to the other? But
this is, as suggested earlier, a nonsense question – men are what
they do and think; there are not two separate worlds, but one.

Over-concentration on the ideas can also lead one to doubt
the existence of *any* common reality. The different perceptions
are of different worlds, and each individual (or group) lives in
his own universe, colliding as in darkness with other individuals
or groups, incapable of communication or mutual understanding.
This is to go to the opposite extreme, to say that because one
man looking at a round flat disc says it is circular and another,
looking from the side, says it is a long thin strip, they must be
looking at different objects. However, substances classified as
'poison' kill whether we believe it or not; rain wets whether a
man accepts it or not; jumping off the Eiffel Tower leads to
certain kinds of result (even if these results vary). There is a
range of possible experience, but it *is* a range, it is determinate,
and its determination is what in part we call 'reality'.

The mistake lies in believing in a 'universe of ideas', for all
ideas are held by people living in a real world. People do not
participate in an autonomous world of ideas in which the ideas
themselves are the active agents independent of people. People
themselves face certain problems and stand in certain relationships to each other, and ideas are a necessary and integral
dimension of this. As society becomes more complex and its

analysis more complicated, its concepts tend to assume a life of their own, so that we forget that terms like society, the economy, bureaucracy, industrial organization, government, and so on, mean no more than people: a particular group of people identified by the relationship in which they stand to the rest of us. 'Reification' as Marx called it, the making of a concept or a relationship into a new and separate thing, is part of the creation of a universe of ideas which seems to tyrannize men, to suggest that men are not responsible for their own acts and decisions, that freedom is impossible and that we must all give up our own freedom to decide to some other external and awe-inspiring authority.

In Marx's hands, this 'tyranny of concepts' was identified as 'false consciousness'. The term 'false consciousness' is problematic for it involves a range of things of very different kinds, all of them relevant to a radical perspective on society. The 'tyranny of concepts' refers to the reduction of a meaningful set of categories for analysis to a series of descriptive nouns – 'society' is not a concept for identifying a system of relationships between people, but a thing that somehow seems to stand over and above people, that is more than they are, that 'tyrannizes' them. In fact, of course, it is only another group of people, calling themselves 'society', who can tyrannize in this way. At a further stage, 'reification' of concepts can lead to more ritual, the repetition of terms, the rhythm and arrangement of which serve artistic purposes, and in themselves, rather than giving meaning to events: the Lord's Prayer can, for example, be seen both as a rhythmic chant, a kind of collective dance without action (which perhaps reactivates feelings of community and solidarity), the meaning of each move no longer being of any significance, or as an actual prayer, a plea to God that summarizes both the human condition and the significance of divine benevolence. On the second interpretation, the actual words are not of great significance – one can enunciate the same idea in a number of different ways without losing the meaning, and, indeed, the archaic language of the Lord's Prayer in its most widespread form might justifiably be seen as an obstacle to modern comprehension. But on the first interpretation, it is the actual sound of particular words which is all-important, and the attached meaning of less significance.

It is the aim of the 'dogmatist' to reduce the most important symbols in which he believes to the level of unthinking accept-ance, a garment to which, like the invisible gown of the emperor, an adequate if unreasoned response will always be due. Unfor-tunately, as the words become less and less useful for meaningful description, even if in the short term they indicate broad loyalty, they die out of ordinary use; men create new subterranean terms to describe their experience, and sooner or later, under the impact of new problems that defy the ability of the inherited tools of comprehension, the ritual fails to contain the feelings of men. Yet, as well, the fragments of belief can continue for a very long time if unchallenged – Weber notes the continuation of the Puri-tan sense of duty in modern times, a sense of one's calling, of one's wholehearted devotion to one's job regardless of the direct cash benefits that result, and this despite the fact that the econo-mic system no longer needs such devotion, indeed cannot accommodate such dedication in conditions where the qualities required in different jobs change so quickly:

Since asceticism undertook to remodel the world ... material goods have gained an increasing and finally an inexorable power over the lives of men as at no previous period in history. ... Victorious capi-talism, since it rests on mechanical foundations, needs its support no longer. The rosy blush of its laughing heir, the Enlightenment, seems also to be irretrievably fading, and the idea of duty in one's calling prowls about in our lives like the ghost of dead religious beliefs. (1930, pp. 181–2)

But this is only one symptom, it seems, of a more generalized phenomenon, 'false consciousness' or, in Marx, ideology. Engels, in a letter to Mehring (14 July 1893, *Selected Works*, I, p. 388), argues that 'Ideology is a process accomplished by the so-called thinker consciously indeed but with a false consciousness. The real motives impelling him remain unknown to him, otherwise it would not be an ideological process at all. Hence he imagines false or apparent motives.' Of course, if someone postulates the existence of things which can be shown not to exist, or not to exist in the way the speaker suggests, or if his scheme cannot accommodate all the elements of the situation, we have a reasonably clear public criterion of 'false consciousness'. But this is possibly an easy case. On the other hand, from the clear and specific perspective from which Engels views the situation his is perhaps a clear criterion, although it probably refers only to a ruling class which, in pursuing certain courses of action, attributes motives to those actions which do not appear adequately to explain those actions in the eyes of the ruled. But the conception does demand for its validity an explicit commitment by the observer; it is not one which can exist in general without that commitment. For if one abandons the perspective involved, one has no criterion for judging true from false consciousness; that is, unless one also defines as explicit a commitment as Engels did. The term 'false consciousness' in context is both a description, and a description from one relative point of view, and therefore one which includes a political position. Theorists who have sought to use the term independently of any perspective can only do so by implying some position, or at least by suggesting that there is a truth over and above the truths men believe which is available to them, by, secretly as it were, using the term to justify a position they are not willing to spell out clearly and specifically.

However, there is a second sense to the term. In so far as the ruled accept the rulers, they too are subject to false consciousness. As Merton formulates it, in so far as the subordinate orders believe that what the ruling class does is in their interests, rather than solely in its own, they are 'ideological'. The difficulty here is that there are so many different kinds of situation and so many reasons why men accept established authority, onerous or not. We have already noted earlier that even the term 'accept' is suspect, since most men do not consider government one of the factors which they can change. It is rather like the weather, and one can neither accept nor reject it for it is not subject to our wills. The study of *The American Voter* (1960) suggests that for many people the information they have available about *national* politics makes participation fairly meaningless; there is 'political impoverishment'.

Thus, acceptance may not be ideological involvement at all, but rather a lack of those concepts and that information which link the active but isolated individual to the national or international framework. However, this is probably only half the truth, for what is perhaps lacking is the incentive to create those links, and this lack of incentive is not itself 'ideologically' conditioned (in the Marxist sense) so much as embodying a possibly realistic appraisal of how far any change is possible. Of course, it might be objected that I am here assuming just the information on which a 'realistic appraisal' would be possible: men decide not to acquire knowledge on the basis of the knowledge they are supposed not to have and need to acquire. But this is not so, for learning and understanding are not single discrete experiences. The experience of a child at school on how far the knowledge he is asked to acquire is useful, on how far he can do things with the knowledge, will in some circumstances condition his future willingness to learn. More boys who learn how a motor car works will continue in the rest of their lives to be interested in motor technology than those who learn Latin will interest themselves in the affairs of the Roman Empire, and this is a trivial observation for no better reason than that motor cars play a much more important role in our lives, people need to know about them in a way no one *needs* to know about Rome.

This is not an argument for philistinism, for 'occupational education for all', let alone 'motor technology' for the masses and Latin for the élite, but is merely intended to illustrate that our needs in part condition what we learn, and that in the area of political and social awareness needs underlie the process of general education. When people speak of popular 'apathy' they indict the rulers as much as the ruled, for the rulers do not present realistic alternatives which will activate people, which will prompt them to try seriously to make a proper choice. The apathetic know it is a game of publicists and ad men, just as much as the politicians, and deserves little serious and sustained attention. But, the reply might come, if it is a game, surely it can only be changed if people really do assert themselves – the freedom of the rulers is only possible so long as the ruled permit, so long as they refrain from laying down strict priorities within which the rulers must operate?

It is here that we return to an earlier point, for what makes the isolated man act is the necessity to survive and the hope of a change. And both factors are only meaningful where many men are prepared to undertake collective action – it is the collectivity alone which can create realistic hope. Thus it is perfectly possible for a man to have a realistic view of his condition and yet to do nothing about it, for nothing can be done by him as an isolated individual. Operative opinion is not necessarily politically significant opinion. And hope rises and falls from day to day. It is not a once-and-for-all spasm, but rather a continuous groping that on some rare occasions, when men are driven by the necessity of immediate events, can coincide in a whole movement that supersedes the isolated individual's problems to search for a general social solution.

One is left with something like the hymn's refrain, 'Only believe and thou shalt see': for the act of faith is the commitment of hope on which ultimately all action depends. 'Apathy' is a lack of socially significant hope, not a positive commitment in favour of the *status quo*.

Thus, just as education is not a single once-and-for-all event, so hope develops slowly in relationship to piecemeal successes: successes and failures that indicate what it is realistic to attempt, what is the line between that capable of achievement and that which necessarily must be accepted. The sole way to observe the rise and fall of hope is actually to see people attempting to achieve limited ends with modest resources. Of course, if someone truly refuses to risk any modicum of hope, nothing can be done. The irreducible act of faith has failed, and may fail even under the most extreme hardship where solutions can easily be perceived. The act of faith, for most people so trivial that it is not noticed, is nevertheless the link between man as the subordinate of his environment and man as the creator of that environment, the link between our perception of objective reality and the purposes we seek to realize. It is this unstable paradox – 'that man,' Meisner puts it, 'the maker of history, is also the object through which the objective laws of history express themselves' (1967, p. 136) – which has been an unresolved thread through most of this account. For each man's relative judgement embodies his act of faith in its truth and requires him to act on that judgement as if it were absolutely true – each relativism is an absolute. No matter what disclaimers and qualifications we may insert about our own fallibility, the tentative nature of our rough approximation, we cannot but commit ourselves in any clear opinion to the implication that other men should accept our opinion as the truth, commit ourselves to striving to convince others.

Thus it is impossible to answer the question we began with – how can we arrive at the right answers? – unless we can assume that we are active participants within society, that we have therefore a particular perspective, a particular experience, already with some modicum of hope that our existence is not meaningless. We cannot assume that there is a god-given answer from outside; there are only the answers men have, and the real question becomes which of these answers is most appropriate for us, thereby rendering all other answers wrong. Goldmann (1964, p. 301) following Pascal describes this initial act of faith as a wager, saying:

... once practical philosophy is no longer centred around an ideal of individual wisdom but comes to deal primarily with external reality, man's life takes on the aspect of a wager on the success of his own action and, consequently, on the existence of a force which transcends the individual. This force must accompany or contribute to the efforts which the individual makes, so that his life becomes a wager that God, Humanity or the Proletariat exists and will triumph.

The wager here embodies a major commitment, a major gesture of hope, even though for most people such a gesture is not required, for education proceeds slowly and piecemeal – the final commitment is only the last phase of a long cumulative experience in which all the small acts of faith have led on from the narrow localized perspective to the ultimate generalities of mankind and world history. The process of generalization is both the process of creating a language and concepts with which to express the ideas concerned and the encompassing of more and more elements – general radical social ideas embody the hope of collective action, and that hope is a precondition for the ultimate commitment.

Thus, the question cannot be separated from the attempt to act, a contention most succinctly expressed in the fragments of Marx's writings called the *Theses on Feuerbach*, the most famous of which is one of the citations at the head of this chapter. Practice, *praxis*, is the sole means available by which we can validate not only our initial act of faith but also the theories we create to relate the purposes embodied in that faith to an objective reality we see, and it is in practice that we sort out the genuine problems from the mere survivals of the past, that reality and consciousness return to a natural interactive relationship. Georg Lukacs, in somewhat obscure language, puts the thought thus: the problem of the relationship between being and consciousness must 'pass beyond the merely theoretical to the problem of practice. For only here, where the core of being is revealed as the social process, can being appear as the product, previously unconscious, of human activity and this activity in its turn as the decisive element in the transformation of "being".' (1966, p. 27.) What we see as existing human nature is no more than the past limits of human activity, and once we perceive those past limits we begin to see how they can be superseded – how our 'being' can itself be changed by the mediation of our 'consciousness'.

Thus, we have no guarantee of divine rectitude. We can only do our best and try. Doing our best involves a wide range of specifications concerning objectivity and also being able to demonstrate in principle that the morality we offer is a universal one, not one which seeks a solution for a minority at the expense of the majority. The precondition for an honest confrontation between opinions is that the protagonists will know clearly what they believe, and that there prevails such democracy as will permit free expression. The argument that wins in any debate cannot be shown to be universally correct, nor located before the debate. But if the debate really does permit free and equal presentation, we can go no further than this. In practice, very few 'free and equal' debates takes place, for insofar as the issue debated is important for established authority, then the terms of the debate will be rigged in favour of authority. In the House of Commons, the important issues are carefully organized so that the government wins the vote, and those issues where a 'free vote' is permitted are the peripheral ones. Even the notion of 'permitting' a free vote indicates where the power lies, for in a 'free and equal' debate no participant should have the power to permit or restrict the participation of others. Outside the Assembly, established authority is armed with the major part of the press, radio, film and television. Its point of view sets the terms of reference for what discussion is possible. Take for example the press reportage of industrial disputes. In the majority of the reports, it is the impact of the strike on production which receives most emphasis, the impact of the strike on the existing *status quo*, rather than the issues at stake, whether or not one side or the other is right. It is presumed in such reportage that the issue of justice is of less importance than that of peace, of keeping production going regardless of the justice involved. Yet is it not most strange that the form of the dispute should loom so much larger than the content, the meaning? Concentrating on the form prompts people to suggest the solution of force – let the police or the army or the law settle the dispute by force – rather than to seek out the reason why the dispute occurs and to endeavour to satisfy the demands of those in dispute. Essentially, the emphasis protects the *status quo* from the demand for meaning, the demand for justification and justice, protects authority from the need to present a point of view on a par with the points of view of the rest of society.

In a 'free and equal' debate, then, the position of the final winner is the best we can hope for, and we can only put his proposals to the test of practice. Thus, objectivity is rather an attitude of mind than a body of methodological tricks that enable one to evade responsibility for a clear choice, to hide behind the authority of some expertise that dare not show itself in public lest it be seen to be inimical to popular interests, that must hide itself in deliberately obscure language. We know that everybody cannot be convinced of the rightness of the same answer, except under conditions of force or dishonesty, but we have to accept the challenge to try to convince, for that is one of the tests of practice and one which is vital in the correction of our own opinions.

It might be objected, quite reasonably, that I have been seeking to describe some of the validating conditions for 'making the right judgements' as if there were a general solution to the problem, whereas the actual proposals I have made are implicitly only radical ones, and, indeed, more than that, Marxist ones. This would be a perfectly legitimate criticism, for the judgements contained in the whole of this book stem from a particular perspective, and implicit in the critique of the beliefs of other people is both a positive political viewpoint, a code of ethics and moral priorities and a strategy for action. It would be less than honest to try to pretend that this was not so. At the beginning of the book, one specific view of 'reality' was arbitrarily presented, and that view includes an account of what is desirable. It is precisely the ambivalent nature of the term 'reality' which makes the term 'ideology' itself ambivalent. 'Ideology' can mean both the views of any and all social groups, and the views of social groups other than my own. Attentive readers will no doubt detect a reluctance in this book to refer to my own views as 'ideology', simply because it is a derogatory term. The Soviet revision of Marx's conception which permitted the Russians to speak of their 'own ideology', and occasional rare Western mentions of Western ideology has not changed the basic derogatory tone of the word. For what is one's own ideology is 'common sense' in most people, simply the obvious truth, so one needs no further word to describe it. It is only other people who have uncommon sense, ideology. The two meanings conjoin, then, an attempt at objective description (the 'views of any social group') and a subjective and purely relative judgement (the 'views of social groups other than my own'). The ambivalence cannot be reconciled except, once again, through the attempt to demonstrate that what one

believes really is in the best interests of all, through practice. At
the point of action one accepts the challenge to try to prove that
one is right, to prove that what one believes is the best that can
be believed, and that beliefs which contradict one's own are false,
are 'ideological'. Thus, in the circle of interdefining concepts –
purpose, interest, survival, reality, ideology must also take its
place. It cannot be defined until we have stated for whom it is to
be defined, what his place in time and society is.

However, what strategy has been implicit in this account? In
the account of religion, the role of religion as a medium for class
struggle was explicitly presented, for popular religion stands con-
strasted with the religion of the rulers. In my account of Marxism-Leninism, it clearly emerges that I hold freedom to be the
most important single ideal and that Russia today in no way
corresponds to even a rough approximation to freedom. Yet if
one identifies freedom with the 'Free World', it will be clear
from my account of Western conservatism that I do not believe
freedom exists in the West. And finally, from the account of
nationalism in the developing countries, it will be clear that I do
not identify freedom with the populist and authoritarian régimes
in many developing countries. The more widespread discussion
of Marxism indicates further that I do identify freedom with
the historic aims of the industrial working classes of the developed countries.

However, although this is not a manifesto and we cannot enter
into topics considered in much greater detail in the publications
of the political Left, it is necessary to bring it down to earth. For
vague talk of 'the industrial working classes' offers no perspective
for action at all and could be, thus, no more than one form of
'false consciousness', ritualizing with empty concepts that have
no implications for the world in which ordinary men lead ordinary lives. One must connect these concepts with what men
actually do, not just in the developed countries, for they are no
self-contained island, nor yet solely in the developing countries.
One must also see what happens today in proper perspective. For
history is, among other things, an account of popular attempts to
secure a greater degree of freedom against the more or less overt

attempts of rulers to subvert that freedom in their own interests. Only sporadic revolt has repulsed the attack and thus temporarily recreated again some small area of freedom. The brutalization of the life of the majority is implicit in societies organized in classes, whether the majority are held to the soil or to the factory bench, whether housed in village hovels or trapped in the tenements of the cities. Society of this kind is organized to expand the wealth and power of those that rule, with the majority whipped or manipulated to contribute the maximum at minimum cost.

But emancipation would be a fraudulent notion if it meant no more than transferring the power held by the old rulers to new ones, if it meant, as it has come to mean for both social democrats and communists, transferring power from private business to the State. For this is emancipation only for those who command the State, and insofar as the State becomes important so will those who command it seek to insulate it from popular wishes, to bury decisions in the secrecy of bureaucracy, to dispense with even the limited significance of 'representative' forms. Emancipation can only properly mean securing a situation in which the majority really does decide what is to be done, in which the power to do things eliminates the apathy of impotence and sustains the demand for control. It is for this reason that the demand for 'workers' control' becomes so important, and this is a demand not for workers' participation (in someone else's society), workers' management or co-partnership, but for the actual control of industry and society by the majority.

It is workers' control which is the creeping threat to advanced society, for in each enterprise continuous warfare is the law of the factory floor. On a multitude of issues ordinary workers press for some greater degree of power, shop-stewards strive for some increased measure of control. Naturally, both employers and established trade unions tend to treat such encroachments as the beginning of anarchy, as the rising tide of barbarism from below, in the same way that Burke and De Maistre treated earlier threats to the *status quo*. Again, it is also true that such uncoordinated and sporadic guerrilla warfare cannot succeed without superseding the bounds of the individual enterprise or industry, without becoming 'political', and forming a coordinated political movement.

Yet, the battle goes on in dozens of factories each day, and it is a battle which provides one element to substantiate a faith in the possibility of popular freedom. The same battle goes on in other spheres – in the attempt of some unions to break a State incomes policy which threatens to freeze the *status quo* by law, in the attempt of tenants to oppose the rising rents generated by rising interest rates. Those rising interest rates represent just such another attempt to change the balance of class power, to shift the distribution of the national income from one class to another. The battle goes on more dramatically in Vietnam or in the ghettos of the great American cities, in the activity of Bolivian tin miners or South African guerrillas.

Playing with concepts tends to prevent one locating in the real world where and how the continuing battle for freedom is being waged. Yet so far established authority has not succeeded in permanently anaesthetizing its population from the effects of exploitation. One must not overestimate the significance of the battle – most of its elements are isolated, fragmentary, rudimentary, and frequently defeated – yet it goes on. And one's attitude to that battle, one's willingness to participate to the full in it, in part determines what one thinks the world is, what 'reality' is.

It was suggested earlier that conservatives who regard the real as, by and large, the ideal, who sacrifice the justice or freedom of others to the peace of themselves, the stability of the *status quo*, have no need to act to validate anything. They do not project a forward aim which is particularly different from the existing situation. *Praxis* dissolves in immediate administration. It is only where men, by reason of their particular situation, need something more than the immediate that the radical perspective becomes appropriate, that we need to find means of validating what we seek – and to do that is to seek.

BIBLIOGRAPHY

Works cited in the text

APTER, DAVID (Ed.) (1964) *Ideology and Discontent* (New York, Free Press of Glencoe).

BAILEY, F. G. (1963) *Politics and Social Change, Orissa in 1959* (Berkeley, California and Oxford University Presses).

BARGHOORN, F. C. (1956) *Soviet Russian Nationalism* (New York, O.U.P.).

BELL, DANIEL (1961) *The End of Ideology, On the Exhaustion of Political Ideas in the Fifties* (New York, Collier).

BELL, DANIEL (1965) 'Soviet Ideology', *Slavic Review*, XXIV, 4 (New York, December 1965).

BENDIX, REINHARD (1956) *Work and Authority in Industry: Ideologies of Management in the Course of Industrialization* (New York, 1956; Harper ed., 1963).

BENDIX, REINHARD (1960) *Max Weber: An Intellectual Portrait* (London, Heinemann).

BENDIX, REINHARD (1964) 'The Age of Ideology: Persistent and Changing', in APTER, D., op. cit., p. 294.

BENDIX, REINHARD (1966) 'A Case Study in Cultural and Educational Mobility: Japan and the Protestant Ethic', in SMELSER, N. J., and LIPSET, S. M. (Eds) *Social Structure and Mobility in Economic Development* (London, Routledge).

BERLE, A. A. (1954) *The Twentieth Century Capitalist Revolution* (New York, Harcourt).

BRANDT, CONRAD (1958) *Stalin's Failure in China, 1924–1927* (Cambridge, Mass., Harvard U.P.).

BUCHANAN, SCOTT (ed.) (1959) *The Corporation in Modern Society* (Cambridge, Mass., Harvard U.P.).

BURKE, EDMUND (1790) *Reflections on the French Revolution* (London, Everyman ed., 1955; Penguin Books, 1970).

BURKE, KENNETH (1941) *The Philosophy of Literary Form: Studies in Symbolic Action* (New York, 1941, Vintage ed., 1957).

CAMPBELL, A., CONVERSE, P. E., MILLER, W. E. and STOKES, D. E. (1960) *The American Voter* (New York, John Wiley).

CARR, E. H. (1957) *The Bolshevik Revolution, 1917–23, I* (London, Macmillan; Penguin Books, 1970).

CHURCHILL, LORD RANDOLPH (1889) *The Speeches of – 1880–89* (ed. Louis J. Jennings) (London, Longmans).

COHN, NORMAN (1957) *The Pursuit of the Millennium* (London, Mercury).

CONVERSE, P. E. (1964) 'The Nature of Belief Systems in Mass Publics', in APTER, D., op. cit., p. 206.

CROSLAND, C. A. R. (1956) *The Future of Socialism* (London, Cape).

DEUTSCHER, ISAAC (1954) *The Prophet Armed, Trotsky 1879–1921* (London, O.U.P.).

DUBOIS, CORA (1949) *Social Forces in South East Asia* (St Paul, University of Minnesota Press).

ENGELS, F. (1850) *The Peasant War in Germany* (Moscow, Foreign Languages Publishing House, 1956).

ERIKSON, E. H. (1958) *Young Man Luther: A Study in Psychoanalysis and History* (London, Norton).

FREUD, S. (1933) *Introductory Lectures* (New York, 1965).

FRIEDRICH, CARL J. (1965) 'Ideology in Politics (Comment on Bell)', *Slavic Review*, XXIV, 4, p. 612.

FRÖLICH, P. (1940) *Rosa Luxemburg* (London, Gollancz, Left Book Club).

GALBRAITH, J. K. (1959) *The Affluent Society* (London, Hamilton).

GEERTZ, CLIFFORD (1960) *The Religion of Java* (New York, Free Press of Glencoe).

GEERTZ, CLIFFORD (ed.) (1963) *Old Societies and New States* (New York, Free Press of Glencoe).

GEERTZ, CLIFFORD (1964) 'Ideology as a Cultural System', in APTER, D., op. cit., p. 47.

GOLDMANN, LUCIEN (1964) *The Hidden God, A Study of the Tragic Vision in the Pensées of Pascal and the Tragedies of Racine (Le Dieu Caché)* (London, Routledge).

GOLDMAN, LUCIEN (1967) 'Ideology and Writing', *The Times Literary Supplement* (28 September 1967, p. 203).

GOLLIN, G. L. (1966) *The Religious Factor in Social Change: Max Weber and the Moravian Paradox*, paper presented to the Sixth World Congress of Sociology, Evian.

GOULD, JULIUS (1964) 'Ideology', *A Dictionary of the Social Sciences*, editors GOULD, J. and KOLB, W. L. (London, Tavistock).

GRAMSCI, ANTONIO (1957) *The Modern Prince and other Writings* (London, Lawrence & Wishart).

GUEVARA, ERNESTO (1960) 'Guerrilla Warfare', translated by J. P. MORRAY, *Monthly Review* (New York, 1961).

GUEVARA, ERNESTO (1961) 'Cuba: Exceptional Case?', *Monthly Review* (New York, July–August 1961).

HARRIS, N. (1963) *Conservatism: the State and Society*, unpublished Ph.D. thesis (University of London).

HOBSBAWM, E. J. (1959) *Primitive Rebels, Studies in Archaic Forms of Social Movement in the 19th and 20th Centuries* (Manchester, Manchester U.P.).

ISAACS, R. HAROLD (1961) *The Tragedy of the Chinese Revolution* (Stanford, California U.P., 2nd rev. ed.).

ISSAWI, CHARLES (1963) *Egypt in Revolution, An Economic Analysis* (London, Royal Institute for International Affairs and O.U.P.).

JORAVSKY, D. (1966) 'Soviet Ideology', *Soviet Studies* (Oxford).

KEYNES, J. M. (1924) 'The End of Laissez-Faire', reprinted in *Essays in Persuasion* (London, Macmillan, 1931).

KEYNES, J. M. (1936) *General Theory of Employment, Interest and Money* (London, Macmillan).

LANTERNARI, V. (1960) *The Religions of the Oppressed, A Study of Modern Messianic Cults* (English translation, 1963, Mentor edition, London, 1965).

LENIN, V. I. (1902) 'What is to be Done?', *Selected Works, I*, p. 149 (London, Lawrence & Wishart, 1937).

LENIN, V. I. (1905) 'Two Tactics of Social Democracy in the Democratic Revolution', *Selected Works, I*, p. 351.

LENIN, V. I. (1933) *State and Revolution* (London, Lawrence & Wishart).

LENIN, V. I. (1937) 'Above the Control of Nature', *Selected Works* (London).

LENIN, V. I. (1960) 'How We Should Reorganize the Workers' and Peasants' Inspectorate', *Collected Works* 9 (Moscow, Foreign Languages Publishing House).

LENIN, V. I. (1960) 'Two Methods of Fighting and Disputing', *Collected Works* 17 (Moscow, Foreign Languages Publishing House).

LENIN, V. I. (1960) 'Some Theses', *Collected Works* 18 (Moscow, Foreign Languages Publishing House).

LENIN, V. I. (1960) Speech, 11 November 1917, *Collected Works* 22 (Moscow, Foreign Languages Publishing House).

LÉVI-STRAUSS, CLAUDE (1962, 1966) *The Savage Mind* (*La Pensée Sauvage*), English translation (London, Weidenfeld & Nicholson).

LI LI-SAN (1949) 'Trade Union Work and Movement in China', *China Digest* (Peking).

LUKÁCS, GEORG (1966), 'What is Orthodox Marxism?', I and II, translated by Mary Phillips from Chapter I of *Geschichte und Klassenbewusstein* (Berlin, 1923) in *International Socialism*, 24, Spring 1966, p. 6, and 25, Summer 1966, p. 24.

MACINTYRE, ALASDAIR (1967) *A Short History of Ethics* (London, Routledge).

MACMILLAN, HAROLD (1938) *The Middle Way: A Study of the Problem of Economic and Social Progress in a Free and Democratic Society* (London, Macmillan).

MAISTRE, JOSEPH DE (1966) The Generative Principles of Political Constitutions, p. 147 in *The Works of Joseph de Maistre*, selected, translated and edited by JACK LIVELY, London, Allen & Unwin.

MANNHEIM, KARL (1936) *Ideology and Utopia, An Introduction to the Sociology of Knowledge* (London, Routledge).

MAO TSE-TUNG (1930) 'A Single Spark can Light a Prairie Fire', January 1930, *Selected Works* 1, p. 117 (New York and Pekin).

MAO TSE-TUNG (1933) 'Re-examination of Land Distribution in the Soviet Districts is the Central Task', *Red Flag*, 31 August 1933.

MAO TSE-TUNG (1938) Report, 6th Plenum, 6th Central Committee, Chinese Communist Party, October 1938. Versions of this appear in *Selected Works* 2, 'Role of the Chinese Communist Party' (p. 195), and 'The Question of Independence and Initiative within the United Front, Problems of War and Strategy'.

MAO TSE-TUNG (1945) 'On Coalition Government', 24 April 1945, *Selected Works* 3, p. 255 (New York).

MAO TSE-TUNG (1954) *Selected Works* 1-4 (New York, International Publishers).

MAO TSE-TUNG (1965) *Selected Works* 1-4 (Pekin, Foreign Languages Press).

MARX, KARL (1845-7) *The German Ideology*, 1845-7 (London, Lawrence & Wishart, 1965).

MARX, KARL (1852) 'The Eighteenth Brumaire of Louis Napoleon',

Selected Works of Marx and Engels, p. 315 (Moscow, Foreign Languages Publishing House, 1933).

MARX, KARL (1845) 'Theses on Feurebach), *Selected Works*, p. 471.

MARX, KARL and ENGELS, F. (1953) *Selected Correspondence* (Moscow).

MEISNER, MAURICE (1965) 'Li Ta-chao and the Chinese Communist Treatment of the Materialist Conception of History', *China Quarterly* 24, October–December 1965, p. 141.

MEISNER, MAURICE (1967) *Li Ta-chao and the Origins of Chinese Marxism* (Cambridge, Mass., Harvard U.P.).

MERTON, R. K. (1957) *Social Theory and Social Structure*, revised ed. (New York, Free Press of Glencoe).

NAESS, ARNE *et al.* (1956) *Democracy, Ideology and Objectivity* (Oxford and Oslo).

NEUMANN, FRANZ (1942) *Behemoth* (London, Gollancz, Left Book Club).

NOLTE, ERNST (1963) *Three Faces of Fascism*, translated (London, Weidenfeld & Nicholson, 1965).

OSSOWSKI, S. (1963) *Class Structure in the Social Consciousness* (London, Routledge).

PARSONS, TALCOTT (1951) *The Social System* (London, Routledge).

PARSONS, TALCOTT (1954) 'The Role of Ideas in Social Action', republished in *Essays in Sociological Theory* (New York, Free Press of Glencoe).

PARSONS, TALCOTT (1959) 'An Approach to the Sociology of Knowledge', *Transactions*, 4th World Congress of Sociology.

REDFIELD, ROBERT (1953) *The Primitive World and Its Transformations* (Ithaca, Cornell U.P.).

SCHRAM, S. R. (1963) *The Political Thought of Mao Tse-Tung* (London, Pall Mall).

SCHWARTZ, B. I. (1958) *Chinese Communism and the Rise of Mao* (Cambridge, Mass., Harvard U.P.).

SHILS, EDWARD (1958) 'Ideology and Civility', *Sewanee Review* 66.

STALIN, J. D. (1926) *On the Problems of Leninism* (Moscow, Foreign Language Publishing House).

STALIN, J. D. (1930) Speech, XVI Congress of the Communist Party of the Soviet Union, *Collected Works* 12 (Moscow).

STALIN, J. D. (1937) Report, Plenary Session, Central Committee, Communist Party of the Soviet Union, translated as *Mastering Bolshevism* (London).

STALIN, J. D. (1938) *History of the C.P.S.U. (B.), (Short Course)* (Moscow, Foreign Languages Publishing House).

STALIN, J. D. (1950) *Concerning Marxism in Linguistics* (Moscow, Foreign Languages Publishing House).

STALIN, J. D. (1952) *Economic Problems of Socialism in the U.S.S.R.* (Moscow, Foreign Languages Publishing House).

STARK, WERNER (1958) *The Sociology of Knowledge* (London, Routledge).

STARK, WERNER (1966) *The Sociology of Religion, 1* (London, Routledge).

STOUFFER, S. A. (1955) *Communism, Conformity and Civil Liberties; A Cross-section of the Nation Speaks Its Mind* (New York, Doubleday).

SUTTON, F. X., *et al.* (1956) *The American Business Creed* (Cambridge, Mass., Harvard U.P.).

THAKUR, B. S., ALLEN, BRADFORD, and THIRTHA, N. V. (1963) *Villagers and the News* (Indian Institute of Public Administration (Andhra Pradesh Regional Branch) and Dept of Journalism, Osmania University, Hyderabad.)

THOMPSON, E. P. (1957) 'Socialist Humanism', *New Reasoner*, 1, Summer 1957.

THOMPSON, E. P. (1963) *The Making of the English Working Class* (London, Gollancz).

TROTSKY, L. D. (1930) *My Life* (Berlin, 1930, translated London, Butterworth, 1930).

TROTSKY, L. D. (1937) *Stalinism and Bolshevism* (Glasgow, Socialist Fight, mimeo.).

TROTSKY, L. D. (1962) *Results and Prospects* (St Petersburg 1906) translated with *Permanent Revolution* by BRIAN PIERCE (London, New Park, 1962).

WALZER, M. (1966) 'Puritanism as a Revolutionary Ideology', *History and Theory III*, 1961, reprinted in SHKLAR, J. N. (ed.), *Political Theory and Ideology* (New York, Macmillan).

WEBER, MAX (1930) *The Protestant Ethic and the Spirit of Capitalism*, translated by Talcott Parsons (London, Allen & Unwin).

WEBER, MAX (1952) *Ancient Judaism*, translated (New York, Free Press of Glencoe).

WEBER, MAX (1965) *The Sociology of Religion*, 1922 (as part of *Wirtschaft und Gesellschaft*), translated (London, Methuen).

WETTER, G. A. (1958) *Dialectical Materialism, A Historical and*

Systematic Survey of Philosophy in the Soviet Union, translated by PETER HEATH (London, Routledge).

WILLIAMS, GEORGE H. (1962) *The Radical Reformation* (Philadelphia/London, Weidenfeld & Nicholson).

Constitution of the Trade Unions of the People's Republic of China (adopted at the Seventh All-China Congress of Trade Unions, 10 May 1953), p. 16 in *Labour Laws and Regulations of the People's Republic of China* (Pekin, Foreign Language Press, 1956).

Selected Bibliography

No bibliography can, within the confines of the space available here, properly encompass the themes touched upon in this book. The works which follow supplement the list of works cited and provide an entry point on a number of different but related topics for the interested reader.

ARON, RAYMOND, *The Opium of the Intellectuals*, 1955, translated by Terence Kilmartin (London, Secker & Warburg, 1957).

BIRNBAUM, NORMAN, 'The Sociological Study of Ideology (1940–60)'. A trend report and bibliography, *Current Sociology*, IX, 2, 1960 (Oxford, Blackwell, 1962).

BIRNBAUM, NORMAN, 'The Rise of Capitalism: Marx and Weber', in SMELSER, N. J. (ed.), *Readings on Economic Sociology* (New Jersey, Prentice-Hall, 1965).

BOTTOMORE, T. B. and RUBEL, M., *Karl Marx, Selected Writings in Sociology and Social Philosophy* (London, Watts, 1961, Penguin Books, 1963).

CORBETT, P., *Ideologies* (London, Hutchison, 1965).

DURKHEIM, E., *The Elementary Forms of Religious Life*, translated by Joseph Ward Swain (London, Allen & Unwin, 1915/57).

EVANS-PRITCHARD, E. E. (ed.), *The Institutions of Primitive Society* (Oxford, Blackwell, 1956).

FREUD, S., *Civilization and its Discontents*, translated by JOAN RIVIERE, International Psycho-analytical Library (No. 17) (London, Hogarth, 1930).

FREUD, S., *Totem and Taboo*, translated by JAMES STRACHEY (London, Routledge, 1948).

GELLNER, E., *Thought and Change* (London, Weidenfeld & Nicholson, 1964).

GERSHENKRON, A., 'Reflections on Ideology as a Methodological and Historical Problem', Part III, p. 179, in HEGELAND, HUGO (ed.), *Money, Growth and Methodology* (Lund, University of Lund, 1961).

HUGHES, H. STUART, *Consciousness and Society: The Reorientation of European Social Thought, 1890–1930* (London, MacGibbon & Kee, 1959).

JORAVSKY, DAVID, *Soviet Marxism and Natural Science, 1917–32* (New York, 1961).

KENNEDY, R. E., 'The Protestant Ethic and the Parsis', in SMELSER, op. cit. (cf. Birnbaum).

LICHTHEIM, G., 'The Concept of Ideology', *History and Theory*, 2, p. 164, 1965.

LUKÁCS, GEORG, *Geschichte und Klassenbewusstsein* (Berlin, Malik-Verlag, 1923), translated by K. AXELOS and J. BOIS, *Histoire et Conscience de Classe* (Paris, Les Editions de Minuit, 1960).

MALINOWSKI, B., *A Scientific Theory of Culture* (North Carolina, University of North Carolina, 1944).

MALINOWSKI, B., *Magic, Science and Religion*, and other essays (New York, Doubleday, 1954).

MEAD, MARGARET, *Cultural Patterns and Technical Change* (UNESCO, 1955; New York, Mentor, 1955).

MEEK, RONALD L., *Economics and Ideology*, and other essays (London, Chapman & Hall, 1967).

MONSEN, R. J., *Modern American Capitalism, Ideologies and Issues* (Boston, Houghton Mifflin, 1963).

MYRDAL, GUNNAR, *The Political Element in the Development of Economic Theory*, translated by PAUL STREETEN (London, Routledge, 1953).

MYRDAL, GUNNAR, *Value in Social Theory: A Selection of Essays on Methodology*, translated, edited and introduced by PAUL STREETEN (London, Routledge, 1958).

PARETO, V., *The Mind and Society*, ed. ARTHUR LIVINGSTON, 4 vols. (New York, Harcourt Brace, 1935).

ROUCEK, J. S., 'A History of the Concept of Ideology', *Journal of the History of Ideas*, V, p. 482, 1944.

SARGANT, WILLIAM, *Battle for the Mind* (London, Heinemann, 1957; Pan, 1959).

SCHER, J. (ed.), Theories of the Mind (New York, 1962).

SCHUMPETER, J. S., *Capitalism, Socialism and Democracy* (New York, Harper, 1942).

SOREL, GEORGES, *Reflections on Violence*, 1908, translated by T. HULME (New York, Collier, 1961).

STARK, WERNER, *The Fundamental Forms of Social Thought* (London, Routledge, 1962).

SUMNER, W. G., *Folkways* (New York, Mentor, 1960).

SWANSON, G. E., *The Birth of the Gods, the Origin of Primitive Beliefs* (Michigan, Ann Arbor, 1964).

TAWNEY, R. H., *Religion and the Rise of Capitalism* (1926, London, Penguin Books, 1938).

WEBER, MAX, *From Max Weber, Essays in Sociology*, translated by H. H. GERTH and C. WRIGHT MILLS (London, Routledge, 1948).

WETTER, G. A., *Soviet Ideology Today*, 1962, translated by PETER HEATH (London, Heinemann, 1966).

WILLIAMS, RAYMOND, *Culture and Society, 1780–1950* (1958, London, Penguin Books, 1961).

WORSLEY, PETER, *The Trumpets Shall Sound, A Study of 'Cargo' Boat Cults in Melanesia* (London, MacGibbon & Kee, 1957).